The Road Out of Debt

Out of Debt

BANKRUPTCY AND OTHER SOLUTIONS TO YOUR FINANCIAL PROBLEMS

Joan N. Feeney
Theodore W. Connolly

WILEY

John Wiley & Sons, Inc.

Published by John Wiley & Sons, Inc., Hoboken, New Jersey.
Published simultaneously in Canada.

Limit of Liability/Disclaimer of Warranty: While the publisher and author have used their best efforts in preparing this book, they make no representations or warranties with respect to the accuracy or completeness of the contents of this book and specifically disclaim any implied warranties of merchantability or fitness for a particular purpose. No warranty may be created or extended by sales representatives or written sales materials. The advice and strategies contained herein may not be suitable for your situation. You should consult with a professional where appropriate. Neither the publisher nor author shall be liable for any loss of profit or any other commercial damages, including but not limited to special, incidental, consequential, or other damages.

For general information on our other products and services or for technical support, please contact our Customer Care Department within the United States at (800) 762-2974, outside the United States at (317) 572-3993 or fax (317) 572-4002.

Wiley also publishes its books in a variety of electronic formats. Some content that appears in print may not be available in electronic books. For more information about Wiley products, visit our Web site at www.wiley.com.

Library of Congress Cataloging-in-Publication Data:
Feeney, Joan N.
   The road out of debt : bankruptcy and other solutions to your financial problems / Joan Feeney, Ted Connolly.
      p. cm.
   Includes index.
      ISBN 978-0-470-49886-6 (hardback); ISBN 978-0-470-87562-9 (ebk);
ISBN 978-0-470-87563-6 (ebk); ISBN 978-0-470-87564-3 (ebk)
      1. Finance, Personal–United States.   2. Debt–United States.   3. Consumer credit–United States. 4. Bankruptcy–United States. I. Connolly, Ted. II. Title.
   HG179.F44 2010
   332.024'02—dc22

                                                                    2010009567

Printed in the United States of America
10   9   8   7   6   5   4   3   2   1

To our parents and especially our fathers,
Judge Joseph F. Feeney and Attorney Matthew T.
Connolly, who taught us by example to help others
in our legal work and in our lives.

Contents

Acknowledgments

Without the assistance and support of many fantastic people, this book may have never come together. We would like to thank Meg Freeborn, Bill Falloon, Chris Gage, Tiffany Charbonier, and the other consummate professionals at John Wiley & Sons for their extraordinary editing, production, advice, recommendations, and endless patience.

Thanks also to David McCormick and his associates at McCormick & Williams for their superb representation; Professor Steve H. Nickles, Professor Jack Williams, Margaret M. Crouch, Molly Sharon, and Ann Fox for their generous support, outstanding review, and editorial analysis; Gerald P. Hendrick, Stuart Brown, Jim McGinley, Charlie Ognibene, John Hughes, Mary-Pat Cormier, Ed Bertozzi, Jean France, Glenn Pudelka, Jennifer O'Leary Cathell, Amy Halloran, Gina Carriuolo, Courtney Jones, Renee Evangelista, and countless other exceptional colleagues at Edwards Angell Palmer & Dodge LLP for their help and guidance; my present and former colleagues, the bankruptcy judges of the District of Massachusetts: Carol J. Kenner, William C. Hillman, Henry J. Boroff, Joel B. Rosenthal, Robert Somma, Frank J. Bailey and Melvin S. Hoffman for their constant and unwavering support and friendship; and for their excellent illustrations, Nicolas A. Coppola and the staff at Corne Cartoons/Enroc Illustration Co. (www.enroc.com and www.corne.com/ar) and Maki and the staff at New Way Solutions (www.newwaysolutions.com).

Special thanks to Sharon whose love and encouragement makes everything possible and to Matt, Maria, Matthew, and Tatiana Connolly and Matthew and Caroline Morton for their love and appreciation.

Preface

The collapse of major corporations, the highest foreclosure rates in history, job losses, staggering unemployment figures, and failing banks have weakened the U.S. economy. In 2009, more than 1.4 million Americans filed for bankruptcy protection and countless others felt overwhelmed by debt. As governments around the world work to fix the global economy, individuals need to concentrate on their own financial issues.

The Road Out of Debt will walk you through the steps you must take to resolve your debts and rebuild your finances. Initially, we discuss your options for avoiding bankruptcy. We then discuss when bankruptcy might be the right decision. If bankruptcy can work for you, we will show you what to do. We will simplify bankruptcy and the bankruptcy process so you can effectively navigate your way through it either on your own or with the help of a lawyer.

Deciding whether to file for bankruptcy is a difficult decision and only you can decide what's best for you. As a bankruptcy judge and bankruptcy lawyer, we have seen thousands and thousands of people go through bankruptcy and we're here to help. Achieving freedom from debt with or without bankruptcy may seem complex and mysterious, but it doesn't have to be. This book will give you the tools, the knowledge, and the ability to free yourself from debt.

With this book, you will take control of your finances. You have suffered the stress of overwhelming debt long enough. We will show you how to fight back and reclaim your life from creditors. We will help you start fresh and live your life on new terms.

The Road Out of Debt is organized into four parts. Part I offers basic information on dealing with debt. You will assess your debt situation, study the solutions available for each problem, and begin to think about resolving your debts.

Part II addresses specific debts, including credit card, mortgage, medical, student loans, auto, and tax debts. This section allows you to concentrate on those debts that are causing you the biggest problems and walks you through the various solutions to them.

Part III discusses the different bankruptcy types and the overall process so you'll know there's nothing to fear. Everyone cringes a little when they think about bankruptcy, but the more you know, the better you will feel about it as a solution.

Finally, Part IV presents stories of hypothetical bankruptcy cases based on real individuals so that you can learn more about what can happen in a bankruptcy case. Although most bankruptcy cases are uneventful and debtors do not see the inside of a bankruptcy court, reading the stories of more complicated bankruptcies is the best way to understand bankruptcy and to remove the mystery that surrounds the process.

At the end of the book, you will find appendices of helpful resources and frequently asked questions, and a glossary of key terms. In addition, links to many of the resources we mention in the book, additional checklists for evaluating your financial situation and dealing with debt, and more can be found on the book's Web sites at www.wiley.com/go/roadoutofdebt and www.roadoutofdebt.com.

The Road Out of Debt provides you with straightforward and essential solutions for taking control and overcoming your personal financial problems. You can now look forward to being free from debt and living the life you want!

TED CONNOLLY

JOAN FEENEY

June 2010

Introduction

If you think nobody cares if you're alive, try missing a couple of car payments.

—Earl Wilson

More than 13 million people have filed for bankruptcy relief over the last 10 years.[1] Millions more each year think about filing for bankruptcy but don't. Should you file? Maybe bankruptcy is the best way to get back on your feet and make a fresh start. But maybe another way out of debt will work better.

Think back to the days, perhaps not so long ago, when you weren't worrying about how you were going to pay your bills each month. The days when you had money left over at the end of the month for a rainy day fund, for retirement, and for your future. You *can* get back to that place . . . with or without bankruptcy.

A Short History of Debt

From the beginning of civilization, people have owed other people. Loans have led to debts that have gone unpaid. Every culture has dealt with debtors in different ways.

In ancient Greece, a man and his entire family could be sold into slavery for unpaid debts. In ancient Rome, a person had to pledge himself, his family, and his property for a loan. If he couldn't pay it back, he became the creditor's slave and the creditor even had the right to kill him. If he had more than one creditor, the creditors could dismember the debtor's body and divide the pieces.

> Ancient Roman law let creditors cut up the body of a debtor and divide him up based on the size of his debt.

In medieval England, the person who didn't pay his debts was strapped by his head and feet into a wooden frame post in the center of town. If he wasn't put in these stocks, the punishment was to cut off his ear.

In 1542, the first bankruptcy laws were passed in England under King Henry VIII. Nonpayment of debt was a criminal offense and the individual could be imprisoned or even sentenced to death for the failure to repay debts.

Debtors' prison crippled many families. Unlike prison for other crimes, people in debtors' prison had to provide their own food and would not be released until the debt was paid off. Unable to work to pay off their debts because they were behind bars, debtors had to rely on family members to work and pay off the debts. At 12 years old, Charles Dickens toiled in a factory to pay off the family debts while his father, mother, and siblings lingered in prison for the debts of his father.

Our Founding Fathers rejected the notion of debtors' prison. However, early bankruptcy laws in the United States were harsh. Before 1833, federal prison awaited the individual who failed to pay back a debt. Throughout the 1800s, numerous bankruptcy laws were passed favoring creditors but none remained as law for long. Finally, in 1898, permanent federal bankruptcy legislation was enacted. During the Great Depression, updated bankruptcy laws were enacted in 1933 and 1934 to offer debtors a "fresh start" and freedom from financial burdens. The laws provided equality of distribution for all creditors and a uniform way to deal with debts. The same purpose underlies the present bankruptcy law.

The same cannot be said in all countries around the world. Dubai, for instance, once hailed as the economic superpower of the Middle East, still jails people for not paying their debts.

United States of Debt

Companies spend huge dollars on television, bus, Internet, and billboard ads all aimed at getting us to buy more and more, whether or not we need the goods and services they are selling.

The United States is in its worst financial condition since the Great Depression of 1929. While the median U.S. household income is currently $43,200, the credit card balance of a typical family is now almost 5 percent of their annual income. Over 8 percent of our households owe more than $9,000 on credit cards. Each year since 2004, consumers have spent more than they made. The last time American consumers had a negative savings rate, where our spending exceeded their income, was during the Great Depression.[2]

In addition, our personal spending has been made much worse by the housing boom and mortgage mess. Over the last several years, banks and mortgage brokers have dramatically changed the ways they lend us money. We have enjoyed easy borrowing through the loosening of lending standards and millions of us find ourselves with little or no equity in our homes. We have used the equity in our homes to refinance and fund expenses, such as credit card debts, college tuitions, and building additions to our houses. Some of us bought more house than we could afford in part because the lender approved such a large mortgage for us, often urging us to borrow more.

Unfortunately, the housing market peaked in 2006 and we are now in the midst of a credit crisis that the world has not seen since the Great Depression in the 1930s. Lenders have now gone to the opposite extreme. Banks and other financial institutions have imposed strict standards in granting mortgage loans. As homes decrease in value, we can no longer refinance to pay off our bills. Banks continue to decline to make any loans except to their most credit worthy clients, leaving the rest of us without the ability to get a loan. Now home foreclosures are at an all-time high and Americans have more debt than equity in their homes for the first time since the Federal Reserve began keeping track in 1945. More than 12 percent of American homeowners are behind on their mortgage payments.[3]

The Credit Trap

Buy now, pay later! No money down! Low monthly payments! Interest free for the first year!

How can anyone refuse an offer to buy and not have to pay anything at the time of purchase? It sounds like a great idea. Just pay with your credit card or sign a paper that says you'll pay later. Easy. If it sounds too good to be true, then it probably is.

Sooner or later, when it's time to make payments, the idea no longer looks so great. You start paying. Month after month and year after year you keep paying. You are now trapped in long-term monthly payments. Before you know it or realize it, old debt combines with new debt until you're imprisoned by a mountain of debt. Then, if something unexpected happens—you or a close family member gets sick, hurt, or loses his or her job—the debt can become overwhelming and all-consuming.

Soon you realize that whatever money you bring in goes to paying your bills and you barely have enough money for your fixed living expenses. You are stuck at home with no extra money for entertainment. You avoid answering the phone and spend far too much of your time each day trying to figure out how to pay the next round of bills. Your mind becomes consumed by your debts and creditors' calls. Your work and your relationships at home suffer from the stress.

You feel that you're working to pay someone else. Creditors hound you by telephone and mail until you pay their bill. They will even go so far as calling your neighbors, your workplace, and your relatives. When your doorbell rings, you want to run and hide. They try to make you feel guilty, to shame or belittle you into paying. The most unscrupulous creditors will even threaten to have you thrown in jail for your failure to pay your debt to them.

The worst part is that you're starting to feel constant stress and worry about what will come next. You even start to wonder how you are going to make it through each day. You feel no joy in life. You cannot get a moment's peace. You see no relief in sight.

STOP!

As bad as it seems, you *can* work your way through your debt problems. You have already taken a step in the right direction by reading this book and showing the desire to solve your financial problems. It may not be as easy or as fun as it was to get into debt but it will be rewarding in so many other ways.

Think about how good it will feel to wake up each morning knowing that you are not going to get any surprise creditor calls or visits.

Your debts will no longer haunt you. You can face the world renewed and empowered. Your debts will no longer control your life.

You *will* be free from the burden of debt.

Owing Money Is Not a Crime

Remember one thing: Owing money is not a crime. No matter what anyone says, you cannot be arrested or jailed for not paying a debt unless you willingly disobey a court order, commit fraud, are convicted of willingly refusing to pay income tax, child support, or hide your property to avoid a judgment against you.

Again, you are not a criminal and cannot go to jail for simply owing a debt.

Creditors can sue you, bring you to court, obtain a lien on your property, and sometimes garnish your wages, but do not believe any threats that you can be jailed unless a court has said you must pay. However, even though you won't be arrested, you will still have to resolve your unpaid debts. Not opening your mail, avoiding phone calls, moving, or changing your phone number will not free you from your debts. Although you may have heard that some of these maneuvers worked for other people, you are only delaying the inevitable. The real result in not facing up to your debts is that you will owe more money and will face more determined and angry creditors.

The time has come for you to take back control and take action. The time to deal with your debts is now. The time to stop ignoring the letters and the calls has come. Only you can take the steps to a better and more enjoyable life. The time to act is now.

You have options. One option is the remedy of bankruptcy. Filing for bankruptcy is nothing to be ashamed of—just look at the millions of people and companies that have benefited from bankruptcy. But, at the outset, let us warn you that bankruptcy can be very difficult emotionally. We want you to know that bankruptcy can be a good option, but we urge you to consider other options first.

You Are Not Alone

As lonely as the contemplation of bankruptcy may feel, you should know that countless others have been and are in your position. From 1994 to 2004, more than 10 million Americans filed for bankruptcy. In 2005, more than 2 million people filed for bankruptcy protection. In fact, more people filed for bankruptcy that year than graduated from college, got divorced, or learned they had cancer.[4] In 2009, more than 1.4 million people filed for bankruptcy.[5]

In 2005, 2,039,214 people filed for bankruptcy—nearly as many people who married (2,230,000) and more than three times the number of people who died from heart disease (652,091).

Source: National Center for Health Statistics, www.cdc.gov/nchs.

Chances are that in any group event or meeting that you have attended in the last month, at least one person there has encountered serious financial difficulties and filed or seriously contemplated filing for bankruptcy. As you drive around your neighborhood, everyone may seem content and secure financially from the outside, but rest assured, many are having issues with bills, bill collectors, and trying to stretch their money just like you.

No matter how far you have come in your life or how much you have accomplished, bankruptcy still might be the right way to achieve a fresh start. Presidents of the United States have filed for bankruptcy, including Thomas Jefferson, Abraham Lincoln, William McKinley, and Harry S. Truman. A president who was general of the U.S. Military, Ulysses S. Grant, also filed, and the most famous traitor to the United States, Benedict Arnold, filed for bankruptcy relief.

Even celebrities need bankruptcy. Having the first R&B record to hit diamond status with 10 million copies sold didn't keep MC Hammer from his share of financial problems. At the height of his success, he was worth an estimated $33 million and even had his own Saturday morning cartoon. MC Hammer made millions with his song "U Can't Touch This." Unfortunately for him, his creditors did touch his property with judgments and liens and Hammer filed for bankruptcy in 1996.[6]

Others in the music business have likewise filed for bankruptcy. In 2006, the famous cofounder and CEO of Death Row Records, Marion Hugh Knight, Jr., filed for bankruptcy protection. Death Row Records had launched the careers of Dr. Dre, Snoop Dogg, Tupac, and many others. Six-time Grammy winner Toni Braxton filed for bankruptcy for herself and three of her companies during the peak of her success in 1998. Mick Fleetwood, of Fleetwood Mac fame, has also filed.

Chrysler Motors, General Motors, United Airlines, Lehman Brothers, Texaco, Delta Air Lines, and Conseco are just a few examples of the many corporations that have restructured in bankruptcy.

Bankruptcy has been a place of refuge for child stars, including Gary Coleman, and the parents of child stars such as Jamie Lynn and Britney Spears. In 2005, Mario Lavandeira, known as Perez Hilton, filed for bankruptcy. He has since become the leading source for celebrity gossip and news. Even the girlfriends of super-heroes have needed the protection of bankruptcy—Kim Basinger, who played Vicki Vale in *Batman*, and Margot Kidder, who played Lois Lane in *Superman*, for example.

"Champions of the World" Joe Louis, John L. Sullivan, Iron Mike Tyson, and Leon Spinks needed bankruptcy. Bankruptcy was the place to rest the "Golden Arm" for Johnny Unitas, who filed in 1991. Three-time Olympic Gold Medalist and three-time WNBA MVP Sheryl Swoopes filed in 2004. More recently, NFL's Michael Vick filed for bankruptcy in 2007.

Even financial guru, talk show host, and author Dave Ramsey sought bankruptcy protection early in his career after the millions he made in real estate evaporated. He continues to thrive today because of the changes he made in his life and lessons learned in bankruptcy.

Although we may never have as much money or fame as these people, the lessons are the same for all of us. As you read through this book and decide whether bankruptcy makes sense for you, remember that countless people have filed bankruptcy. They have made the changes in their lives to become stronger both financially and personally and have found more success in the end.

Consider the life of this man: At age 22, he lost his job. At 23, he lost the election for the state legislature. At 25, his general store failed, but he won a seat on the state legislature. At 26, his sweet-heart died and he fell into a deep depression. At 29, his candidacy for Speaker of the state House of Representatives failed. After being reelected twice for the state legislature, he failed to become his party's nominee for Congress. At 37, he won a seat in Congress. Two years later, he stepped down from Congress and was rejected as a federal land officer. Between 45 and 50, he twice fell short in obtaining a seat in the U.S. Senate and did not succeed in his nomination as Vice President of the United States. Plus, throughout these days, he suffered through the ups and downs of a law practice.

Who is this man? He is none other than Abraham Lincoln, arguably the best president in the history of the United States. The rollercoaster ride that was the life of Honest Abe shows that failures, both financial and emotional, can be just minor setbacks on the long journey of life.[7]

Greater Things to Come

We know you will find it difficult to imagine now, but even if you do file bankruptcy, it will have no impact on how far you can go and how much you can accomplish with the rest of your life. Great successes routinely arise out of financial failure.

Mickey Mouse brings a smile to everyone's face, both young and old. Who hasn't daydreamed about enjoying a day at Disney World or Disney Land? Yet the world may have never known a ride on Space Mountain or the high-pitched giggle of Mickey Mouse if Walt Disney himself did not have the chance for a fresh start through bankruptcy. Upon returning from his job as a volunteer ambulance driver in World War I, Walt Disney began an animation company with a friend. But when the company failed to make sufficient income to pay employees, Walt Disney said good-bye to his staff, filed for bankruptcy, and bought a one-way ticket to California. Soon after, with only $40 to his name, Walt and his brother Roy started Disney Brothers Productions, which later became Walt Disney Studios.[8] Without perseverance and the ability to file bankruptcy, Walt Disney may never have been able to fulfill his vision of bringing joy and happiness to countless children and adults around the world.

Eighty percent of Americans admit they are stressed about their personal finances and the economy, according to the American Psychological Association. In fact, most studies find personal finances the leading cause of stress in a person's life and the biggest factor behind divorce.[9] If you are having trouble sleeping at night, always feel angry, or always feel fatigued, too much debt may be your problem. Resolving your financial worries will lift a giant weight off your chest. You will feel better in all aspects of your life.

Millions have come out of bankruptcy relieved that they have shed a huge burden and are now optimistic of the bright days ahead. Bankruptcy is available to everyone—individuals and businesses. Bankruptcy is a part of the American way of life. Our Founding Fathers made sure of this. The U.S. Constitution granted Congress the power to establish bankruptcy laws. When you successfully navigate a bankruptcy or choose another nonbankruptcy solution to your financial debt, your best years are yet to come. Live them debt free!

PART I

A ROAD MAP TO DEBT RELIEF

1

Getting Started

Forewarned, forearmed; to be prepared is half the victory.

—Miguel de Cervantes

There's an old expression that says, "When you're in a hole and trying to get out, stop digging." This means stop doing the things you've been doing that caused you to get in a hole in the first place. If you keep digging, you're only going deeper. Deciding to stop is a turning point where you put down the shovel and decide what to do next.

You have reached a turning point. You have decided to do something about your financial situation. That is why you are reading this book. This is the point where you fight back, the time in your life when you start over. You've had turning points before, even if you didn't recognize them at the time.

Think back to the times in your life when you reached turning points. What about the time you were involved in a personal relationship that didn't work out? Did you stop living your life? No, you left the relationship or it left you. You got over it, moved on, and probably became stronger because of it.

Or think about a time when you decided to move. You reached a turning point. You did something about it. You moved to another place. Maybe it was moving out of the family home or back into the family home, but it was a turning point. You made that decision and went on with your life. The same thing happened when you decided to change jobs, go back to school, or leave school.

You might feel like things haven't gone along exactly as you planned (they rarely do). You haven't reached all of your goals, but you still have hope. When you approach roadblocks in a career, relationship, or even in the place you live, you can quit your job, end the relationship, or move. You can make the changes you need to make in order to fix what is bothering you. You can start fresh with a new job, a new love interest, or a new place to live.

It's time to do the same in your financial life. Getting free from debt gives you the chance to start fresh. You can break free from the bad choices you have made in the past. You can get away from the harassing phone calls and feelings of dread about your debts. You can turn your life and finances around. You *can* fight back.

"I THINK I'M MAKING SOME PROGRESS"

None of us ever planned to get into debt we couldn't manage. We never thought that our bills or debt would become an all-encompassing, dominating part of our lives. And we never, ever thought that we would owe more debt than we'd be able to pay.

But in these times, more and more people are finding themselves with too many bills and not enough income and asking themselves how they're going to make it through the month—or worse, the day. The nagging question is: "How did I get into this situation in the first place?"

Unfortunately, it's easier to get into debt than out of it.

How Debt Happens: An American Story

Rob and Jean are hardworking, middle-class Americans. Rob is a fireman in the city and Jean is a real estate broker who earns commissions based on sales. They have two kids and live modestly. They own a house in a modest suburb where the schools are known for their strong scores.

Rob and Jean bought their home in 2001. After a couple of years, they realized that the value of their house and their equity in it had grown substantially. On top of this increased equity, interest rates had dropped. They heard from friends that they could refinance their mortgage, pay off their cars and credit card bills, but still pay less for their mortgage every month than they were paying. They called a mortgage broker who confirmed it was true.

The mortgage broker explained that with a lower interest rate, Rob and Jean could use the increased equity in their home to take on more debt and a bigger mortgage while paying the same or lower monthly payments. Because the value of the house would continue to rise, they could then refinance again in the future to cover any new debts.

Rob and Jean couldn't believe their luck. They refinanced. They paid off their credit card debts and one of their cars, bought the season tickets Rob always wanted (lower section), and even upgraded their kitchen with stainless-steel appliances and granite countertops. The best part was that their monthly payments would be considerably lower for the next three years.

Rob and Jean then became a little looser in their spending. The kids' clothes came from the mall, not just the discount chains. Dinners and nights out became more frequent. Soon the credit card balances began to grow again. They didn't worry because they figured they could just refinance again as the mortgage broker represented.

But then Jean's sales slowed throughout 2008. Worse still, the value of their house had not appreciated like it had in the past. No bank would accept their application to refinance. Then the rate on their three-year adjustable rate mortgage increased dramatically. Now, more money than they could afford had to go to the mortgage each month. They had to start picking which bills they could afford to pay and which bills they would try to pay next month.

Soon the calls started coming. The mailbox was filled with stacks of letters that neither of them wanted to open. Rob and Jean felt tension between them like never before. Even the kids began to worry. The worst part was the persistent and harassing phone calls and visitors at all times of the day, any day of the week.

They felt depressed and inadequate because they were unable to provide for their family. They both felt that they were the subject of whispers wherever they went.

For Rob and Jean, the downturn of the economy and the housing market and the decline in Jean's commissions caused them to fall behind in paying their debts. For others, it could be job loss, sickness, medical emergency, the need to care for a family member, years of spending too much, or simply the slowdown in a business or the economy overall. While the underlying reasons may differ, the results are the same. The bills aren't getting paid on time.

Getting Started on the Road

Being behind on the bills should not strip you of your dignity. There are many things you can do to take the pressure off and to restore your peace of mind.

Stop the Harassment

The first thing you need to do is to stop all the annoying creditor calls and other harassments. No one can get ahead when the phone keeps ringing about his or her debts. It doesn't matter how strong a person you are. You cannot live your life under the constant anxiety that a bill collector is calling you, your work, or even your neighbors. You have to make the calls and letters stop.

You, by yourself, can make these harassing calls stop. You don't need to hire a company to help (they can't do anything you can't do yourself). You do it by writing a simple letter. We cover how to write that letter and other rights you have in Chapter 3.

Know Your Options

Stopping the harassment is the first step. The next step is dealing with the underlying problem of the debt that the collectors called about. You have many options to get out of debt and many resources to assist you in evaluating what options are best for you.

Sometimes, you will be able to handle one debt in one way but your other debts require a different set of strategies. Always remember that if one way is not working, you can always try another way. Two things always to keep in mind when dealing with your debts: Be flexible and be ready for anything. You may use one or more methods to conquer your debts. The pros and cons of several options are shown in Table 1.1.

Table 1.1   Options for Getting Out of Debt

Option	Pros	Cons
Negotiate (Deal with the Creditors on Your Own)	Inexpensive You control the process, for better or worse You can access government programs	Time consuming Not very effective due to unfamiliarity with law and regulations Frustrating Uneven playing field
Get Debt Counseling	Experience dealing with creditors Payment plans within your budget Works out debts	Many are scams May end up in worse shape than when you began Can be costly Frequent defaults
Adopt a Debt Management Plan	Payment plans are proposed Consolidates debt Can lower interest rates	Many are scams May end up in worse shape than when you began Can be costly Damages credit Long-term commitment

(Continued)

Table 1.1 *Continued*

Hire an Attorney	Experience	Long process
	Effective due to knowledge of laws	Expensive (unless done on retainer)
	Shows you're serious	May pick a bad or inefficient attorney
	Creditors want to avoid hassle of lawsuits	
Obtain Legal Assistance (Legal Aid)	May be free if you qualify	Long process
	Effective due to knowledge of laws	Too many cases, not enough staff/funding
	Shows you're serious	Hard to qualify
	Creditors want to avoid hassle of lawsuits	
Contact a Government Agency	Knowledgeable	Bureaucratic red tape
	Free advice	May not take an individual case
	Can deal with all debts, such as house, car, credit cards, etc.	Busy with other cases
File for Bankruptcy	One stop for most debts	Potential loss of some assets
	Liberating	Emotional and financial expense
	Fresh start	Needs to be done properly or results may be harsh
	Keep certain assets	

Now that you know there are many options available for debt relief, it's time to determine which one is right for *you*. The next section will guide you through evaluating your financial situation and determining if bankruptcy will help.

Evaluate Your Situation: Do You Need to File for Bankruptcy?

Just as the U.S. Department of Homeland Security has levels of security threats, we've created levels to assess your financial situation and determine how best to handle your debt problems and whether bankruptcy is your best option.

Two terms you should know for this evaluation are *secured debt* and *unsecured debt*. Secured debt means a lender has security so that the lender can take certain property if you stop paying your bills. Examples include mortgages (your house is at risk) and car loans (your car is at risk). Unsecured debt, on the other hand, does not come with a security interest and no property is involved. Examples include credit cards and medical bills.

Green Level: No Need for Bankruptcy

The green level is where we all strive to be. At this level, you have minimal credit card debts and other unsecured debts and manageable secured debts. Your income exceeds your expenses. You are not worried about your bills, tuitions, and mortgage payments. Your job is secure and you have sufficient savings and assets to get through any crisis. Working with the ideas in this book will help you reach the green level.

You are in the green level if you:

- Pay all your bills on time.
- Have assets, including health coverage, to carry you through any crisis.
- Have secure and steady employment for the foreseeable future.
- Have no balance or you're paying off the balances on your credit cards monthly.
- Save money at the end of each month.

Blue Level: You Might Need to Consider Financial Changes

At the blue level, you start cutting back on expenses and shifting priorities. Bankruptcy is not on your radar but your finances could use some changes. Your emphasis should be on budgeting and watching your spending (see Chapters 4 and 5).

You are in the blue level if you:

- Fear losing your job.
- Can't pay off the total monthly balance on your credit cards.
- Have increasing debts and you're dipping into your assets to meet your expenses.
- Have both unsecured and secured debts.
- Do not save money each month.

Yellow Level: Consider Bankruptcy

At the yellow level, you should start to consider strategies involving negotiating with your creditors to restructure your personal finances and reduce your debt. You must seriously start to work on improving your situation. If you don't work on improving it, your situation will only get worse and may lead to the necessity of filing bankruptcy. You should start working through the next several chapters to reduce your debt and change your expenses.

You are in the yellow level if you:

- Fall behind in some payments of secured and unsecured debts.
- Only pay some bills each month and wait to pay others.
- Get calls from collection agencies.
- Have little or no savings and your assets have diminished in value.
- Have been out of work for one month or more.
- Do not have health insurance.

Orange Level: Strongly Consider Bankruptcy

If you are at the orange level, you have to get very serious about your debts, house, cars, credit cards, and all other expenses. You are not always making even the minimum payments on your secured and unsecured debts. Bankruptcy is an option you should strongly consider. But first, work through the alternatives and see if you can solve these issues without bankruptcy (see Chapters 7 through 12).

You are in the orange level if you:

- Are more than 60 days behind on paying more than one bill.
- Use new credit cards to pay the minimums on other credit cards.
- Have pending lawsuits against you.
- Have total debt (excluding car and home) that can't be paid off in full over three to five years.
- Have high medical bills not covered by insurance.
- Owe taxes you can't pay.
- Have been out of work more than three months.

Red Level: File for Bankruptcy Immediately

Consider filing for bankruptcy immediately if much of the orange level and any of the points in the red level apply to you. The time for negotiation has passed. You should file bankruptcy as soon as possible.

You are in the red level if your:

- Unsecured and secured debts can't be paid.
- Wages have been garnished.
- Bank account has been subject of a court order of attachment.
- Car has been repossessed (or will be within days).
- Home is set for a foreclosure sale.
- Unemployment benefits are ending or you have no income.

If this is your situation, skip to the bankruptcy chapters (Chapters 13 through 20). You could improve your situation and your life tremendously by filing for bankruptcy as soon as possible.

It Can Get Better

What you are going through now—the uncertainty and fear—is as bad as it will get for you. If you have taken steps to stop the calls, letters, and other harassments, you have already turned a corner to getting your life back. You've stopped digging and started to figure out how you are going to climb out of the hole. You are past the worst of it. Whether you find yourself in the blue level, the red level, or somewhere in between, the rest of the book will lead you, step-by-step, to a new start. You will again be in control.

Points to Remember

- Recognize your financial trouble.
- Know you have to make changes.
- Develop a strategy for turning your personal finances around.
- Study your options for dealing with your debts, and remember that bankruptcy is just one of those options.
- Take the time to evaluate your financial situation and your level of need for bankruptcy.

CHAPTER

Negotiating Your Way Out of Debt

If you want peace, prepare for war.
—Flavius Vegetius Renatus, circa 375 A.D.

Creditors talk to you for only one reason: They want your money. They will stop at nothing until they are sure they won't get any money from you or until you stop them.

You are the only person who will look out for your interests. You may be able to solve all your issues through negotiations so we encourage you to give it a try. Through negotiations, you may be able to improve your financial condition.

There's a little-known secret in the credit industry: Creditors may accept a lesser payment than what they are owed, through negotiations. The trick is knowing when and how to offer it.

Learn from Donald Trump

Donald Trump negotiates; that's what he does. The Donald is a billionaire, real estate mogul extraordinaire, and host of the television show *The Apprentice*. Before he reached the height of the wealth and fame he now enjoys, Donald Trump had his share of financial problems.

During the 1980s, Donald Trump continually bought buildings, yachts, hotels, and casinos and even owned his own airline. The recession of the early 1990s, however, hit him very hard. At its worst, his companies reportedly carried debts of $11.4 billion. He was forced to place some of his casinos and other businesses in bankruptcy. And because he had personally guaranteed $1.3 billion of his companies' debt, Donald Trump was on the verge of his own personal bankruptcy. He once said this: "You can't give up. You are going to have times when you feel there's no light at the end of the tunnel. I had times like that and I had a choice: I could sit in the corner with my thumb in my mouth, or I could fight. My advice to you is: Punch like hell and don't take no for an answer." (*St. Petersburg Times*, May 7, 1996)

Donald Trump did not hide. He did not run from his creditors. He did not sit back and hope things got better. No, he fought back. He used all his negotiation and business skills to resolve hundreds of millions of dollars of debt. He didn't take "no" for an answer. He worked hard to talk to the right people and get to the decision makers. He remained flexible, offering a little here, taking a little away there. He was always alert to his actions and knew where he wanted to go. He made people at the 99 banks he owed money to his allies so that he could work out his issues with them. He made sure the creditors realized they were getting the best offers that he could make at that time.

Donald Trump has said that those lean times helped him learn that he could handle pressure. Donald Trump is now the 278th richest man in the world, with a net worth estimated by *Forbes Magazine* to be $2.6 billion. And there is something that Donald Trump didn't tell you. You'll always notice he has a little twinkle in his eyes. Donald Trump did not approach his negotiations with fear, even though it seemed the whole world was collapsing around him. He made his negotiations a competitive experience.

You're probably thinking that of course Donald Trump could negotiate out of his personal debt. He's a famous millionaire. Banks and creditors listen to him. You're right. He does have the money and the status. But also think about how much more debt he had (millions and millions). Plus, you can picture yourself as a mini Donald Trump. You can still use the same techniques and ideas he used. Banks and creditors will listen to you if you offer something they don't think they'll get easily on their own or that they could lose completely if you file for bankruptcy.

Negotiating and not taking no for an answer is your first move to get out of debt. If you make the calls and talk to the right people, you may find your financial problems will diminish simply by making an offer that the creditors won't want to refuse.

Keep in mind that you have to be flexible and straightforward in your dealings. But you must also approach the negotiations with no fear. Work your way to financial health. Practice and hone your negotiation skills. Don't get intimidated, get out of debt.

20 Keys to Successful Negotiations

Here are 20 keys to successful negotiations. These keys will assist you in gaining level ground with the professional debt collectors. The road out of debt begins with negotiations backed by these negotiation tips and strategies.

Key #1: Get Prepared: The More You Know, the Better

Creditors do not like dealing with knowledgeable consumers. The more you know about your debt, your financial position, and your rights, the better negotiating position you will have. Create a budget (we walk you through one in Chapter 4). Become familiar with your rights under the Fair Debt Collection Practices Act (see Chapter 3). Understand your loan terms. This is particularly important when you negotiate your mortgage (as we discuss later).

The more you know about your situation and the debts you are calling about, the more effective the phone call will be. Most important, get your bills, letters, records, and all other information about your finances organized. Keep thorough records!

Key #2: Be on Guard When Dealing with Creditors

Bottom line: Credit companies are in the business of making money. They communicate with you in order to get your money, not your friendship. You want to keep your money. You are at odds. No matter what they say, they do not want to help you unless they are helping themselves even more.

Remember, though, to remain friendly but serious. In fact, there's no harm in letting them think they are becoming your friend in order to get what *you* want as long as you always bear in mind that the person on the other end of the phone has one goal: to get your money. If you didn't owe them something, they wouldn't be talking to you.

Key #3: Remember That No Two Creditors Are the Same

All creditors and collection agencies are different. Each has different strategies, methods, and tipping points. What works for one person will not necessarily work for the next person. Persistent effort is the key. Every creditor has particular requirements and limits on how much it will negotiate. It is important for you to push those limits.

Key #4: Communicate

All of us naturally try to avoid any contact with bill collectors and creditors. We don't open our mail and don't answer the phone unless we know the sender or incoming number. After all, who wants to be reminded about what they owe? Unfortunately, the worst thing we can do is run away from all contact. Instead of avoiding them, get rid of them.

Key #5: Make Collectors Stop Calling and Writing

Negotiations should be on your terms. You will learn about the Fair Debt Collection Practices Act in Chapter 3. You will stop the calls and letters so you can negotiate on your terms (as described in Chapter 3). If the creditor continues to contact you, contact the attorney general of your state and consider hiring a lawyer who will take your case on a contingency basis. Chapter 3 includes sample letters you can use to stop creditors' calls. The attorney general of your state has a consumer protection department to deal with creditors who ignore your rights.

Key #6: Make Offers to Your Creditors

Your creditors will respond to reasonable offers if they think your offer is their best chance at recovering some of the debt. They are especially willing if the offer is close to their projected return on the debt. If creditors believe that you are conscientious about your debt and intend to repay, they will work with you. You may have to talk to a supervisor, or the supervisor's supervisor. Never be afraid

Copyright © 2010 Corne Cartoons/Enroc Illustrations Co., www.enroc.com and www
.corne.com/ar.

about asking to talk to someone else. See Chapter 3 for example
letters offering settlements.

Key #7: Remain in Control

When dealing with creditors, you are in control. You have something
they want: your money. You may owe it to them but they still have to
get it from you. They also want to put forth as little effort as possible
to get the money from you. Make an offer. If you don't get what you
want, let some time pass. Time is your friend in your negotiations.
Negotiate at the end of the month. Creditors have deadlines, quotas,
and bonuses that depend on monthly collections. They are more willing
to settle at the end of the month to meet those deadlines and quotas.

   The more difficult you make it seem that it will be for them to
get the money from you, the more willing your creditors will be
to renegotiate and reduce interest rate or payments.

Key #8: Be Patient and Persistent

Keep your composure when talking with creditors or collection agencies. Call customer service and explain your situation. If you get nowhere, call back. See if the next person will be more receptive. Ask for the supervisor or the supervisor's supervisor if you must. Customer service will discourage you and say the supervisor won't offer anything different. Still, sometimes supervisors do. You have to find out for yourself.

Wait for the supervisor. Credit collection companies hope that you hang up. If you make no progress with the supervisor, ask for another supervisor or ask for the legal department. The squeaky wheel gets the grease.

Key #9: Have No Fear

Do not be intimidated by anyone you talk to about your debts. Remember, you are in charge. You cannot go to jail for simply not paying a debt. Even if creditors or collection agencies say they are going to sue, they probably don't want to pay lawyers and court costs. They want money coming in and they don't like it going out. So they rarely sue. Some less reputable won't want a judge to hear about their collection practices and they don't want a judge interfering.

If the creditors do sue, not much changes. It's still an issue of money (which you know). If you are sued, contest the case. You can do this without a lawyer, although it is always preferable to have a lawyer in any civil case because a lawyer will know the intricacies and local rules and customs that can greatly impact a case. And even after you are sued, you still can negotiate a settlement. Sometimes, you can go before a judge and tell her or him that you offered money to settle it and the judge may facilitate. All we are telling you here is if you are sued, which is unlikely, it does not change anything too much.

If they sue, so what? The worst that will happen is that you'll still owe them money. If the creditors try and repossess your property, you have an ace in your pocket that stops them in their tracks: bankruptcy. Even if they get a court judgment saying you owe the money, bankruptcy may protect you.

Key #10: Threaten to File for Bankruptcy

The threat of bankruptcy is a powerful weapon. The supervisor and legal department of a loan collection agency do not want to hear the word *bankruptcy*. So, we suggest you say the following: "Without a sharp reduction in my rate so I can afford to pay, I will have to consider bankruptcy." You likely need at least a 50 percent reduction in your interest rate if your rate is over 10 percent.

The debt collectors and creditors do not want you to file bankruptcy. Make them aware that you are teetering on the edge of bankruptcy and that this is their last chance before you file. They likely will listen because once you file, they may get nothing.

Be careful after using this threat. Do not take on new debt after this threat because a credit company could argue that you took on debt that you didn't plan on paying back, which might have adverse consequences if you file for bankruptcy.

Key #11: Call Once, Then Use Certified Mail

It's best not to talk to a collection agency by phone except for your initial contact. Restrict your communications to certified mail.

Get the creditor's address when you make this call—before you talk about anything else. Communicating via certified mail costs more, but you will have the necessary signatures and receipts for your records. You may need them later on. Keep good records and copies of all correspondence. Keep a log of every call and response.

Key #12: Get It in Writing

When a creditor makes you an offer, get it in writing before you pay anything. Agree to a creditor's terms only if they send you the modifications in writing, whether by e-mail or U.S. Postal Service. If you don't get it in writing, don't be surprised if the creditor has no memory of the changes or the agreements that you made. They conveniently forget because forgetting gets them more of your money.

Creditors will recite facts that best suit them and keep records of those. You want proof that what you have said is correct.

Key #13: Only Agree to Terms You Can Afford

Even if they sound terrific, if you can't afford the new terms and payments, don't take them. You need better terms. Or you need a different solution. You have to remain in your budget, otherwise you will have gained nothing. You'll be facing the same problem a few months down the road.

Key #14: Never Agree to Pay a Debt You Don't Owe

Never agree to pay a debt that you don't think you owe. If you do, you may have created a new debt that you didn't owe before. Make the creditor prove to you, in writing, that you owe it. Immediately send a Validate and Cease Letter (discussed in Chapter 3). Don't do any more negotiation until it is proven in writing that the debt is truly owed and it is not barred by the statute of limitations (a "zombie debt").

Key #15: Use Time to Your Advantage

Debt loses value over time. In addition, after a certain period of time (when the statute of limitations expires), the debt no longer exists. The more time that passes, the more incentive a creditor has to settle and the better your chances are for getting a good deal. Take your time in negotiation so that your creditor starts to worry. Never take the first settlement offer. If they've made one, they are willing to negotiate. Creditors are more willing to deal and compromise at the end of the month.

Key #16: Uncover Your Creditor's Bottom Line

Many creditors sell their debts to debt collection companies. Often the debt collectors are the people calling you. These debt collection companies buy millions of dollars worth of debts for pennies on the dollar. They will normally spend between $0.02 and $0.08 for each $1.00 of debt. That means if your balance is $1,000, a debt collector spent between $20.00 and $80.00 for the right to collect that debt from you.

> Debt collection companies buy millions of dollars worth of debts for pennies on the dollar. They will normally spend between $0.02 to $0.08 for each $1.00 of debt.

Do your best to uncover your creditor's bottom line, such as the amount they bought your debt for or the amount they would sell your debt to another company for. You should offer to pay back a little more than the bottom line and only a percentage of your debt, as much as you can afford. Don't be surprised to find that collectors and creditors accept 50 to 70 percent of the original debt as settlement.

Key #17: Don't Let Legal Jargon Trip You Up

You are dealing with people who collect debts every day for their job. They will try to confuse you and get you to agree to things you cannot afford or do not want. They may use legal terms and/or discuss legal actions with you that you do not understand. Listen very carefully and ask them to explain what they've said if you don't understand. Don't be embarrassed!

Far too many people did not understand the financial instruments that caused the current financial crisis but they invested anyway because they were too embarrassed to ask for explanations. The results have been catastrophic for them and the economy as a whole. Don't be afraid to have someone explain something to you. If you don't understand, ask again. Very often you'll find that hidden behind a big word is a simple concept. And remember, never agree to anything unless it is in writing and you understand it fully.

Key #18: Be Honest in Your Dealings

Don't lie about your intentions to pay a creditor, your income, or other debts. If you lie, the creditor will have an upper hand in any court proceeding, including bankruptcy court, and will accuse you of fraud. Never give a creditor, or anyone else, that power over your finances. Never allow a creditor to gain access to your checking account and never give your Social Security number to a bill collector. You should send a check or money order. Write on the check that cashing this check equals payment in full of the debt you owe.

Never write a check that you can't cover, even if the creditor says they won't cash it until you tell them. Even if they promise you that they will hold the check, they could cash it right away and cause you overdraft fees and other penalties. Wait until you have the money in an account before you write any checks.

Key #19: Never Assume Another Person's Debt

Don't ever agree in any negotiations to assume the debt of another person or make another person responsible for your debt.

The creditor is looking for another source. You can negotiate on behalf of another person but you must never agree to assume that person's debt.

Remember, when you cosign, you're on the line. If that person you are cosigning for doesn't pay, you're on the hook. The creditor will look to you for payment. For the same reason, don't let any of your family members or close friends put their necks on the line for you when you are having trouble paying.

Key #20: Use Honey, Not Vinegar

Like the old expression "you catch more flies with honey than vinegar," you'll get further in your negotiations if you can offer something the creditor wants. It doesn't have to be much but if you can make the creditor think that they are getting something that they would not get otherwise, you are going to be successful in your negotiations.

Points to Remember

- Attempt to negotiate a consensual settlement of your debts with your creditors or their debt collectors.
- Disclose your assets and liabilities to your creditors, and advise creditors that you will have to file a bankruptcy petition if an agreement is not reached.
- Offer a one-time, lump-sum payment toward your debt or payment plan based on your ability to pay in exchange for forgiveness of debt.
- Communicate with your creditors and their debt collectors only in writing and keep copies of all letters organized!

CHAPTER

Fighting Back

There is not a person alive who isn't going to have some awfully
bad days in their lives. . . . What are you going to do? Most people
just lie down and quit. Well, I want my people to fight back.
　　　　　　　—Paul "Bear" Bryant, former University of
　　　　　　　　　　　　　　Alabama football coach

Y ou've read this far because you want to fight back. This chapter gives you the first step to do just that.

Make no mistake about it: Creditors do not want to be your
friends. They won't even tell you their last name. If they do, expect
to hear Jones or Smith. Almost all are probably using pseudonyms.
Ask yourself, do you want to disclose personal information to a person who has to give you a fake name? The same person rarely calls
you more than once.

Some creditors are nice. Some creditors are cordial. Some creditors are downright nasty. Don't be fooled if they act nice, friendly,
sympathetic, or understanding. No matter how they act toward you,
creditors have one objective when they call: They want your money.
They will try anything to reach that goal. Don't ever let creditors
make you feel bad about yourself.

Most creditors hide their identities by using pseudonyms. They have one objective when they call: They want to collect your money.

Keep in mind, the debt collectors that call deal with debt collection as their job. They spend their working hours trying to collect debts. Most earn commissions on how much debt they collect. Many debt collectors thoroughly enjoy the business they are in—some consider it "one of the sexiest, one of the most financially lucrative businesses you can get into." They know all the tricks so you won't be able to outwit them. You won't have an excuse that they have not heard a thousand times before. When you deal with them, you are stepping into the ring with a professional. But if you keep that in mind and deal with them honestly, forthrightly, and without fear, you'll come out on top.

Some may try to intimidate or humiliate you into paying. The bad news is that some creditors know no limitation to the level of harassment they will engage in. The good news is that you do not have to take any of it. A "cease" letter to a bill collector requires them to stop calling you. You never should be put in the position that Nina faced.

Nina: An American Tragedy

Nina[1] had a long history of mental illness. She also had a penchant for manic shopping sprees. Nina opened three credit card accounts in her own and her husband's name. She hid these accounts from her husband, Don, by opening a post office box to receive the cards and the correspondences. She used the cards to purchase a number of items, from gas to exotic cats.

After finding a letter that was sent to the house rather than the post office box, Don confronted Nina about the credit cards. Two days after the confrontation, Nina attempted to kill herself. Nina was hospitalized and then returned home under a psychiatrist's care. Don promptly canceled all the cards and informed each bank, in writing, that the cards had been fraudulently obtained in his name.

Throughout this time, debt collectors working for a credit card company accused Nina of committing credit card fraud and threatened her with jail time. The pressure from the debt collectors caused her to feel like she was on the verge of a nervous breakdown, with shakes and numbness throughout her body. In addition to their threats to Nina, the debt collectors threatened Don with lies such as:

- The district attorney's office said he was legally liable for his wife's charge card.
- They had filed a report with the county sheriff's office.
- Because Don was aware of his wife's problem, he "should keep a better eye on her" and "keep her away from the Internet."

After four months of threats and harassments, Nina purchased a handgun and killed herself. She wrote to Don that she could not "take this kind of pressure and humiliation any longer." According to Nina's treating psychiatrist, her fear of incarceration was the primary reason that led to her suicide. He stated that in his professional opinion, the statements of the credit card debt collectors were the "significant precipitating factor" in her suicide. The Sixth Circuit Court of Appeals found the credit card company's behavior to be "outrageous" within the meaning of Tennessee common law, even though there was no question that Nina owed the debt.

You *Can* Fight Back

Never allow creditors to drive you to the state that Nina reached. You owe money. That is it. You are still a good person. You are not going to jail over any of your debts just because you simply owe the money. Do not believe anyone who tells you differently.

You know you owe and you don't need to be reminded constantly by creditors. It's time to make them stop and it's easier than you think. You just need to know what to do and what to say.

The creditors and bill collectors play on a very uneven playing field. They collect debts every day, all day. They know all the tricks and pressure points of thousands of people just like you. You've had very little experience, if any, dealing with creditors.

Remember, you don't have to talk to anyone who calls. Hang up. If they call back, hang up again. Some are just vultures who will do anything to get you to pay, even if you no longer owe the money. But you have the law on your side. You have rights and powers that no creditor wants you to know. You will learn them in this chapter.

The tactics used against Nina and her husband are business as usual for some debt collectors. Disreputable debt collectors have been making illegal and immoral threats for years. Some collectors are basically phone thugs. They'll call and tell you:

"Don't be surprised to find the sheriff knocking on your door."

"You will be thrown in jail if you don't pay."

"What will your neighbors think?"

"Wait until your boss finds out."

All of these statements, and many more, are not just immoral; they are illegal. Bill collectors cannot threaten dire circumstances for you not paying. They cannot call your neighbors except to find out your location or your work, and they cannot call before 8 A.M. or after 9 P.M.

Worse still, bill collectors may never call you to collect debts that you never owed or that have expired. Once a debt is incurred, the statute of limitations is the amount of time a creditor has to try and collect on that debt. The statute of limitations in most states is six years; be sure to check on your state's statute.

Creditors will call you names, make up "facts," and do anything else to beat you up so that you'll send them your money. And they are going to keep doing these things until you stop them. It's time to fight back.

The Law Is on Your Side

You have powerful rights under the Fair Debt Collection Practices Act (FDCPA). Bill collectors routinely violate the FDCPA when they contact people. They rely on people not knowing their rights. But the FDCPA ensures that we all have debts collected from us in a civil manner and that we are protected from abusive debt collectors.

Please note: The FDCPA applies to the companies that buy the rights to collect your debts from your original creditor and it does not apply to the creditor that originally gave you your loan. Congress has excluded original creditors from the restrictions of the FDCPA. Fortunately, your state's attorney general provides the same protection as the FDCPA against your original creditors, but these protections are under state law. Deal with your original creditors

ANOTHER VIOLATION OF FDCPA

in the same way, but if they violate your rights, you will use your state laws to handle them.

Here's what you need to remember when dealing with bill collectors (we'll explain more later):

1. Ask them to stop (write a letter).
2. Write down any violations.
3. File a complaint with the attorney general's office.
4. Hire a lawyer and then sue.

Ask Them to Stop

You know what you owe and you don't need to be reminded every day, and especially not several times a day. In fact, you know you owe, so you don't need to be reminded at all. Guess what? A simple letter may do the trick. You can make the bill collectors stop. Remember, the law is on your side.

How? Write a letter. It's that simple. Don't ever pay anyone who promises to make creditors stop calling you because they cannot do anything more than what you can do for yourself.

Collection agencies cannot contact you after you have written them requesting that they stop except to advise you that they will not contact you again, notify you that they may take certain steps they normally take under these circumstances (such as filing a debt collection lawsuit or reporting your debt to the credit reporting agencies), or tell you that they are indeed taking such steps. Once you have written your Cease Letter, federal law is on your side.

We provide five letters that match different circumstances; choose the one that best suits your needs and send it to your creditor (see the following Example: Write a Letter to Your Creditor).

- *Lump sum payoff letter.* Use this letter if you want to pay off your debt with a lump sum payment at a lesser value than what you owe. Cash on the barrelhead means immediate cash to the creditor. It is a rare creditor that can refuse a decent cash offer. Offer a one-time, lump sum payment. Many creditors cannot refuse when money is offered in a large sum. Start low. Make sure that you can afford what you offer. Make the offer in writing.
- *Changed circumstances, lower payments letter.* Send the second letter if something has happened in your life (e.g., job loss, medical emergency) and you have some means to pay, but you want to lower your payments.
- *Freeze payments letter.* Use this letter if you want to freeze payments while you recover from an unfortunate event in your life but you still plan to pay once you recover from the bad happening event.
- *Cease and validate letter.* These letters must be sent within 30 days of the creditor's initial contact with you to make the creditor legally bound to validate. After 30 days, the debt collector is no longer legally compelled to produce verification of the debt under this provision of the FDCPA. But you should still demand validation in writing. If the creditor is reputable, they will validate the debt. If they are not, you know you are dealing with a sleazy collector.

If the creditor has filed a court action against you and you did not show up to court or lost in court, you should be prepared to file for bankruptcy (Orange Level as mentioned in Chapter 1). The creditor probably got a judgment against you that allows them to collect the debt from your property or your wages even if it was a bad debt from the start. You may need to file bankruptcy to stop their actions and make them prove the debt. You should also consider contacting a lawyer to help you straighten out the debt outside of bankruptcy.

Example: Write a Letter to Your Creditor

Lump Sum Payoff Letter

Dear Sir or Madam:

As of my last monthly statement, I owe [$___] on my Account #___. Changes in my life [provide explanation if you choose] have made it impossible for me to continue to make monthly payments, and I will not be able to pay off my debt to you in full. Please agree to accept $___ as a one-time, lump sum payment in full satisfaction of my debt. Please freeze interest and any other charges. If you do not accept, I may have to file bankruptcy.

Please reply to me in writing on whether you accept my offer.

Changed Circumstances, Lower Payments Letter

Dear Sir or Madam:

Since making the previous payment agreement my circumstances have changed. I cannot now afford the agreed monthly payments because [explain your unique circumstance – lost job, separation, divorce, sickness]. I only have $___ a month available for my creditors. [Enclose your budget if you can.] I have worked out offers with other creditors and am waiting for responses to accept the reduced amounts. Because of my circumstances, please agree to accept $___ a month. If you are adding interest, I would appreciate it if you would freeze these charges. If you do not accept, I may have to file bankruptcy.

If my circumstances change, I will contact you again.

Thank you for your help. Please reply to me in writing on whether you accept my offer. I look forward to hearing from you as soon as possible.

(Continued)

Freeze Payments Letter

Dear Sir or Madam:

I can no longer make the agreed monthly payments to you because [state reason]. My budget no longer allows me to continue to make payments. Please agree to suspend payments for six months or accept a token payment of $1.00 for the next six months. Please freeze interest and any other charges as well for the same six-month period. If you do not accept, I may have to file bankruptcy.

Cease Letter

Dear Sir or Madam:

Please cease all communications with me except the limited correspondences provided under the Fair Debt Collection Practices Act (FDCPA).

According to the FDCPA, 15 USC 1692c, Section 805(c) entitled "Ceasing Communications" and the laws of [insert your state], you must cease all communication with me after I write to you stating that I no longer wish to communicate with you. Therefore, immediately cease *all* communications with me. Do not call or write to me. Do not call my home, my work, my cell phone, or any other location.

Please be advised that I am well aware of my rights under state law and the FDCPA. Any future contact by you or your company violates the law.

Be advised that I am keeping complete records of all correspondence from you and your company. I will contact my state's attorney general and pursue legal action should contact continue.

Validate and Cease Letter

If you don't believe you owe the debt or you think it is an old debt that has expired (exceeds the statute of limitations), send a letter like this by certified mail:

Dear Sir or Madam:

This letter is sent in response to a [choose one: phone call [letter] I received from you on [insert the date of the phone call or letter]]. Pursuant to my rights under the Fair Debt Collection Practices Act (FDCPA) and the laws of [insert your state], I am requesting that you validate this debt and the laws of evidence that I have a legal obligation to pay you. In particular, I demand that at a minimum you provide the documentation of the amount you assert I owe, the date the debt was originally incurred, the name and address of the original creditor, payment history, the assignment to you of the debt, and your license to collect debts in my state.

In addition, after providing me with the requested information, please cease all communication with me except the limited correspondences provided under the FDCPA.

According to the FDCPA, 15 USC 1692c, Section 805(c) entitled "Ceasing Communications" and the laws of [insert your state], you must cease all communication with me after I write to you stating that I no longer wish to communicate with you. Therefore, immediately cease *all* communications with me. Do not call me. Do not call my home, my work, my cell phone, or any other location. Do not write to me.

You are hereby notified that if you do not comply with this request, I will immediately file a complaint and pursue such other legal remedies as I see fit.

For these and other letters, see www.debt-n-credit-letters.com and www.fair-debt-collection.com/disputing-debt-collections.html.

If your offer is accepted, write back to that creditor to memorialize the deal. Then, use your agreement with this creditor as additional ammunition to ask other creditors to waive other fees.

If creditors refuse your offer of compromise, do not give up. If you wrote the Lump Sum Payoff Letter, pay the amount you stated in the letter as goodwill (or a portion of the lump sum payment). Ask the creditor to reconsider your offer by letter, and mention that other creditors have agreed to reduce payments.

Send these letters by certified mail and keep a copy of both the certified-mail receipt and the letter. Start a file for each creditor. Keep organized.

Write Down Any Violations

If creditors continue to call after they have received your Cease Letter or Validate and Cease Letter they are breaking the law. You should keep a record and write down every time they call. Put these call records in the same place you are keeping the certified-mail receipt of the letter you sent. Contact their trade organizations or your state's attorney general to report creditors that act irresponsibly.

Even if you don't write a cease letter, you still have rights that no collection agent can violate (but many do). Following is a list of violations under the FDCPA.

Communication Violations

When communicating with you, your rights have been violated if the collector:

- Gives you a false impression of the type, amount, or legal status of your debt (such as saying you will be arrested).
- Says they are calling from an attorney's office, a credit reporting agency, or that they are affiliated with the federal or state government when they are not. Some will also claim to have sent official court or government documents.
- Threatens legal action they do not plan to bring.
- Attempts to embarrass you.
- Calls after 9:00 P.M. or before 8:00 A.M.
- Calls or visits you at work when he or she knows it's inconvenient for you or that your employer doesn't allow such calls or visits.
- Continues to talk to you once you've said you have a lawyer.
- Continues to contact you after you have sent a letter disputing the debt or requesting that all communication cease.
- Contacts your family or friends and discusses or publicizes the alleged debt or threatens to collect from them.

Collection Violations

When trying to collect the debt, your rights have been violated if the collector:

- Attempts to collect more money than is allowed under the original contract.
- Asks for, accepts, deposits, or threatens to deposit a postdated check.
- Causes you to incur financial charges, such as the cost of accepting collect calls or travel expenses.
- Publicizes the debt by placing derogatory symbols or words on the outside of an envelope or uses a postcard.
- Unlawfully repossesses, levies, or disables any of your personal property.

- Attempts to collect on an old debt (beyond the statute of limitations).
- Acts in any other unfair or outrageous way.

Harassment Violations

Your rights have been violated if the collector harasses you by:

- Using or threatening to use violence or some other criminal means to collect the debt.
- Using obscene, profane, or other abusive language.
- Calling endlessly or engaging you in conversations repeatedly.
- Calling without properly identifying himself or herself.
- Publishing a "dead beat list" of consumers who supposedly do not pay their debts.
- Engaging in any other conduct that is meant to or results in harassment, oppression, or abuse.

The FDCPA applies to your consumer debts (not debt from a business) and protects you chiefly against third-party debt collectors (not the original creditor). State laws that are usually very similar to the FDCPA likely protect you from the original creditor if the original creditor violates your rights.

If you have suffered any of these indignities, keep track of them. Write down the date and time of the call and what the collector said. The more detail, the better. You want to have an in-depth record of as many violations as possible. Add these to your files. Tell the callers that you know your rights. After keeping track of these violations, it's time to file a complaint.

File a Complaint with the Attorney General's Office

You should consider reporting any problems you have with debt collectors to your state's attorney general's office and to the Federal Trade Commission (FTC). These are strong organizations that are interested in looking out for and protecting your rights. The staffs of both agencies are knowledgeable and have a great deal of experience with the harassment issues you are experiencing. They are the professionals you want fighting back for you against the professional debt collectors.

Many states have their own debt collection laws. The staff at your state's attorney general's office can help you determine your rights. (See Appendix A for more information.) The FTC is the federal agency that works for the consumer to prevent fraudulent, deceptive, and unfair business practices in the marketplace. The FTC provides information to help consumers spot, stop, and avoid them. The FTC won't handle your individual case but it will use your information to determine a pattern of abuse by a creditor.

Some people have complained about the effectiveness of the attorney generals and the FTC in combating harassment by debt collectors. You may have to take matters into your own hands. You may have to sue.

> The Federal Trade Commission (FTC) received more than 78,000 complaints against debt collectors in 2008 alleging violations of the FDCPA.

Hire a Lawyer, Then Sue

Whether you file a complaint with the FTC or your state's attorney general, you should consider hiring a lawyer. This is the sure way to stop the harassment. The best part is that it likely won't cost you anything. You may be able to find a lawyer to take your case on a contingency basis (the lawyer gets paid only if he or she wins the case). Make sure you've kept a good, detailed file.

Lawyers like taking cases involving violations of the FDCPA brought by an honest person with a well-kept record of the debt collector's violations. Under the FDCPA, you can sue the debt collector for up to $1,000 for statutory damages plus actual damages (e.g., mental anguish, phone charges, and mailing costs) and attorneys' fees. You have one year from the date the law was violated to bring legal action.

Plus, if the creditor is harassing you, they are probably harassing others. Debt collection agencies find themselves the subject of class action lawsuits all the time.

Don't Give Up! Keep Fighting

Many debt collection agencies rely on heavy pressure and intimidation to collect from you. They are accustomed to bullying and getting their way. Stand up for your rights and your family's rights. Don't succumb to harassment.

Points to Remember

- Know your legal rights under the Fair Debt Collection Practices Act including the illegal practices in communicating and collecting debts from you.
- Keep a detailed record of all debt collection activity against you and keep copies of all written communications.
- Take steps to protect yourself from unfair debt collection practices by demanding in writing that creditors and their debt collectors cease illegal practices.
- If illegal practices continue after a demand to cease, notify the attorney general of your state, the Federal Trade Commission, and the Federal Consumer Protection Agency and hire an attorney to file a complaint in court against the creditor and/or debt collector seeking damages, attorneys' fees, and other appropriate relief.
- Understand your legal rights and fight for them!

CHAPTER

4

Budgeting Your Way Out of Debt

*Annual income twenty pounds, annual expenditure nineteen six,
result happiness.
Annual income twenty pounds, annual expenditure twenty pounds
and six, result misery.*

—Charles Dickens's *David Copperfield*

How well do you know your finances? The next step on the road
out of debt is to know your financial situation and how to use your
money to your benefit. Knowledge is power. Without an understanding of your financial situation, even if you get out of debt this time,
it will only be a matter of months or years until you find yourself in
the same situation. See how well you spend by taking the quiz "Are
You a Smart or Sorry Spender?"

Quiz: Are You a Smart or Sorry Spender?

1. If you are given $100, what is the first thing you would do?
   A. Pay your credit card balance
   B. Go out to dinner

(Continued)

   C. Shop for new clothes
   D. Pay your rent or mortgage

2. If the next day you are given $500, how would you spend it?
   A. Celebrate with friends
   B. Buy lottery tickets
   C. Put it in the bank
   D. Make a car payment

3. If on the third day you find $20 blowing down the street and no one is around, what would you do?
   A. Buy a big lunch
   B. Buy an extra cup of coffee
   C. Put it in your purse or wallet for later
   D. Put a lost-and-found ad on Craigslist

What's Your Score?

Question 1: 4 points for A, 1 point for B or C, 3 points for D
Question 2: 1 point for A or B, 3 points for C, 4 points for D
Question 3: 1 point for A or B, 3 points for C, 0 points for D (We don't believe you!)

If you scored 9 or higher: Congratulations! You are making the right choices on your budgeting. Read on to learn how to continue making good choices, even through rough times.

If you scored 8 or lower: You have some bad spending habits, but you can still make changes that will allow you to budget out of debt. Read on to learn what you should do.

Understand Your Situation

If you are ever going to solve your debt problems, the first step is to know your income and expenses. As important as knowing how much money is coming in, you must know how and where your money is spent. If you don't know where your cash flow stands, you may someday be the next person who buys the world's most expensive cup of coffee and bagel!

No one would argue with you if you said five dollars for a cup of coffee at Starbucks or Dunkin' Donuts is rather expensive. Well, almost no one. Jake Dreher might.

The one thing Jake looked forward to each day was a hot cup of coffee in the morning, even in the summer heat. It would not be a good day unless Jake started it off with his coffee. One Monday near the end of the month, Jake walked to the counter at his favorite coffee shop. He knew that he had written a few checks that month and that the balance in his checking account may be running low. He had some cash in his wallet and expected his paycheck would be directly deposited into his checking account that day, so he paid with his debit card. If the debit card were declined, he'd pay cash.

He was pleasantly surprised, thinking his paycheck had cleared, when the cost of his coffee was put on his debit card. He then ordered a bagel and paid for that with his debit card. Two or three days later he received overdraft notices from the bank. Each transaction caused an overdraft in his checking account. Not only was he assessed a fine for each overdraft but he was charged a fee for the bank covering his transactions. Because of the two fines and two bank fees, Jake's coffee and bagel cost over $120!

Jake's experience is an extreme one, but it is not uncommon. There are endless ways to lose track of our finances. When we do lose track, we put ourselves in peril of being hit with fees and fines that cause bigger and bigger problems.

We lose track because we all tend to overestimate how much money we have and underestimate how much we are spending. We do this because our spending sneaks up on us. Plus, it's amazing how little everyday expenses add up over the year.

> One medium Dunkin' Donuts or Starbucks coffee and plain bagel on your way to work each day adds up to more than $687 over the course of one year.

Everyday purchases have a greater impact on your overall expenses than you'd think. So nothing is as important as keeping track of what's coming in and what's going out.

Recognize the Warning Signs

Many warning signs can tell you if you're heading toward financial difficulty, and some are more obvious than others. Human nature causes us to exaggerate how much money we can spend. We want to get things. We don't like to tell ourselves no. We think we have more money than we do. Overestimating your finances is a big warning sign. Other warning signs include the following:

- You don't know how much you owe each month.
- You pay your bills late.

- You get new credit cards or new loans (sometimes at worse rates than you've been offered before) to pay for old credit cards and old loans.
- You pay only the minimum balances on credit cards.
- You spend more than 20 percent of net income on debt (excluding rent or mortgage).
- You have little or no savings and no emergency fund (emergency credit cards don't count).

Check the number of warning signs you recognized to see where you are on the color spectrum introduced in Chapter 1.

- One warning sign = blue level. Pay attention.
- Two warning signs = yellow level. Be careful.
- Three or more warning signs = orange level. You have lost control of your finances and spending and need to make changes.

Set a Budget

The best way to reduce the warning signs in your life and put your financial house in order is to set up a budget. A budget is the simplest way to make sure what you take home each month exceeds what you spend. When you achieve that balance, you can then start saving that extra money to put yourself on the road to financial security.

To set up a budget, you must take a hard look at what you bring in and your expenses. Sit down and calculate it. We know it sounds hard, but it really isn't. We make it easy. In fact, you can do it in front of the television. Start by writing your daily expenses in a journal when you get home at night. You will be surprised by the little things you spend your money on and how much they add up to. You'll find that keeping a journal of your expenses is worth it in the end because it will help you understand where you stand financially. Then you can decide your financial options. You will be able to better decide whether bankruptcy is your best option.

Start budgeting by looking at these three areas of your finances:

- *Monthly take home.* Your revenue (e.g., salary, benefits, Social Security, pension, and so on).
- *Essential fixed expenses.* Expenses you cannot avoid for your home, health, and safety.

- *Other expenses.* Expenses that your home, health, and safety do not depend on.

The goal of your budget is to put money away as savings every month. Only with savings are you ready to handle emergencies and other major life events.

Monthly Take Home

The first step to budgeting is to determine how much income you receive each month. Your income determines your maximum spending limit. Your monthly salary is probably your main source of income. Look at your actual take-home pay on your paycheck. This is your spending limit for the month.

We suggest setting a monthly amount because most of our expenses, like rent, mortgages, credit cards, utilities, and insurance, are billed monthly.

"JUST THIRTY MORE WEEKS AND I'LL PAY OFF MY CREDIT CARDS FROM SPRING BREAK LAST YEAR"

That means if you are paid:

A salary or fixed amount weekly: Multiply your take-home pay
by 52 then divide by 12 (or just multiply by 4.33).

Every other week: Multiply your take-home pay by 26 then divide
by 12 (or just multiply by 2.67).

Twice a month: Multiply your take-home pay by 2.

Monthly: You have your number.

Memorize your number. This is the most important number for
you to know. This is your monthly take-home pay. This is your starting point.

If you receive other monthly payments that you can rely on,
such as Social Security, disability insurance, alimony, or child care,
add this amount to your number. Conversely, if you have to pay
alimony or child support, subtract this amount from your number.

> Little purchases add up. If you stopped a pack-a-day cigarette habit, you
> would save over $2,500 a year (and your lungs).

If you are self-employed, make sure you do not include operating expenses, estimated taxes, or other favorable increases in your
monthly number. Your spending limit is just what you can count on
to spend each month that you won't owe to the government or anyone else later in the year.

If you're not employed or do not have a steady and reliable
income, do not budget on a hypothetical or hoped-for income.
Remember this advice from Proverbs in the Bible: "The poor man's
budget is full of schemes." Develop a realistic budget.

Your monthly take home is your starting point.

Essential Fixed Expenses

Next, figure out your essential fixed expenses. Essential fixed expenses
are those that you cannot do without—expenses for home, health,
and safety. These are the expenses you incur each month in order
to just get by. If you cannot meet your essential fixed expenses, you

will threaten your well-being and your family's well-being, or land yourself in jail. Essential fixed expenses fall into five major groups: food, shelter, utilities, safety, and clothing.

> *Food.* This is what it costs you to feed your family and yourself at a minimum level to maintain everyone's health. The cost of this can be affected by where you shop and how wise a shopper you are. But for now, figure out as well as you can what you actually spend on food.
>
> *Shelter.* This is what you pay to keep a roof over your head, such as for your mortgage or rent expenses, including taxes and insurance if you own your own house.
>
> *Utilities.* This is what it costs to have heat, to cook your food, to light your house, to have water, to discharge your waste and trash, and to reach out to other people by telephone. This too can vary greatly depending on your living style. How high do you keep your thermostat in the winter or how often do you need air-conditioning? Do you shut off unnecessary lights? Do you continually run the water while you are washing dishes? Do you have a landline and cell phone? Figure out what you are actually spending to see if you can cut back but look at your lifestyle.
>
> *Safety.* This is what you pay for expenses such as child care. It is also how much you pay for insurance (e.g., home, car, life) and to ensure you have transportation for your necessary commitments.
>
> *Clothing.* These are your expenses for minimum essential clothing and does not include your "night-on-the-town" clothes. You should primarily be thinking about clothes for your children as they grow out of their current size.

Add these up and write this number down. This is your essential fixed expenses number.

If your essential fixed expenses exceed your monthly take-home amount and you have other expenses that you cannot pay, Orange Level! Your choice on filing bankruptcy is easy: Unless you can reduce your essential fixed expenses, you have to seriously consider filing for bankruptcy as soon as possible. Somewhere in your life, something has gone wrong; you cannot support your lifestyle anymore, and it's time to overhaul your life. Bankruptcy may be the help you need to fix things so seriously consider filing.

Don't even think about using your credit cards to make up for gaps in your budget! Using your credit cards in this way is a quick fix that only delays the inevitable. Plus, using credit cards increases your chances of overspending and making your budget problems worse.

Other Expenses

Provided that your monthly take-home exceeds your essential fixed expenses, you can begin to work on the rest of your budget. For this, you have to determine the rest of your spending each month. Again, your goal is to have more coming in than going out. Your goal is for your monthly take-home to exceed both your essential fixed expenses and your other expenses.

Think about where all your money is spent throughout your day, week, and month. Other expenses are monthly expenses that you can live without. You can manipulate other expenses so that failure to pay them in any given month won't severely impact your everyday life, cause the loss of your home, or land you in jail because you stop paying things such as alimony and child support. You cannot stop making payments on some of these items, such as on your car, but you can eliminate some or slide a month on others. Reducing other expenses is a way to give your spending some wiggle room.

Other expenses include: credit card payments; cable or satellite bills; membership dues; cell phone bills; condo fees; gym and health club memberships; nail, hair, and spa appointments; cleaning services; dry cleaning; dining out; taxis; vacations; coffee; education; recreation; personal items; donations; gifts; landscaping; snow removal; and the like.

We understand that you are probably thinking, "I'll never be able to figure that out." But there is a way, an easy way.

If you really want to know what you spend, think back over what you have spent over the last week. Think about *every* expense. We want you to sit down and jot down your usual daily expenses, including what you spend over the weekend. This will give you a general idea of the ways your money escapes. Sometimes just recognizing the little drains and stopping them is all you need to get yourself back on your financial feet.

Record your whole picture when budgeting. Do not fool yourself by leaving out, expenses and spending habits that you deny or don't like to admit to yourself, such as clothes, shopping, special-occasion gifts, cigarettes, and a quick ice cream on the way home.

As a safety factor, we suggest that you consider adding 10 percent to your other expenses as a cushion. Our experience shows that most people underestimate what they spend by at least 10 percent or more. Once you have your number for your other expenses (with an added 10 percent), add it to your essential fixed expenses. This is your total expenses number.

Do your total expenses exceed your monthly take-home amount? If not, good! Read on to learn how to increase the difference and ensure that your total expenses never exceed your monthly take-home number.

If they do, you have to make cuts, find more income, restructure your debts, or a combination of all three. You are not the U.S. government. The only way for you to live well is with a balanced budget. You have to make changes so that your monthly take-home amount exceeds your total expenses.

The following changes are helpful even if your monthly take-home number exceeds your total expenses. Sometimes small changes can make a big impact, put you back on the right spending track, and let you put this book back on your shelf. Budget changes combined with changes to your debts (discussed in Chapters 4, 5, and 6) can put you in a great financial place.

Do the exercises "Calculate Your Monthly Total Income" and "Calculate Your Monthly Total Expenses," which will help you understand how well your current budget works for you. Fill in the blanks by inserting the amount requested for the last month; or better yet, use the average amount for the last six months if you can calculate it.

Exercise: Calculate Your Monthly Total Income

1. Monthly gross wages, salary, and commissions $ _____
2. Estimated monthly overtime $ _____
3. SUBTOTAL $ _____
4. LESS PAYROLL DEDUCTIONS
   a. Payroll taxes and Social Security $ _____
   b. Insurance $ _____
   c. Union dues $ _____
   d. Other $ _____

(Continued)

5. SUBTOTAL OF PAYROLL DEDUCTIONS $ _____
6. TOTAL NET MONTHLY TAKE-HOME PAY $ _____
7. Regular income from business $ _____
8. Income from real property $ _____
9. Interest and dividends from investments $ _____
10. Alimony or support paid to you $ _____
11. Social Security or government assistance $ _____
12. Pension or retirement income $ _____
13. Other monthly income $ _____
14. SUBTOTAL OF LINES 7 THROUGH 13: $ _____
15. MONTHLY INCOME (Lines 6 plus 14) $ _____

Exercise: Calculate Your Monthly Total Expenses

1. Rent or home mortgage payment $ _____
    a. Real estate taxes $ _____
    b. Property insurance $ _____
2. Utilities
    a. Electricity and heating fuel $ _____
    b. Water and sewer $ _____
    c. Home phone $ _____
    d. Cell phone $ _____
    e. Cable $ _____
3. Home repairs and maintenance $ _____
4. Food $ _____
5. Clothing $ _____
6. Laundry and dry cleaning $ _____
7. Medical and dental expenses $ _____
8. Transportation (not car payments) $ _____
9. Recreation/Entertainment $ _____
10. Charitable contributions $ _____
11. Insurance
    a. Homeowner's or renter's $ _____
    b. Life $ _____
    c. Health, if not deducted in your pay check $ _____
    d. Auto $ _____
    e. Other $ _____
12. Out-of-pocket taxes $ _____
13. Car payments $ _____
    a. Other vehicle payments $ _____
14. Alimony and support paid to others $ _____
15. Other monthly payments $ _____
TOTAL: $ _____

Fix a Broken Budget

If your budget needs some help, there are some easy changes that you can make to fix it. Some of the suggested changes will affect your income, others will affect your spending, but all will help put you on the road to maintaining a healthy budget.

Earn Extra Income

Can you work extra hours? Pick up a second job? Do handyman work? Landscape on weekends? Plow or shovel? Teach? Teach English as a second language? Tutor? Coach? Write articles? Temp? Cook meals for others? Perform housekeeping duties? Have you thought of and explored all additional ways to bring in some extra money each month? Get creative. Any and every extra dollar can help.

Here's a suggestion: If you are getting a refund from the IRS at the end of the year, change your deductions on the IRS form W4. IRS form W4 is what you signed at work so your employer can calculate the taxes to withhold from your paycheck. If you get money back, you are giving the government an interest-free loan. An increase in deductions will give you extra money each pay period increasing your monthly take-home amount.

A word of caution: Experience teaches us that it is best to increase your deductions and not wait for the yearly tax refund check. When someone gets a good chunk of money at one time, the person is more likely to go on a spending spree than pay down debts or save it. That's why the government sent out stimulus checks rather than lowering the amount it took from our pay: it hoped we would all go out and spend it.

Reduce Your Expenses

Can you eliminate or lower any of the following costs: commuting, housekeeping, lawn maintenance, salon services, or sports club memberships? Can you eat at home more often or bring your lunch? Drink less coffee?

If you decide to make cuts to balance your budget, attack the nonessentials first. We suggest you consider making cuts in four waves. The following sections include "waves" that we think are nonessential; however, you may disagree. Jake Dreher thought his morning coffee bought at a coffee shop was essential. You may

Copyright © 2010 New Way Solutions, www.newwaysolutions.com.

find making a cup at home or doing without will take its place. In our wave system, the higher the wave, the more serious are your financial issues.

When you make the cuts to balance your budget, remember two unbreakable rules:

1. Don't use credit cards to "tide you over."
2. Always pay your mortgage or rent, alimony, child support, and taxes.

First Wave of Cuts   The first wave of cuts is the easiest and the hardest at the same time. They are the easiest because they have the least impact on your life. But they are also the hardest because you are not used to making cuts and because these cuts usually affect the more enjoyable activities in your life. Don't worry. After you take your road out of debt, you will enjoy these things even more.

The first wave of cuts are to donations, eating out (strictly limit it), specialty coffee drinks, subscriptions to magazines, club memberships, premium cable, vacations, movies at the cinema, cell phone or home phone, long-distance service, cable/DSL Internet, life insurance (change universal whole life insurance to a term policy), student loan forbearance, and traveling (drive less and take public transportation).

If after making cuts in the first wave your monthly take-home exceeds your total expenses, you are in the Blue Level. If not, you enter your second wave of cuts.

Second Wave of Cuts   For the second wave of cuts, consider not buying books, newspapers, and magazines; stretch out hair appointments, nail appointments, and spa treatments; cancel gym memberships (hit the streets and jog); stop extra classes, reduce alcohol purchases and cigarettes; shop at discount clothing stores for essentials; cancel home services such as landscaping and cleaning services; take no outside lunches; no longer eat out; and halt your savings (but savings should be the first thing you start again).

If after making cuts in the second wave your monthly take-home exceeds your total expenses, you are in the yellow level. If not, you enter your third wave of cuts.

Third Wave of Cuts   The third wave of cuts requires that you re-adjust insurance amounts; cut out any cable; do not rent movies/DVDs; no Internet; put off home repairs; and find the cheapest transportation to work, even if it is inconvenient. The bottom line: Stop all unnecessary spending.

If after making cuts in the third wave your monthly take-home amount exceeds your total expenses, you are in the Orange Level. You are making deep cuts that are borderline dangerous, and you have to make sure that they do not harm the health, safety, or welfare of you or your family.

Fourth Wave of Cuts   Sorry, there is no fourth wave. If you have gone through the first three waves, you are in the Red Level. Seek immediate assistance and strongly consider bankruptcy. You are down to your bare essentials. Your last alternatives are to sell your house and car and get cheaper alternatives (e.g., a cheaper apartment and a used car).

Major Life Events   Reaching the third or fourth wave of cuts means drastic measures have been taken and bankruptcy is a strong possibility. Any of the following major life events will also place you in the Red Level:

- Job loss.
- An illness of you or a loved one can put a major financial strain on you and your family.
- A sudden disabling injury is similar to the problems caused by illness.
- Divorce or separation.
- Death of a loved one or family member is an unexpected and large expense that can have repercussions for months.
- An emergency of any kind—blown transmission, broken furnace or other appliances, family member demanding assistance, involvement in a crime—can create major money troubles.

When you reach the third or fourth wave of cuts or suffer a major life event, you must carefully prioritize expenses. You have to make sure that you take care of your essentials first. See the emergency expenditure in Table 4.1 to help you prioritize your spending. In the table, money flows from the top to the bottom like a pyramid and no money reaches the next level until the higher level is satisfied.

Figure out how long you can stay ahead of your debts before your situation threatens your first four levels. If your first four levels are threatened: red level. Bankruptcy is most likely your best

Table 4.1   Emergency Expenditures

Level	Expenditure
Level 1	Shelter and food
Level 2	Utilities
Level 3	Essential vehicle and all insurance policies, including life insurance: don't hurt the family if you die. Reevaluate medical and auto insurance and shop around
Level 4	Fines that could land you in jail: child support and alimony
Level 5	Taxes, student loans, and school payments
Level 6	Minimum savings
Level 7	Other expenses
Level 8	Entertainment

option, so skip ahead to Chapter 12 to understand the bankruptcy process and your bankruptcy options.

Stick to Your Budget

Once you have done your budget, you should continue to keep track throughout your life—through the good times and the bad. Having a budget and sticking to it is a skill that can benefit you more than you can imagine.

Experts recommend that you stick to the following guidelines on how your money should be spent each month. The further away you find yourself from these guidelines, the closer you will find yourself to financial troubles. Table 4.2 shows a list of monthly expenses and the percent of income that each should safely fulfill.

Start Saving: Pay Yourself First

The most important thing you can do with your money each month is to save it. The best way to ensure that you save each month is an automatic withdrawal from your paycheck. You'll probably never miss the money and you'll have a nice safety net before you know it. Start your savings now. Pay yourself first. Only you can look out for yourself, and the best way to do that is to have savings you can rely on. America used to be a nation of savers, but the country has changed. Now we spend and charge. It is time the country changes back to the way it was. Savings equal security and peace of mind.

Table 4.2   How Much Should I Spend on That?

Monthly Expense	Percent of Income
Housing, including taxes	30 (not to exceed 35%)
Transportation	15
Food	15
Clothing	5
Medical	5
Recreation	5
Utilities	5
Other debts	5
Savings	5
Miscellaneous	10

Savings are the best way to be prepared for any major life event. Savings bring happiness.

It is amazing how savings can add up over time. You can think of savings as an inverted pyramid. You start with very little (the tip) but as you continue to save the platform becomes bigger and more stable, just as you will feel better and more stable.

Start saving now because the numbers get bigger and bigger the more and the longer you save. For example:

- $25 saved a month with no interest for four years = $1,200.
- $50 saved a month with no interest for four years = $2,400.
- $100 saved a month with no interest for four years = $4,800.

An amazing study chronicled in *The Millionaire Next Door* by Thomas J. Stanley and William D. Danko demonstrates the power of savings.[1] They found that the typical millionaire is not the flamboyant person we see on television but rather a frugal, everyday person who is smart with his money, lives below his means, and concentrates on savings first. These people are persistent in making sure that they pay themselves first and put money away that is untouchable for their personal spending.

Beware of Unsolicited Advice

When it comes to budgeting, you will get a lot of advice from friends and strangers and you will hear all different kinds of advertisements offering to free you from your debts. Beware: There are no shortcuts.

If you think you cannot budget on your own or would like help, contact the National Foundation for Credit Counseling (NFCC). The NFCC offers information on financial and consumer topics. It offers expenses and income reviews and it can help you set up a realistic budget. The NFCC may even contact creditors and help arrange reduced payments. The NFCC will help you create a budget for future expenses with reasonable or no fees. Appendix A contains contact information for the NFCC.

Points to Remember

- Understand your income and expenses by analyzing exactly how much you earn and spend each month.
- Pay attention to the warning signs to keep yourself from running into budget troubles.
- Analyze your expenses and learn which you can cut (discretionary) and which you cannot (fixed).
- Explore ways to supplement your income.
- Make the hard choices to reduce expenses by applying our strategies and guidelines and learn to make budget cuts in waves.
- Implement a realistic budget.
- Stick to your budget and save money each month to build a rainy-day fund and a nest egg for your future.
- Remember to pay yourself first!

The Danger of Quick Fixes

Never spend your money before you have it.

—Thomas Jefferson

W hen you try to solve your financial problems, you will come across a number of seemingly quick and easy solutions that promise fast cash and credit. These promises will bombard you through a flood of television commercials, radio commercials, newspaper ads, flyers, billboards, and the Internet. Desperate for cash, the ads and commercials sound great. But these alleged solutions are dangerous and fraught with risks. Remember, if it sounds too good to be true, it probably is. Beware of quick and easy fixes; they don't exist. The following story is, unfortunately, not unusual.

Katie's Lesson

Katie Silver needed some extra money for a trip to New York City to attend a friend's wedding and buy a present. Every day on her way to work, Katie drove by a storefront with a sign that read "Get Money Fast: No Credit Check." She especially liked the "no credit check" part because she feared the review of her credit score, so she decided to stop in.

Katie walked out of the store with $400. She had paid a $50 fee for the loan and given them a check for $400 that she dated for the next Friday when she would get her next paycheck. She knew the interest rate and the fees were high but she knew she'd have the money to pay back the loan on her next payday.

Katie enjoyed the wedding more than she could have imagined, so she spent an extra night at the hotel and dined with both old and new friends the next night. When payday came, she didn't think she'd have enough money to pay back the loan. She called the lender, who allowed her to roll over her loan for another two weeks provided she paid the $50 fee again. In the weeks that followed, something always seemed to come up when Katie had to pay back the loan and the lender always seemed willing to let it slide. The loan continued to roll over; after five months, Katie had paid $550 in fees and still owed the original $400!

How They Draw You In

What happened to Katie is not uncommon. She got caught in a trap that will cost her more than she ever imagined. Her loan, usually called a *payday* loan, is one of several loans we strongly recommend that you avoid except for in the most extreme circumstances. The next sections discuss these payday loans, vehicle title loans, pawn shop loans, and tax refund anticipation loans. Also in this category are the get-rich schemes you hear about in the media. While not technically loans, these schemes likewise seek to scam you out of your money. If you ever find yourself caught in an emergency and get drawn in by one of these quick fixes, make sure you get out immediately and pay back what you owe.

Payday Loans

Payday loans go by different names. They are called *payday loans, cash advance loans, check advance loans, postdated check loans,* and *deferred-deposit check loans.* No matter what they are called: Stay away!

A payday loan can be approved within a matter of hours with typically no credit check. Usually, you write a personal check payable to the lender for the amount you wish to borrow plus a fee. You date the check for your next payday or another agreeable date within the next couple of weeks when you figure you'll be able to repay the loan. The idea is that you have the money coming to you at that time so you'll be able to pay the loan.

When the day arrives that you have to pay the loan, you usually have two options: pay off the loan either by letting the lender deposit the check or paying the amount of the check in cash; or pay a fee and roll over the loan for another two weeks, as we saw with Katie.

A typical borrower pays $793 for a $325 payday loan, and 90 percent of payday borrowers roll over their loan at least once.

Source: Uriah King, et al., *Financial Quicksand: Payday Lending Sinks Borrowers in Debt with $4.2 Billion in Predatory Fees Every Year* (2006), www.responsiblelending.org/payday-lending/research-analysis/rr012-Financial_Quicksand-1106.pdf.

If at all possible, you should never go to a payday lender. The typical fee for a $100 two-week payday loan is $15. That is almost a 400 percent annual percentage rate. Even your 30 percent annual interest rate on your credit card looks good compared to a payday lender's rate. Debt created by payday loans will often quadruple in just one year because of interest and fees. One tiny mistake can mean a lifelong debt, so it is very important to get out of the loan, and to get out quickly.

There are 23,417 payday lenders in America, almost twice the number of McDonald's.

Source: "Think Payday Lending isn't out of control in the United States?" 2006 (California State University, Northridge, www.csun.edu/~sg4002/research/mcdonalds_by_state.htm).

Remember Katie? She may become trapped in an endless cycle of paying fees and then never be able to pay back the original amount. Katie's interest rate on her $400 loan may become as high as 1,000 percent at the rate she's going. How would you like to be able to lend some money at a rate of 1,000 percent?

If you put $1,000 in the bank and received 1,000 percent simple interest, at the end of the year you would have $10,000. At the end of two years, that $10,000 becomes enough to buy a small house: $100,000. The reason there are almost double the payday lenders as there are McDonald's is obvious. It's a great business for the lender, but it's a horrible deal for the borrower.

Have you ever noticed where payday lenders are located? They are often found in neighborhoods where a significant number of the residents cannot qualify for more conventional, mainstream loans. They capitalize on people fearful of or discouraged by their credit scores. Keep in mind that you *do* have to pay for a lender to overlook your credit score—accepting money with no credit check has its price, and it's called interest.

Once you write a check, make sure you have sufficient funds in your bank account to cover it. If you don't, both your bank and your payday lender will probably charge you a bounced-check fee. Some states consider it a crime to write a check when you don't have sufficient funds to cover it. In those states, writing a "bad" check gives the payday lender the ability to threaten you with a lawsuit if you fall behind. Dealing with debt rarely involves criminal charges, but writing checks this way may be a criminal act. Remember, payday lenders know they have this powerful tool in their back pockets.

Do not be fooled by a claim that a $15 fee on a two-week $100 loan is a 15 percent rate of interest. Interest rates are determined annually by annual percentage rate (APR) of interest so all loans can be evaluated equally. This two-week loan has a 390 percent APR. The average credit card has a 12.71 percent APR.

Source: www.foxbusiness.com/story/personal-finance/bofa-rate-hikes-push-national-average-credit-card-apr-higher/.

Payday loans are structured in such a way that you can easily be trapped into paying fees for a very long time. You will most likely end up paying three, four, or even ten times the amount you originally borrowed. Consider alternatives to payday loans, including:

- Get a paycheck advance from your employer.
- Take out a small, short-term loan from a credit union.
- Use an unsecured line of credit from a finance lender. These credit lines range from $2,000–$5,000 with interest rates from 25 to 35 percent annual percentage rate APR.

Whatever you do, avoid payday loans!

Vehicle Title Loans

Like payday loans, you can get a title loan and obtain quick cash without a credit check or test to see if you can pay. You will find these loans in the same stores where you can get payday loans. The signs that announce them echo payday loans, saying "Get Cash Now" and "No Credit, No Problem." Just like payday loans, avoid title loans at all costs if possible.

Typically, to obtain this type of loan, you will be asked to sign over the title to your vehicle, give them a copy of your keys, and agree that the vehicle can be repossessed if you fail to make a payment on time and in full. The title on your car, truck, SUV, or sometimes even your boat or RV secures your payment on title loans. The amount you can borrow is based on a percentage of your vehicle's value. Title loans usually run for a 30-day term and the interest rate varies by state; needless to say, most lenders charge the maximum allowed in that state. Interest rates for title loans reach astronomical levels, like payday loans.

In addition, fees for processing the loan are also substantial, including document fees, title fees, and security fees. Many vehicle title loans come with a 25 percent finance charge for the 30-day loan. That means that the loan has an annual interest rate of 300 percent. Plus, lenders will encourage you to roll over your loans until the loan and your interest rates reach absurd levels.

But the extraordinarily high interest rate is only one problem with a title loan; the lender will repossess your vehicle if you don't keep up with the interest charges or cannot pay the entire sum back at the end of the 30-day period. We have even heard of lenders selling cars after two missed payments. If your car is repossessed, you will likely owe the money you borrowed in addition to the cost of the repossession and the legal costs of the lender in doing the repossession. These costs will amount to much more money than you originally borrowed. In some states, the lender can keep the total amount of money the car is sold for even if it was more than you owed plus the repossession costs. Beware, even a small amount of money borrowed on a title loan can quickly turn into large amount and deprive you of your vehicle even while you may still be liable for making car payments.

Your car is much too valuable to you and your family to risk in a title loan. Like payday loans, these loans are stacked heavily in the lender's favor and the likely outcome is the loss of your car. Avoid title loans!

You will sometimes hear interest rates quoted monthly in order to make them seem lower. In Georgia, title loans often have a monthly interest rate of 25 percent—that's an annual APR of 300 percent or three times your original loan!

Source: www.ajc.com/services/content/metro/stories/2009/01/25/title_pawn_loans.html%3F cxtype%3Drss%26cxsvc%3D7%26cxcat%3D13.

Hard Money Lenders

Hard money lenders (also known as loan sharks) offer money without a credit check and will give you cash on the spot. You may be tempted to go this route, but don't. The horror stories about lost cars, lost homes—not to mention broken body parts and other acts of violence—are not myths but fact. Avoid hard money loans at all costs.

CONSEQUENCES OF LATE PAYMENTS
TO HARD MONEY LENDERS AND LOAN SHARKS

Pawn Shop Loans

Vehicle title loans are a variation of the type of loan that you can expect to receive from pawn shops. Pawn shops offer quick money for the valuable possessions you bring to the shop. You can get these possessions back when you pay back the loan. But the rates are usually too high and it is unrealistic to think that you will actually get your property back because pawnbrokers use the same tactics as lenders who give payday loans and vehicle title loans. There are between 10,000 and 15,000 pawn shops in the United States.[1]

Pawnbrokers make loans on personal property left as collateral. The property can be redeemed when the loan and all interest is repaid. The interest rates for pawn shop loans may range from 4 to 8 percent a month or from 48 to 96 percent on a yearly basis. Some states regulate the interest rate. Loans can usually be renewed, but only if the interest for the original period has been paid.[2]

Pawnbrokers will accept a variety of personal property as collateral and won't lend more money than they think they can get if the pledged item is not redeemed and has to be sold.

When a pledged item is not redeemed, some states require pawnbrokers to notify the customer that the loan period has expired so that he or she has a final opportunity to pay off the entire loan and get back their personal property. If the customer cannot or does not, the pawnbroker has the right to sell the item. Depending on where you live, pawnbrokers can either keep all the money received from the sale of the item or only keep the original loan and any interest due and return the excess from the sale back to the customer. But you can likely bet the sale will not exceed the debt.

The pawnbroker is interested in getting back the amount advanced, along with interest and costs incurred. This usually requires that the item you pawned be sold at a price far less than its fair market value. It's also difficult to ascertain whether the pawnbroker tried to sell the article fairly or whether it was sold to a friend or friendly business.

When the pawnbroker works with a friend or friendly business, here's what happens: You have a nice watch worth $600 that you don't want to sell. But you need a couple hundred dollars, so you go to the pawnbroker who knows the value of the watch and gives you $200. You are given the option of redeeming it within 60 days for around $225. After 60 days pass, you can't pull that money together, so the pawnbroker takes possession of it. His options are to sell it for $600, keep the $225, and return the $375 to you *or* sell it to a friend or friendly business for $250 and call it even with you. The friend or friendly business will sell it for the $600 and will split the $175 difference with the pawnbroker.

Online pawn shops work the same way. You enter your personal information on the pawn shop's Web site and mail in your personal items for collateral. Obviously, making pawn deals online increases the risks involved pawning goods; you do not know if your personal information will be compromised, if your property will arrive safely, or whether the pawn shop is even legitimate. Plus, you can expect that if you default on your contract you will never see your item again nor will you receive anything close to fair market value for the item pawned. Moreover, some online pawn shops traffic stolen goods, which leaves you without any legal protections.

Top pawned items include:

- Gold chains, rings, silverware
- Televisions, computers, digital cameras, DVD players
- CDs and DVDs
- Electric saws and drills
- Rifles and shotguns

Just like payday loans and vehicle title loans, pawn shop loans are stacked heavily in the lender's favor. The likely outcome is the

Cash for Gold

Advertisements about turning your cash into gold are prevalent in these economic times. If you have gold jewelry or coins that you no longer wear or value, selling these items may be a good idea. However, make sure you go to a reputable jeweler who will give you a fair price. Do not mail your gold. You will not get fair value. The television show "Good Morning America" tested this in an episode that aired on March 20, 2009. They mailed $350 worth of gold jewelry to three different mail-order jewelers. The prices they were initially offered were $206.00, $89.71, and $66.05.

Source: "Gold Rush: People Rush to Sell Gold Instead of Finding It: 'Good Morning America' Tested Mail-Order Gold Companies," March 20, 2009, http://abcnews .go.com/GMA/story?id=7125707&page=1.

loss of your possession for much less than what it is worth. Consider selling the property outright and avoid pawn shops.

Tax Refund Anticipation Loans

You've seen the advertisements: People smiling as they walk out of the tax preparer's office. The voiceover states that you too can get your refund right away. The advertisements will promise loans for up to $5,000 against your upcoming tax return. What they don't show you is the interest rate you'll pay for this loan. Both independent tax offices and national chains offer these refund anticipation loans at annual percentage rates in the hundreds of percentage points. A person will be hit with huge interest rates just to receive their tax refund a couple of weeks or even just a few days earlier.

When a tax filer pays to have his or her taxes done, the tax preparer determines whether the person will be receiving a tax refund. If the tax preparer finds the tax filer is entitled to a refund, the tax preparer then offers the tax filer the opportunity to receive the refund immediately or in the next couple of days from the tax preparer.

The tax preparer is actually offering a loan on the tax return for a fee—in the form of an actual fee, a commission, or in interest. If the tax filer accepts the loan, the tax preparer submits the form to the IRS. The IRS confirms that the filing is free of mathematical errors and that the filer had no liens or delinquent federal student loans. After the tax preparer gets this confirmation, the tax preparer gives the tax filer the loan. The IRS issues the tax refund to the tax preparer who then issues a check for the refund to the tax filer, minus the fee and interest.

Checks in the Mail

Have you ever received a real check in the mail for thousands of dollars? These are tempting ways to put quick cash in your checking accounts. All you have to do is deposit the check and your cash flow problems are cured. Don't do it! Various low-level lenders send these disguised loans that feature exorbitant interest rates and huge penalties.

If the tax preparer determines that you will receive $1,000 from the IRS, he might offer you a loan of $900 that you will receive in the next couple of days. However, if you file your taxes electronically, you will receive the whole $1,000 in two weeks at most. Why only get most of your money, when you can wait a week and get all your money?

The typical time period for this type of loan is less than 10 days, with the loan being repaid when your actual refund check from the IRS arrives. Fees for an average tax refund loan range from 40 percent to more than 700 percent APR.

Don't let your impatience get the best of you. If the tax preparer says that you are eligible for a tax refund anticipation loan, your tax return has already been basically approved by the IRS, meaning that you could receive your tax refund in a couple of weeks if you file electronically. Money from the IRS will be deposited in your bank account in 10 to 14 days if you file electronically. The IRS is currently working on speeding up the process to two to three days.

Wait the extra days so you'll have extra money for yourself. The refund is your money that you worked hard to get. You've been waiting part of a year for it already. Be smart. Don't give your money away. Car dealerships and even furniture stores have started to join in on the tax refund anticipation loan business by allowing you to put up your tax return for a down payment on your vehicle or furniture purchase. Beware: Car dealers and other retailers charge the same fees and exorbitant rates that tax preparers charge for a very short-term benefit to the customer. Avoid these loans at all costs!

"Work at Home" Scams

Offers to "work at home" and run a "home-based business" fill the Internet. Who of us hasn't been tempted by the thought of easy money while working at home on our computer? The problem is, however, that countless scam artists know how tempting the lure of big money for little work is to people.[3]

The lure of a convenient work arrangement and high compensation catches the eye of the computer user either from an e-mail or an advertisement on a Web site that he or she visits. The description of the work or the rewards entices the person to pay for a service, set-up fee, or products that will get the person started in business.

There are two basic types of scams: "work at home" and "start a home-based business." Work at home scams will offer you money to stuff envelopes, assemble an item such as baby booties or plastic signs, make copies of chain letters, or process medical and insurance claims. You will have to pay for the customer lists and products in advance. Supposedly, you will be doing these jobs for a company that will pay you for your completed work. However, there is no company to pay you!

You can recognize a work at home scam by any one of these signs:

- It's not an offer of regular employment or salary.
- It advertises fantastic pay for short hours.
- It requires money up-front for instructions or merchandise.
- It promises huge markets and demand for your products and services.
- There is no experience required.

Offers to help you start your home-owned business will have you become a "mystery shopper," Internet travel agent, or a "network marketer" who recruits other people to sell products. The problem is that the only money that ever gets exchanged is from you to the scammer.

E-Mail Winnings

Don't be fooled by e-mails that tell you that you have won the Nigerian Lottery, that some foreigner is having trouble clearing customs and needs you to cash money orders for them, or some other way that a stranger wants to give you money for little or no work. No one is so lucky! These are scams that seek to steal money from you.

Look for the following warning signs: exaggerated claims of potential earnings, profits, or part-time earnings, claims of inside information, overstated claims of product effectiveness, you have to pay for instructions or products before you learn how things work, or claims that you don't need experience.

Besides wasting countless hours, you could lose substantial money, ruin your reputation, or become the target of legal prosecution if you get involved in some of these Internet scams. Avoid Internet work at home scams!

Safer Loan Options (but Tread Carefully!)

If you are desperate for money and you've tried all of the budget fixes mentioned in Chapter 4, you may consider one or more of the following options. We do not recommend these methods to help your budget, but we do not put them in the "avoid at all costs" category. If you must, use these methods only to fill in gaps in your budget under limited circumstances; using them long-term can have a serious downside.

Family and Friends

A tempting place to look for money is a loan from a close friend or family member. These loans may be fine as a temporary answer to your problems but you have to treat them with as much or more respect as you would a bank loan.

Only accept a loan from a family member or close friend if he or she can easily afford to lend you money and will not expect to be paid anytime soon. Loans among family members, as with all money transactions with family, can easily cause hard feelings and resentment. People change when they are owed money. Sometimes they change back when they are repaid, but sometimes, they are never the same person you once knew.

The dynamic of the relationship also changes. The person who lent the money is looking for a word or two about when repayment will be made; the person who borrowed the money resents the person expecting some explanation. Soon their interaction is one more of avoiding each other than speaking to each other. One complains the other stiffed him; one complains the other treats him poorly just because he borrowed money from him. Family functions can become cold and awkward when one family member owes another family member money and is not paying back as expected.

You can probably think about an example in your family. Your debts are not worth losing a relationship with a loved one. Your family relationships and friendships greatly outweigh any money you owe.

The same advice applies when a close friend or family member asks you for money. Don't lend it unless you can afford to never see that money again. Better yet, give it to the person as a gift. Not only will it feel good, but you will have spared yourself from many potentially uncomfortable moments with that person in the future.

Your 401(k) or Pension

Your 401(k) plan constitutes your retirement savings. You may think it a good idea to borrow from it. After all, you are borrowing from yourself. You are entitled to access up to $50,000 or half of your balance, whichever is less, with minimal paperwork and no credit check. However, unless you are really in a pinch, borrowing from your 401(k) to pay off debts creates risks that you should likely avoid.

Your 401(k) plan likely makes up the cornerstone of your retirement money and you count on the growth in assets from the growth in the stock market. By taking a loan, you withdraw funds you will have to pay back. But, while you hold those funds, if you borrowed in a down market, you will miss out on any recovery the stock market makes and you take a big bite out of the compound interest and the investment potential of the money you have withdrawn.

In addition, you have to pay back the loan with your post-tax dollars, which means you have lost the pretax component of the 401(k) that makes it so appealing. Although the money you contributed from your pay to your 401(k) was not taxed, the money with which you will have to repay the loan comes from money you hold after taxes.

Moreover, should you leave your job or get fired, the balance of any outstanding 401(k) loan comes due immediately. If the balance is not paid off within three months of your departure from your job, the loan becomes a taxable withdrawal. Finally, and most important, money in your 401(k) is protected in a bankruptcy filing but the money you borrow from it is not. You are putting your retirement at risk by borrowing from your 401(k) when a bankruptcy filing may be in your future. Instead, you could consider temporarily halting your 401(k) contributions and implement your budget fixes, or one of the other alternatives we suggest in Chapter 4.

As with borrowing from your 401(k) plan, you may have the ability to borrow from your pension. Consider this option carefully. You rely on these funds being there when you retire, so preserve and protect them as best you can.

Home Equity Lines and Second Mortgages

Many lenders encourage individuals who owe credit card debts to consolidate their loans into a home equity line of credit or a home equity loan (a second mortgage). The lenders will give you these loans based on the amount of equity that the lender calculates that you have in your home. Your total home equity equals the total fair market value of your home minus the amount you owe on the home.

If your home is valued at $500,000 and you owe $400,000 then you have $100,000 equity in your home. Both second mortgages and home equity lines of credit give the borrower a good portion of that $100,000 to use. In return, the lender gets a lien on the house so that if you stop paying or cannot pay on the amount you owe, the lender has the right to put the house into foreclosure. Foreclosure, which is discussed at length in Chapter 8, could lead to the sale of your house by your lender.

You should know this: When you borrow money to buy a house, whether initially, or on top of the initial amount, you sign what is called a *promissory note*. The note sets out the terms of the loan and the conditions concerning repayment. To secure the note, or another way of saying it, to make sure it gets paid, the lender will then require that you grant a mortgage on the house to secure repayment. The mortgage is the way the lender makes sure that it will be paid because a house with a mortgage cannot be sold without the mortgage being paid off. The mortgage is paid off by paying the terms of the note.

Home Equity Loans versus Home Equity Lines of Credit

Home equity loans, also known as second mortgages, come as a lump sum payment from the lender usually at a fixed interest rate that includes costs to close the loan, although lenders may waive the closing costs.

Home equity lines of credit are like credit cards and almost always have a variable rate of interest. The lender sets a limit that you can borrow, and you can write checks up to that limit. For instance, you have $100,000 equity in your house. The lender may give you the option to write checks so that you can borrow up to $80,000 of that amount. If you write out a check for $30,000, you still have $50,000 against which you can write out checks. You pay interest on the $30,000 you took out.

Any amount that you borrow reduces the amount you have left to borrow. Once an amount you have borrowed is repaid, you can borrow it again. If you paid back the $30,000 plus the interest, you would again be able to borrow up to $80,000. The longer you take to repay, the more you will pay in interest and the less you will likely be able to borrow because some lenders will automatically add the interest to the amount you borrow.

Still, if the new loan is on better terms than debts being refinanced, the new loan terms are reasonable, and you can afford to make the payments, a consolidation loan may be a good option.

Plus, you may also get a tax advantage from these products. Still, you must be aware that you are pledging your home and putting it at risk.

History repeated itself in 2008 when housing prices took a downturn. Taking out a home equity line to pay off your credit cards, medical bills, or other unsecured debts makes the debt secured by your house. This is a very risky maneuver. You should understand that in agreeing to refinance your home to pay previously unsecured debt (debt with no property associated with it), lenders are converting this unsecured debt to secured debt and pledging your home as collateral, and you are depleting your equity and risking foreclosure and loss of your home in the event of default on the mortgage.

You have the added risk of falling into the trap of running up your credit cards again because you have brought their balances down to zero. It may be too big of a temptation not to use them. Consider carefully the risks before taking a home equity line of credit or a home equity loan/second mortgage.

Reverse Mortgages

If you are at least 62 years of age, a possibility for you is the reverse mortgage. A *reverse mortgage* is a transaction in which the lender pays off the homeowner's current mortgage, advances cash or makes credit available to the homeowner, but does not collect monthly payments as it would with a traditional mortgage. Instead, the lender collects when the property is sold or the homeowner dies. Reverse mortgages enable senior citizens to remain in their home when they cannot afford regular monthly mortgage payments.

All borrowers must be at least 62 years of age and generally must occupy the home as a principal residence (live there more than six months of the year). The property must be a single family, one-unit dwelling in order to be eligible for a reverse mortgage. Some programs also accept two- to four-unit owner-occupied dwellings, along with some condominiums, cooperatives, planned unit developments, and manufactured homes. Generally, mobile homes and some cooperatives are not eligible.

A reverse mortgage is a home loan that you do not have to pay back for as long as you live in your home. It is similar to an equity loan or a second mortgage, only you don't have to make any payments. It can be paid to you in one lump sum, like a second mortgage; as regular monthly income, like you issuing yourself monthly checks from your equity loan; or at the times and in the amounts you want, like an equity loan.

According to the AARP, most borrowers of reverse mortgages choose the line of credit option rather than a lump sum payment or monthly checks.

Source: http://assets.aarp.org/www.aarp.org_/articles/money/financial_pdfs/hmm_hires_nocrops .pdf.

Repayment is due only after the last home owner moves out or dies, at which point the home can be sold to pay off the debt. Because you make no monthly payments, the interest and fees cause the amount the borrower owes to increase over time. As the debt grows, the amount of cash left after selling and paying off the loan generally decreases. The loan repayment can never exceed the home's market value (even if it declines), absolving heirs of any liability.

Congress raised the reverse-mortgage loan limit to $625,500 through the end of 2010. After that, the lending limit reverts to $417,000, unless Congress intervenes. A rough idea of how much a borrower can take out in a reverse mortgage depends on the borrower's age: a 65-year-old can borrow up to approximately 35 percent of his or her home's value; 45 percent for a 75-year-old; and 55 percent for an 85-year-old.[4]

But look at the numbers and the fees. Suppose you are 62 years old and you own your home outright. Its fair market value is $500,000. That means you can borrow up to $175,000. Great! you say. You borrow that amount. Ten years later, what do you owe? It depends on the rate and fees. But assuming a normal 1 percent monthly rate compounded, you'd owe about $350,000. Aside from this, you probably would have paid an application fee up front along with closing costs including a title search. If your house depreciated like many others did in the downturn, you could find that for the $175,000 you borrowed, you now have no equity in your house.

Reverse mortgage borrowers continue to own their homes and are still responsible for property taxes, insurance, and repairs. If the borrower fails to pay these, the lender can use the loan to make payments or require the borrower to pay the loan in full. Similarly, if the borrower is out of the house for more than 12 consecutive months, the reverse mortgage could convert to a 30-year fixed rate mortgage.

The biggest risk with a reverse mortgage is that you are dealing with, and potentially parting with, a significant asset. Entering into a reverse mortgage could leave you without a nest egg or income should you need it later to pay for other living arrangements, such as assisted living or a nursing home. Plus, you will not have your house to pass on to your heirs at your death.

Second, you have to consider the up-front costs of a reverse mortgage. Payments of up-front costs are added on to the final payment of the mortgage. If you are not planning to stay in your house for the long-term, a reverse mortgage is a very expensive proposition. The up-front costs on a $200,000 reverse mortgage could likely exceed $20,000. In addition, interest, fees, and costs then take a bigger bite of your home equity the longer you hold the mortgage. Up-front costs include:

- The origination fee
- Mortgage insurance
- Title insurance
- Initial insurance premium equal to 2 percent of the home's value (up to the reverse-mortgage loan limit) plus 0.5 percent per month of the mortgage balance
- Hour-long training session required by the lender that can cost around $125
- Closing costs and other fees

A reverse mortgage only works for the right person of a certain age who wants to stay in the property and needs an increase in monthly income. But understand this: You are giving up your nest egg. If property taxes are the reason behind your desire to get a reverse mortgage, you may be better off searching out a local program that can help you. You might also be better served by a home repair program from a local program, if repairs or maintenance are the issue; or prescription drug assistance from Medicare, if medical costs are a problem for you.

A note of caution: You will hear that reverse mortgages are a federal program or have a federal guarantee. That's true. But the guarantee does not help you; it is a guarantee to the lender. That's right. The federal government guarantees the lender will not lose money on the loan to you. The government does not guarantee that the lender has given you a good deal.

Before agreeing to a reverse mortgage, understand that the money you will receive from the lender is coming at a stiff cost. If you have no heirs you are concerned with, no children or grandchildren you'd like to leave something to; you are only interested in spending on yourself, as we see on some bumper stickers "I'm spending my kids' inheritance"; and you have no other sources of income, then a reverse mortgage may be the right option for you. But if that's not your goal, consult with a lawyer or trusted family member or friend who is financially savvy before making a decision.

As mentioned, reverse mortgages aren't all bad for the person in the right financial situation. You might be the target market for a reverse mortgage if you want to:

- Enjoy retirement
- Remain independent
- Stay in your home
- Avoid a monthly mortgage payment
- Keep tax-free money
- Spend without restrictions

But do you really need a reverse mortgage? The answer is no if you:

- Want to use the money for vacation
- Want to use the money for investments
- Need to buy something that's not for the house, such as a boat or RV
- Have been contacted by someone who has suggested that you get a reverse mortgage for something they are selling

Federal programs now exist to help you and assist in refinancing your mortgage. We discuss them in Chapter 10.

Lower Interest Rate Credit Card

You could consolidate all your credit cards on a credit card with a lower rate to bring down your credit card debt. If you can then make payments above the minimum to this lower rate card and not use your other cards, great. Get to work.

The major problem with this method is that some people only make the minimum payment on the new credit card while continuing to use old credit cards. Better solutions to your credit card debt can be found in Chapter 7.

Beware of Bad Advice

If you need help to get your budget in order you may want to consult a credit counselor, debt relief organization, or other debt management professional. However, these carry high risks. Some organizations will scam you and many will make your situation worse. Because these organizations can have much to offer if you're careful, we discuss them in more detail in Chapter 6.

Points to Remember

- Be wary of people who offer cash or credit to you without a credit check. Payday loans and vehicle title loans are traps.
- Pawn shops exist to take your good items and give you pennies on the dollar. Sell your item yourself and get what it's worth.
- Tax refund loans give you money you have already earned—money you are going to get soon anyway. Don't let others take a piece of it.
- If you own property and have equity in it, think first of a home equity loan or a second mortgage.
- When dealing with your home, get advice. You worked hard to own your home, so take the time to make sure you do what's best for you and your family.
- Retirement accounts (401[k]), pension plans, and family and friends are safer loan options but tread carefully.
- There are no quick fixes. What you borrow just adds to what you owe. "Borrowing made easy" comes at a stiff price.

CHAPTER

Debt Counselors: How to Tell the Bad from the Good

It's a foolish sheep that makes the wolf his counselor.
—John Ray, *A Collection of English Proverbs* (1678)

om Brown had been having trouble sleeping through the night because his financial troubles were building up. One fateful night after a couple hours of tossing and turning, he got up. He went to the living room and turned on the television. He heard these words: "Wouldn't it be nice not to have any debt? Think about how great your life would be! If you have over $10,000 in credit card debts, we can help you."

Knowing his growing debt load was responsible for his restless night, he figured he'd call the toll-free number and give it a chance. After all, what did he have to lose?

It's too bad Tom didn't see a December 2002 CBS news program on credit counseling.[1] The program discussed how a credit counseling company, Financial Freedom, promised Romanita Berrios that she could eliminate her debt with one easy monthly payment. At the time Berrios, a registered nurse, had a perfect credit rating and was an on-time payer. But she soon faced hardship: she required open-heart surgery and the medical bills began piling up. Desperate, she signed up. As she said, "I did my part. I gave them the money every month."

The credit counselor promised he would lower her rates on her credit cards and pay them off. She soon saw her cards were not being paid; instead, her interest rates and late fees were adding up. Then collection calls started to come in. Worried, she called the company, Financial Freedom. It assured her everything was fine and she shouldn't worry.

Financial Freedom transferred her to another agency that kept taking her money and promising her results. However, nothing was ever paid by these companies. Not one bill. She lost thousands and was on the verge of getting her wages garnished. Her debt became unmanageable and she filed for bankruptcy.

Or maybe Tom would have been more cautious had he read a July 2009 posting by a Cleveland man, JF, on the RipoffReport.com, a Web site where consumers can post fraud reports. JF's story was about how the credit counseling company he dealt with kept taking money out of his checking account, after all of his balances were paid off.[2] Another poster, Lauren from Illinois, wrote about how she paid $121 a month for 12 months and couldn't even get a return call from the credit counseling service, never mind having her debts paid off.[3] There are hundreds of other stories by people who paid money to companies to pay their bills that never followed through.[4]

But Tom was tired and desperate. The advertisement promised that the company would negotiate his debt, work with his lenders, and make deals that only it, with its extensive experience, could negotiate.

Tom entered the program and did exactly what it said to do. He stopped making payments to his creditors so that he could make the one monthly payment to the debt negotiation company. The company promised that soon after he entered the debt repayment program, his credit would begin to improve. Several months after he had started in the debt repayment program, he still continued to receive bills from his creditors, but he was assured that this was normal and it would all be cleared up in the end.

It was only when his credit card was denied at the supermarket that he called his credit card companies. All three of them said he was over 180 days late on payments. He had been assessed late and over-the-limit fees so that his balances had increased from a little over $10,000 to over $16,000.

Now really worried, Tom investigated further. He found out that none of his creditors had received a payment since he had entered into the program. Despite making $1,400 in payments to the debt negotiation company, his debt had increased dramatically. Worse still, his credit score dropped severely. When he called the debt negotiation program, the representative informed him that the company was still in the process of negotiating his accounts and he should continue to make payments.

Tom had had enough. He realized he was on his own to fix his debt issues made dramatically worse by the company on which he had relied. He hung up the phone and began calling his credit card companies. After he made these calls, he phoned his state's attorney general and the Better Business Bureau. Though it took considerable time and effort for Tom to dig himself out from under his financial debt, he found that managing the debt himself was the only way to know exactly how his money was being used. And you know what? He found that he slept much better.

Don't Fall for the Slick Talker

Financial problems do not differ from other life problems. You may find that you need a person who will listen to your story and offer to help you get your debt reduced or under control. Predatory business people find people in debt easy prey. Debt wears down the best people so they grasp at any glimmer of hope.

A recent poll showed that over one-third of parents who had children under 18 years of age living with them have suffered from insomnia caused by money or debt problems and 20 percent of them suffered from depression. Among parents with an income of under $25,000 a year, these figures rise to 47 percent and 40 percent, respectively.

Source: www.thinkmoney.com/debt/news/debt-problems-causing-insomnia-and-depression-0-2062.htm.

Debt wears people down to such a degree that according to one survey nearly one-third of the respondents (an estimated 10 million to 16 million people have debt problems in the United States) reported suffering from severe anxiety because of their debt problems and almost one-quarter reported suffering from severe depression.[5] The respondents attributed their health issues such as ulcers, muscle tension (lower back in particular), migraines, and even heart attacks to stress, caused by their debt problems. Excessive debt equals increased stress, which may cause depression and the inability to see one's situation clearly.

Unscrupulous advisors know that financially strapped people have been weakened and are spending so much time worrying about it that their defenses are down. Professional rip-off artists know the words to say and tricks to play on these people to swindle them out of the rest of their money. The worst part is that these offenders masquerade among honest businesspeople.

Most people cannot pull themselves out of their financial issues on their own. Everyone faces times in their life when they need help with their problems, whether medical, emotional, or physical. You should seek out a trustworthy, honest person who will give you the hard advice that you cannot expect to hear from your friends, family, or even yourself.

At the same time, you must protect yourself from the crooks. Thieves come with all different personalities and from all walks of life. You cannot tell if a person is honest just because he or she *seems* honest. We cannot tell you how many times we hear people say that they cannot believe they were ripped off and taken for a ride because the man (or woman) seemed so sincere, trustworthy, or honest. Thousands of people trusted Bernie Madoff, a prominent man on Wall Street, to handle their money. His fraud lost over $60 billion of these trusting people's money.

Please do not think the person whom you like best is the one you should trust with your finances. Protect yourself by taking the steps we suggest. Remember, you've already dug yourself into a hole—you don't want someone jumping in with another shovel to dig you in deeper.

Help with your financial problems comes in three types:

- Credit counselors
- Debt management plans
- Debt negotiators

As you now know, some debt and credit counselors are good and can give you a hand, and some are bad and they just want to take your money. We've told you why you should not fall for the slick talker; now we'll tell you the other steps to protect yourself, and they are quite easy. If you decide to turn to one of these sources for assistance, it's important to understand what each one may do for you.

Credit Counselors

When you're not making progress on your diet, one of the things you can do is to join a program that provides you with a food and nutritional/diet counselor. When you are having marital problems, you know that you can visit a marriage counselor for help. A credit counselor is the person to turn to when you want help handling your debt problems. The counselor can be your confidant and your support through the storm—as long as you find an honest and competent one.[6]

Credit counseling agencies were originally molded in a social service tradition, and most were reputable nonprofits known as consumer credit counseling services (CCCS) affiliated with the National Foundation for Credit Counseling (NFCC). In recent years, however, more and more businesses have moved away from the social service tradition. More businesses seek benefit and profit rather than helping you with credit counseling.

The type of good and reputable credit counseling organizations that you must look for will advise you on managing your money and debts, help you develop a budget, and usually offer free (or very low-cost) educational materials and workshops. Their credit counselors are certified and trained in the areas of consumer credit, budgeting, and money and debt management by an outside organization.

The trustworthy credit counselor will discuss your entire financial situation with you. The counselor will take the time to understand not just your debts but your entire financial situation. A good counselor will seek to understand how you got into the financial situation you now find yourself in and help you develop solutions to solve your money problems. An initial counseling session typically lasts an hour. Counselors need an hour to fully understand your financial condition. The counselor will take the information you provide, study and work on it, and then offer one or more follow-up sessions to discuss your situation. A reputable credit counseling agency should send you free information about itself and its services without requiring the details of your situation.

Most credit counselors receive at least some financial support from creditors and credit card companies. If these companies are their sole source of funding, however, proceed with caution: You might not be receiving the full loyalty of your counselor.

Creditor counseling organizations offer different services. You may want to shop around to find the one that fits your situation best. Some offer advice on how to repay or handle your debts but put the burden on you to do this. Others may go a little further and offer advice on how a consumer should negotiate with creditors. Then there are others that will undertake the negotiations for you. A general rule of thumb is the more you expect the counselor to do for you, the more costly the service.

Some credit counseling organizations will go beyond the counseling aspects and involve themselves in collecting money from you and distributing it to creditors for a fee. If you reach this point, you should be involved in the formulation of a debt management plan (DMP). We discuss DMPs in depth in the next section.

Even among the honest credit counselors, you will find some individual counselors are better than others, or you may find that you do not "click" with an individual counselor. If you feel that the counselor does not understand your situation or is unable to address your needs and concerns, do not hesitate to suggest to the counselor that you are not satisfied. A good company will provide you with a different counselor because reputable companies know that the same counselor is not right for each person. If you are not comfortable with the counselor you are dealing with and do not have an option to choose another then it is sometimes better to walk away and find another company that will have a counselor who will be better able to address your concerns.

You should know that some so-called nonprofit credit counseling organizations charge high fees, which may be hidden or presented as "voluntary" contributions for their "nonprofit" services. Heed our advice: Run away from any counselor who asks for voluntary contributions. Just because an organization designates itself as a nonprofit organization does not mean you are dealing with a reputable or legitimate business interested in helping you. In fact, a company may not be making a profit because the take-home pay of its officers is so great that it could not possibly make a profit. Many use the term to fool you into thinking that they have your interests foremost in mind; whereas, in truth, their profits at your expense are their true driving force.

Credit counselors affiliated with CCCS and NFCC will charge fees in the following range: $20 to $30 for a counseling session; $30 to $40 to set up an account; and $25 to $30 as a monthly service fee. In addition, members of another reputable organization like CCCS and NFCC called the Association of Independent Consumer Credit Counseling Agencies (AICCCA) may not charge more than $75 to set up a DMP account or more than $50 in monthly service fees.

With so many people ready and waiting to take advantage of you, how do you know that the credit counselor you are dealing with is legitimate? We have put together a series of questions to help you decide. (See Table 6.1.)

Table 6.1   How to Spot a Legitimate Credit Counselor

Question to Ask	Good Answer	Bad Answer = Red Flag
What services do you offer?	A range of services, including budget counseling and savings and debt management classes.	We enroll you in a debt management plan.
What information do you provide?	Free educational materials, including free workshops. Books at low cost.	We provide a pamphlet and classes for additional fees.
Will you help me avoid additional problems?	Services include understanding what went wrong so you do not make the same mistakes.	We free you from debt. If new debts arise, we will take care of them in the future.
Where can I see your fees?	Our fees are in writing and posted on our Web site.	We can negotiate those later but expect you to make a "voluntary contribution."
What if I can't afford to pay your fees?	We will provide you with assistance.	Try to get a loan from a friend or relative.
Will I have a formal written agreement or contract with you?	Yes, we will enter into a simple contract that you should read before any money is exchanged.	You won't need one. I can answer all your questions over the phone. Or, we have a contract. You won't need to read it, but it's long and protects your rights.

(Continued)

Table 6.1 *Continued*

Question to Ask	Good Answer	Bad Answer = Red Flag
Are you licensed to offer your services in my state?	Yes.	It's pending.
Are your counselors accredited or certified by an outside organization?	Yes, we are accredited by the AICCCA or the NFCC.	We train them in house.
How do I know that information about me will be kept confidential and secure?	We provide details of our policies on confidentiality in writing.	You can trust me.
How are your employees compensated?	Annual salary.	Salary plus commissions for certain services you sign up for or additional fees you pay. (They won't tell you this but if they try to upsell these fees and services, you can be sure they are.)
Will you provide me detailed information about your services?	Sure, we will send that right out.	Sure, after you send your statements and detailed information of your debts.
What are your fees?	They are all listed and include a small one-time set-up fee, a low monthly maintenance fee, and a small fee to enroll in a DMP, if we decide one will be good for you.	They vary. In addition to a set-up, monthly maintenance, and DMP fee, we charge an application fee, a membership fee, an up-front fee (often called a "voluntary contribution" or per-creditor fee).
Can I come to your offices?	Yes, we are open during normal business hours.	We are based solely on the phone and Internet.
How long is the initial interview?	Usually, an hour. But we may have a follow-up meeting before we take any actions.	I'll have you on your way in a DMP in 20 minutes.
Will you continue to give me budgeting advice if I don't enter into the DMP?	Yes.	No. The DMP will cover everything. You won't need it.

Even if you are comfortable with all of the answers you get from your prospective credit counselor, you would be wise to check out the business with your Better Business Bureau, your local consumer protection agency, and your state's attorney general. They can tell you about any complaints filed against the business.

Watch out for credit counselors who:

- Charge high up-front or monthly fees for counseling.
- Pressure you to make "voluntary contributions."
- Will not provide you a fee schedule in writing.
- Won't send you free information about their services without your personal information.
- Immediately try to enroll you in a debt management plan (DMP).
- Charge monthly fees for a DMP.
- Enroll you in a DMP without discussing budgeting or changes to your money management.
- Demand payments into a DMP before your creditors have agreed to be in the program.
- Ask for your checking account information so that they can withdraw money from it.

Most credit counselors offer services through local offices, the Internet, or on the telephone. If possible, find an organization that offers in-person counseling. Many universities, military bases, credit unions, housing authorities, and branches of the U.S. Cooperative Extension Service operate reputable nonprofit credit counseling programs. Finally, make sure the credit counselor can help you with all your unsecured debts, not just a couple of creditors with which they have a relationship.

Debt Management Plans

Both reputable and disreputable credit counselors could advise you to enter into a DMP. Good creditor counselors will point you to a DMP to help you resolve your debt issues. Bad credit counselors, on the other hand, use DMPs as a vehicle to receive additional fees and payments from you. As with credit counselors, you have to be alert if you enter into a DMP. Become educated about the plan and if you don't understand something, ask a question.

DMPs allow you to make one monthly payment to pay your unsecured debts. A good DMP will cover all of your unsecured debts (e.g., credit card, medical, or student loans) and will pay them according to a schedule. At its best, a DMP can get you a reduction in interest rates, an elimination of finance charges, lower monthly payments, "re-aged" accounts to make you current, relief from collection agents, and one-stop bill paying on your unsecured debts.

In a DMP, you deposit money each month with the credit counseling organization that will direct your money to pay the creditors of your unsecured debts. Your credit counselor will develop a payment schedule about which both you and your creditors agree. In some instances, your creditors may agree to lower your interest rates and/or waive certain fees.

A successful DMP requires you to make regular, timely payments and could take 48 months or more to complete. Your credit counselor should be able to estimate how long it will take for you to complete the plan. Note that you may have to agree not to apply for—or use—any additional credit while you're participating in the DMP.

Never under any circumstance enter a DMP in which the credit counseling organization requires you to give it the right to access your bank account.

We recommend that you should only sign up for a DMP after you have made changes to your budget and spending habits so you can avoid the same debt problems in the future. Also, you should only pursue a DMP after a reputable credit counselor has spent time thoroughly reviewing your financial situation and has offered you customized advice on managing your money.

Many people have lost considerable money and ruined their credit because they entered into a DMP that was set up by dishonest people. Therefore, take the following precautions when entering into or participating in a DMP:

1. Before making any payments to the DMP, double check to make sure you are enrolled in the plan and they have offered the concessions that the credit counseling organization described to you.
2. Continue making payments to your creditors until they confirm they are receiving payments from the DMP.

3. Only enter into a DMP that has an affordable monthly payment.
4. Make regular, timely payments.
5. Make sure the payments from the DMP will reach your creditors before they are due each month.
6. Read your monthly statements from your creditors to ensure that they are being paid according to the DMP.
7. Contact your credit counselor immediately if you cannot make the regular payment or if the creditor is not being paid as planned.

Your debt and credit are at risk when you enter into a DMP, so you have to be the one who monitors the situation. If the payments from the DMP are not made on time, you may lose all of the concessions from the creditors, including the lower interest rates and fee waivers. You could then be hit with late fees and "late" payment remarks on your credit report.

Remember the advertisements for the credit counselors AmeriDebt, Inc. and DebtWorks, Inc. in the mid-2000s? You don't hear these ads anymore. The Federal Trade Commission filed charges against them for deceptive practices in their credit counseling and debt management plans. More than 460,000 consumers were victims of the abusive practices of these and their affiliated companies.

Source: www.ftc.gov/opa/2005/03/ameridebt.shtm.

DMPs can be very advantageous if done correctly and set up by a good and reputable credit counseling agency. Initially, a DMP may lower your credit score, but will then, over time, improve it. With determination, you can fix your debt problems through a good DMP with a reputable agency. But they take time (four years or more for some people) and perseverance. Make sure you are up for the task.

Debt Negotiators

We have all heard the claims: "See up to 50 percent of your debt negotiated away!" "Gain your financial freedom in as little as 12 months," "Service-fee money back guarantee!"

We have all seen the commercials that promise that our debt
will be cut in half. We immediately ask ourselves: "How can they
do it?" "How can they make these claims?" It would be great if
these claims were true. Who wouldn't want their debt cut in half?
Unfortunately, most, if not all, of these companies cannot live up to
these claims. In fact, they probably don't even try to once they have
some of your money.

Debt negotiation companies (also known as debt settlement
companies) initially sound like credit counselors with DMPs on
steroids, but they're usually bad news. They claim to work with
creditors to reduce debt, set up DMPs, and collect and distribute
payments to creditors. But that's just half of what they propose to
do. These companies advertise that they'll cut your debt by as much
as half. They tell you that your debts will be paid off in a quarter of
the time of a DMP. It all sounds too good to be true, and in fact, it
is too good to be true.

Debt negotiation firms make their extravagant claims to entice you to pick up the phone or e-mail to contact them. Just like car dealers who advertise cars that you won't find on their lots, debt negotiation companies thrive on unsubstantiated claims. They draw consumers to them through their sensationalism. Many of these debt negotiation firms may claim that they are nonprofits, but as we've learned, that does not mean they will act in your interest.

They may claim that they can arrange for your unsecured debt, credit cards in particular, to be paid off for 50 percent or less of the balance owed. They suggest, for example, that they can arrange to pay off your $17,000 credit card balance for $8,000.

These firms may claim that using their services will have little or no negative impact on your ability to get credit in the future or any negative information can be removed from your credit report when you complete their programs. They will tell you that they are saving you from bankruptcy and tell you to stop making payments to your creditors but instead send the payments to them. However, these companies cannot support these bogus claims.

> On one day in the spring of 2009, the New York Attorney General issued 14 subpoenas to debt settlement companies and the law firm that counseled them in order to stop the abusive practices of these companies.
>
> ---
>
> *Source*: "Attorney General Cuomo Sues Debt Settlement Companies for Deceiving and Harming Consumers." May 19, 2009. http://www.ag.ny.gov/media-center/2009/may/may19b_09.html.

Debt negotiation companies will likely charge you large fees or sell you services and products you don't need. They may even tack on a fee that they will claim to be a percentage of what they saved you. Debt negotiation companies can be very risky, have a long-term negative impact on your credit report, and greatly impact your ability to get credit.

> When the Federal Trade Commission shut down the National Consumer Council in 2004 for misleading advertising, it learned that only 638 of the company's 44,844 clients (1.4 percent!) completed the debt settlement program. Worse, 43 percent of the clients dropped out of the program after paying an average of $1,780 in fees.

Debt negotiation and debt settlement companies will suggest (and sometimes require) that you stop making payments on credit card and other unsecured debt so that you have enough money to save up for their program (and pay their fees) before the plan is in place. However, there is no guarantee that a creditor will accept partial payment of a legitimate debt or that the creditor will agree to participate in the program. In fact, if you stop making payments, late fees and interest usually are added to the debt each month. If the nonpayment and the fees cause you to exceed your credit limit, additional fees and charges also can be added. Bottom line: This can cause your original debt to go up. Moreover, although creditors have no obligation to agree to negotiate the amount a consumer owes, creditors do have a legal obligation to provide accurate information to the credit reporting agencies, including your failure to make monthly payments (even if you are not paying at the command of your debt negotiation or debt settlement company). Late payments and nonpayments can result in negative entries on your credit report.

Creditors could also have the right to sue you for the money you owe. In some cases in which creditors have won lawsuits based on the borrower's nonpayment (even when the borrower paid the debt negotiator monthly), creditors have been allowed to put liens on homes to collect debt.

You will receive very little upside in entering into a relationship with a debt negotiation or debt settlement company. You will likely lose money, not impact your debt, and expose yourself to bigger debts and bigger financial problems.

Tip-offs to bad debt negotiators include:

- Guarantees that they can eliminate your unsecured debt.
- Promises that your unsecured debts can be paid off with pennies on the dollar.
- Charges for substantial monthly service fees or a percentage of what they "save" you. They may also require you to make monthly payments before any arrangements are set up.
- Instructions to stop making payments to or communicating with your creditors.
- Promises that working with them will have no negative impact on your credit report.
- Claims that they can remove all negative information from your credit report.

No matter how down and out you feel, and no matter how difficult it may be for you to get things together, remember that crooked businesses are mixed in with honest ones. Credit counselors can offer good advice to help you with your debt, but you have to be careful in choosing where you take your advice.

Points to Remember

- Don't settle for just any credit counselor. If you are uncomfortable with your individual counselor, request a new one.
- Ask questions of the company and check it out on the Internet to see if it is legitimate.
- Avoid high-profile companies that make big promises about wiping out your debt.
- DMPs may serve you well when done in conjunction with a reputable and honest credit counselor.
- Stay away from credit repair firms. No company can repair, restore, or clean up your bad credit report no matter how much you pay unless the report contains inaccuracies (and those you can fix yourself). Only time and good credit behavior can repair a bad credit report.

PART

II

FINDING YOUR WAY USING NONBANKRUPTCY SOLUTIONS

7

The Way Out of Credit Card, Medical, and Student Loan Debt

You want 21 percent risk free? Pay off your credit cards.
—Andrew Tobias, American journalist

Different types of debt require different solutions and the strategies that you will adopt will result in different outcomes. Some debts are secured by collateral, such as the mortgage on your house and the auto loan to your car. These secured debts require you to pledge some security to back them up. If you stop paying secured debts, you will put at risk, and likely lose, the possessions that you have pledged to secure the debt. Other debts, such as child support and taxes, though not secured, can be enforced by federal or state governments. You can suffer harsh penalties, including incarceration, if you don't pay these debts. The third major type of debts is your ordinary, everyday debts that are backed solely by your promise to repay them. Unsecured debts include credit cards, medical bills, and student loans.

Up till now, we have discussed generally how to deal with all your debts. In the next few chapters, we provide specific advice on how to handle different types of debt. But just as every debt has its unique properties and characteristics, so do each of your creditors. You won't know what will work with your specific creditors until you try. This chapter provides the approaches you should use when you want to get out of your credit card, medical, personal, and other unsecured debt.

The average credit card debt per household in the United States was $8,329 in 2008. For households that had one or more credit cards, the average outstanding credit card debt was $10,679 in 2008.

Source: The Nilson Report, April 2009

Credit card debt is perhaps the most dangerous type of debt. Readily available in your purse or wallet, credit cards satisfy the impulse of the moment. Whether you desire an ice cream cone, concert tickets, new shoes, or a piece of beautiful jewelry in the display cabinet, you can have it immediately by paying with a credit card. Credit cards are attractive because you only have to pay two or three percent of what you spend each month and you can continue to buy until you reach your maximum spending limit. You then pay your minimum payment on time and need make only a minimum payment to retain the credit line and not go into default. But even after reaching a maximum spending limit, you can always get another credit card so that the spending spree can go on. Credit cards have replaced cash. They have become a crutch that continually traps more and more people.

The Credit Card Trap

The credit card industry, much like the tobacco industry, knows that if you hook a customer when he or she is young, you have a customer for life. Because of this, the credit card industry has engaged in a form of predatory marketing practices in targeting college students, although government legislation seeks to stop these practices. One young man named Sean O'Donnell (a 22-year-old National Merit Scholarship Finalist who planned to become a lawyer) stepped into the trap.

Sean's mother, Jane, tells how she had a long talk with him about his credit card debt. He had 12 credit cards: 3 from major banks, 8 from retail stores, and 1 from a national gas station chain. She knew he had been to credit counseling and that he had transferred from the University of Dallas back to live at his home in Oklahoma to cut down on his expenses. Sean had enrolled in the University of Oklahoma and he was holding down two jobs while attending college.

In 2009, 84 percent of the student population overall had credit cards, an increase of approximately 11 percent since the fall of 2004.

Source: Sallie Mae, "How Undergraduate Students Use Credit Cards," April 2009.

Both of Sean's parents had been helping him as much as they could. But their help did little to make Sean responsible for his debts. With their resources limited and another son ready to enter college, Sean's parents were greatly constrained in what they could do for him. Sean could see no way out from the stress of the overwhelming debt. He wanted to go to law school but knew that there was no feasible way of paying the tuition and attaining his goals. His mother tried to help him figure out what to do, but he was really depressed. A week later he committed suicide.

Another example is Mark Harris, whose credit card problems also started in college. He bought his textbooks at the university store at the beginning of his freshman year. At the bottom of the bookstore bag, he found numerous credit card offers. Mark had heard that establishing a credit history would benefit him when he a rented an apartment or wanted to buy a car or house later in life. Plus, he thought it would be nice to have a little extra spending money throughout the semester. So Mark applied for one credit card and used it sparingly throughout his freshman year.

However, sophomore year was a different story for Mark. First, he signed up for a credit card in order to get a free T-shirt at a football game. Next, he signed up for another credit card on the quad because of the free beach towels and beer mugs. He began buying new clothes, CDs, and dinners and drinks at the bar for all of his friends. Before he knew it, he had accumulated more than $10,000 in credit card debt by the end of junior year. Mark worked part-time at school but could not bring down his debt by paying only the minimum payment and attempted suicide.

Sadly, many people have chosen to take their own lives over debt problems. We relate these extreme cases of credit card problems to show the extreme impact credit card debt has on people. You must keep the following in mind: No debt is worth your life. If you are feeling overwhelmed by debt, talk to someone whom you trust to discuss your issues. This person may be someone in your religious community or a good friend. Talking your situation through will help you put your debt in proper perspective. Never keep your debts a secret. Never consider taking your own life because you owe money.

No matter how large your credit card or other unsecured debt, you can get relief. The amount of your debt, your determination, and the willingness of your creditors to work with you will determine which of the following roads out of credit card debt you should take. You may have to take more than one step to free yourself from credit card, medical, and other unsecured debts. The six turns, or steps, we suggest are to negotiate, evaluate and plan, discover new ways to pay, make changes to your budget, seek outside help, and consider bankruptcy.

Negotiate

Creditors want your money. They all hold this goal in common. In Chapter 2, you learned how to negotiate with creditors. Unsecured debt, such as credit cards and medical bills, may be the easiest to negotiate because you have the greatest leverage—repayment of these debts is almost entirely in your hands, and your creditors cannot take any of your property if you don't pay. Plus, you have the ability to completely wipe out most or all of your unsecured debt if you file for bankruptcy (one exception, however, is student loan debt). The first step of getting out of unsecured debt is to negotiate because you will never get anything if you don't ask for something. There's no harm in asking—you won't be punished by a higher interest rate or shorter payment periods.

Be aware that whenever you extend a payment plan and lower your monthly payment, you are increasing the amount of interest you will pay over the life of the loan. Sometimes, this greater amount of interest you will pay can equal tens of thousands of dollars, depending on the balance and length of time.

Barbara Meyers learned the hard way. She mailed her payment to one credit card company on time but it was received late and her interest rate spiked to 29.99 percent. While dealing with that, another credit card company hit her with a 29.99 percent rate on the money she owed them because the company changed the due date of her payment from the fourth of the month to the third of each month and she did not realize it. Late payments triggered the default rate. She cried herself to sleep when this happened and woke up with a feeling of dread and despair.

She called each company, explained her dilemma, and asked for a lower interest rate. If they told her no, she asked for a supervisor. She persisted even though they told it would take three or four days to get back to her. If they didn't call her back by the next day, she called them. Her result was that the first credit card company lowered the interest rate to 12 percent with a schedule of payments for the life of the loan; the other credit card company set the rate at 5 percent as long as she provided payments directly from her checking account on the first day of each month. She made a wise choice to fight for herself instead of giving up.

Credit Card Debt

Because of the U.S. government's crackdown in the Credit CARD Act of 2009 on certain practices of the credit card industry—via the Credit CARD Act of 2009—many credit card companies are imposing and enforcing new fees and penalties. Some of these new fees include:

- Inactivity fees for accounts that have not been used in the last 12 months
- Fees for purchases made outside the country

- Over-the-limit fees for increasing a credit line
- Cross-default fees (If you default on one credit card, another credit card can increase your interest rate because of that default.)
- Reinstatement fees for late payers attempting to collect rewards
- Annual fees on credit cards that never previously had annual fees

Even as they introduce new fees, credit card companies are still trying hard to acquire new customers and to retain old customers. They won't tell you this, but it's easier for them to keep you than it is to get someone to replace you. You have heard the adage "a bird in the hand is worth two in the bush." That's how the credit card companies think. They do not want to lose customers.

You can use their desire to retain you as a customer to your advantage. In addition to the suggestions provided in Chapter 2, we suggest you do the following when negotiating a settlement of your credit card:

1. Examine credit card offers that you receive in the mail or that you find on the Internet.
2. Determine the best introductory (teaser) and long-term interest rates that banks are offering.
3. Call your credit card company:
   - Tell them that you have been a good customer and mention the number of years you have been with them.
   - Mention you have received new offers with lower rates.
   - Tell them that you hate to leave them because you love their card.
   - Explain you don't wish to terminate the relationship but by staying you are losing money.
   - Ask them whether they can lower your interest rate to keep your business.
   - Mention the specific rates and actual offers you have received or found.
4. Mention that with a lower interest rate you will find it easier to make payments for which you now find it difficult. You will capitalize on most companies wanting to avoid writing off debts.

5. **Threaten bankruptcy.** Tell them you have prepared a bankruptcy petition and that the creditor will receive no dividend. Follow up with a letter stating your intention to file bankruptcy and include a check to the creditor with a note written in the bottom left corner that reads "in full settlement."

If the credit card companies will not change your interest rates or fees, you may want to consider transferring your balances to a lower interest rate card. If they agree, you will have gained yourself some breathing room but you will have to keep working to get rid of the debt completely. Keep moving down the road out of credit card debt.

High medical expenses are the cause for 62.1 percent of all bankruptcy cases filed. The share of bankruptcy cases attributable to medical problems rose by 50 percent between 2001 and 2007.

Source: David U. Himmelstein et al, "Medical Bankruptcy in the United States, 2007: Results of a National Study." Elsevier, Inc., 2009.

Medical Debt

Like credit card debt, medical debt can be *discharged,* meaning released or extinguished, in bankruptcy. Your ability to discharge medical debt gives you extra leverage in negotiating because you can drastically reduce the creditor's recovery if you file for bankruptcy. In addition to the suggestions in Chapter 2, you can take the following steps when negotiating medical debt:

1. Make sure you are only paying for the services you received. Examine your detailed bill.
2. Call your insurance company and/or Medicaid to ensure that you were not covered for any of the services for which you are being billed in full. Also, ensure that they have received bills for the proper services.

3. Call the hospital or service provider and explain your situation. Express that you cannot afford the bill or the payments.
4. Be explicit in the relief you seek. Ask for interest-free forbearance for a certain period of time, a payment plan, or a reduction in your bill.

You will likely find hospitals and medical providers are willing to help you restructure your payments and that they will be fairly sensitive to your needs. However, if your loans have been sent to collection agencies, you most likely won't find a sympathetic ear and will have to negotiate as you would with a hostile lender. But remember, collection agencies get paid a percentage of what they collect. You can negotiate with them but don't be shy—demand that they work something out with you.

Student Loan Debt

Student loan debt is different from credit card and medical debt because you cannot discharge it in bankruptcy. Plus, not paying and defaulting on student loans can cause substantial fees and penalties.

For example, on federal student loans, if you fail to make payments for 270 days, the government can garnish your wages up to 15 percent and a portion of your Social Security may be withheld. The government can intercept your federal and state income tax returns and direct them to your loan. You may be prevented from renewing your state professional license and you could be sued for the immediate payment of the full loan amount. Plus, you could be hit with collection charges of up to 25 percent.

Two out of every three undergraduates walk off the graduation stage with some form of student debt, according to a 2008 College Board study. The average amount is $22,700 per graduate.

Source: David K. Randall. "Tips on Consolidating Student Loans," www.forbes.com/2009/04/15/student-loans-moneybuilder-personal-finance-consolidate.html.

Your lender, despite these different regulations, may be willing to work with you. In addition to the suggestions in Chapter 2, here are steps you can take specifically for negotiating student loan debt:

1. Explain the situation to your lender.
2. Ask for a lower interest rate. You could qualify for lower rates if you:
   - Have payments automatically deducted from your bank account
   - Make a preset number of on-time payments
   - Maintain good grades in school
3. Change your payment plan. Repayment plan options include:
   - *Extended repayment.* Monthly payments begin at a minimum of $50 with payment terms up to 25 years.
   - *Graduated repayment.* Monthly payments start as low as $25 and increase over time with payment terms of 10 to 30 years.
   - *Income or income-based contingent repayment.* Monthly payments are capped at a percentage of your discretionary income (income based on your income and family size, not the total amount you borrowed).
   - *Federal student loan repayment.* Federal agencies repay federally issued students loan as a recruitment or retention incentive for candidates or current employees of the agency.
4. Consolidate your loan. This option is available on federal loans only. Consolidation may extend your payment period but it may not reduce your interest rate.
5. Ask for loan forgiveness. Under certain circumstances, the federal government will cancel all or part of your student loans. To qualify, you must:
   - Perform volunteer work such as AmeriCorp, Peace Corps, or Volunteer in Service to America (VISTA)
   - Perform military service such as the National Guard
   - Teach or practice medicine in certain types of communities; or
   - Meet other criteria specified by the forgiveness program.
6. See if your loans can be canceled. Certain federal education loans can be canceled for fire fighters, certain law enforcement and correction officers, and victims of 9/11. Other reasons a loan might be canceled include school closing, disability, or death.
7. Seek an economic hardship deferment or forbearance that suspends or reduces your monthly payments. Under a *deferment,*

your lender will allow you to skip payments, generally for up to a year at a time, and your payment period is extended. *Forbearance* mirrors deferment in that your lender will allow you to skip payments for a set period of time. However, the lender does not extend your payment deadline. You will have to make larger payments to pay off the loan by your original deadline once the deferment period is over. Keep in mind that interest continues to grow when you stop making payments under a hardship deferment or forbearance.

Student loans have no statute of limitations, which means *lenders* may have the right to pursue you to collect past-due student loans even after you are retired. Deal with them now because you wouldn't want your Social Security checks to be garnished.

If you don't know whether you qualify for any of these repayment options, call your lender and ask. Student loan lenders can be very helpful and accommodating.

Evaluate and Plan

Do you know how many credit cards you have? Do you know what percentage interest rate you are paying on each credit card?

If you are like most Americans, you cannot answer these two questions precisely. In fact, you would likely have to guess on both questions. Credit card companies do not want you to know. But by not knowing, you are throwing away money. It is time to fight back.

If you charge $2,000 on a card with a $40 annual fee plus 19.8 percent interest and then pay only your minimum balance, you will pay $8,202 in additional finance charges and it will take you 31 years and two months to pay off the card.

First, cut up all but two of your credit cards. There are two reasons for this: first, the more credit cards that you have, the more trouble that you will naturally get into; and second, it's nearly impossible to follow all the changes your lenders make to your accounts. You should dispose of the cards even if you cannot pay off the balances right away. Let's start evaluating:

- Get rid of department store or other retail cards. Credit cards from retail and department stores usually have the highest interest rates and often include annual fees. The coupons and discounts you receive on the credit cards from retail stores rarely exceed the amount you will pay in fees and interest.
- Cut up any card with an annual fee. If you have any credit cards without an annual fee, why are you paying extra money for those other cards? Annual fees are a waste of money. No credit card is that impressive or has such great benefits that you should give a credit card company extra money in the form of an annual fee.
- Look at your credit card statements to figure out which credit cards have the lowest interest rates. Choose the two credit cards that charge the lowest interest rates and that do not charge annual fees. Make sure you know if there is any charge for transferring balances before you make your decision. Also, beware of cards that offer low introductory rates that skyrocket after the promotional period ends unless you can get the balance paid off before that point.
- Close out your newest accounts. One of the components of your FICO score is the length of your credit history, which is negatively affected each time you open a new account. By closing these newer cards, you are effectively making the average age of your credit history older.

Finally, transfer as much debt as you can to your two remaining intact credit cards that you identified as having the lowest interest rates, no annual fees, and no charge or minimal charge for balance transfers; also, if they offer low introductory rates, you are certain that you can pay the balance off before the introductory period ends; and preferably they are older accounts. We will discuss how to make payments on credit card debts in the next section.

Approximately 91.1 million American households had one or more credit cards at the end of 2008.[*] The U.S. Census Bureau determined that there were nearly 1.5 billion credit cards in use in the United States. A stack of all these credit cards would reach more than 70 miles into space and be almost as tall as thirteen Mount Everests.[**]

Sources: [*]*The Nilson Report*, April 2009; [**]*The New York Times*, February 23, 2009.

Discover New Ways to Pay

The third step in finding your way out of unsecured debt is to discover new ways to pay. You may have heard of the Snowball Method as a way to dig yourself out of credit card debt. The Snowball Method is commonly suggested by financial management experts, including Dave Ramsey. We agree wholeheartedly with this method but have added to it to cover the great variances in interest rates on credit cards. We call our method the Excavation Method.

The Excavation Method

What is the Excavation Method? The simple answer: It is a way to start paying your debt so that you build momentum and dig yourself out of your credit card hole or your other unsecured debt holes as quickly as possible. (See "The Excavation Method: Paying Off Your Debts.")

If you have a balance of $15,000 on a credit card with a 20 percent interest rate and a minimum monthly payment of 2.5 percent, it will take you almost 42 years to pay off the debt, and you will pay an incredible $29,500 in interest. One in six families in the United States with credit cards pay only the minimum due every month.

Source: Experian National Score Index Study, February 2007.

No matter how many credit cards you have, you can use this method to get rid of your credit card debt. In addition, if you have other unsecured debt, such as medical bills or student loans, you can incorporate them into this method.

1. Determine what your minimum payment is on all your credit cards.
2. Be certain that you will have sufficient money each month to pay the total of all your minimum payments plus at least an extra $50 but as much as you can afford. You must be able to do this every month.
3. Rank your credit cards by the amount of the outstanding balance. The credit card with the lowest balance is ranked number one. If the balance on two credit cards is within

$1,000, the credit card with the higher interest rate should be the one that you pay off first.

4. Pay the minimum to each card each month but add an extra $50 (or more if you can afford it each month) to the payment of the credit card with the lowest outstanding balance, credit card #1.

5. Continue to make payments in this manner until credit card #1 is paid off completely. Then pay the minimum to all the remaining credit cards, except now pay the extra $50 and the amount you had been paying as your minimum payment on credit card #1 to credit card #2.

6. Continue paying in this way each month until credit card #2 is paid off. Then start paying the minimum of the remaining cards plus the amounts you had been paying as minimums on credit cards #1 and #2 *plus* the extra $50.

7. Follow this method until all credit cards or other unsecured debts are paid off.

The Excavation Method: Paying Off Your Debts

To explain how the Excavation Method works, we will use a simplified example dealing with four credit cards.

1. Determine the minimum payment on each card.

Credit Card	Balance	Minimum Payment	Interest Rate
Bank credit card #1	$1,000	$ 50	18.9%
Bank credit card #2	$3,000	$150	20.9%
Bank credit card #3	$4,000	$200	28.9%
Department store card	$ 500	$ 25	24.9%
Total Debt	$8,500		

2. Evaluate your monthly income.
   Make sure you have at least an extra $50.
3. Rank your cards.
   Card #1 = Department store card
   Card #2 = Bank credit card #1
   Card #3 = Bank credit card #3 (although it has the larger balance, it has the higher interest rate and is within $1,000 of bank credit card #2)
   Card #4 = Bank credit card #2

(Continued)

4. Start excavation payments.
   In the first month, you pay:
   $75 to card #1 (minimum payment plus extra $50)
   $50 to card #2 (minimum payment)
   $200 to card #3 (minimum payment)
   $150 to card #4 (minimum payment)
   Total = $475

5. Start Excavation Level Two.
   After you have paid off card #1 (approximately 8 months), then pay:
   $125 to card #2 ($50 minimum payment plus $25 minimum payment you were paying on card #1, and the extra $50)
   $200 to card #3 ($200 minimum payment)
   $150 to card #4 ($150 minimum payment)
   Total = $475

6. Start Excavation Level Three.
   After you have paid off card # 2 (approximately 8 months after card #1 was paid off), then pay:
   $325 to card #3 ($200 minimum payment plus $25 minimum payment you were paying on card #1, $50 minimum payment on card #2, and the extra $50)
   $150 to card #4 ($150 minimum payment)
   Total = $475

7. Continue Excavation Plan.
   After you have paid off card #3 (approximately 15 months after card #2 was paid off), then pay:
   $475 to card #4 ($150 minimum payment plus $25 minimum payment you were paying on card #1, $50 minimum payment on card #2, $200 minimum payment on card #3, and the extra $50)
   Total = $475

8. Finish Excavation Method and be free from credit card debt!

Make all of your payments and do not incur new credit card debt. In approximately four years, you will have paid off all four credit cards, $8,500 in debt, by making only $50 dollars over the minimum payments.

If you only make minimum payments, it would take you approximately 12 years to pay off the same $8,500 in credit card debt and you would pay more than $4,000 in interest.

If you miss payments or have some other default that causes a big jump in interest rates on one card, call that credit card lender to complain and negotiate the rates back down. If that lender refuses to restore the lower rate, reexamine the order of your credit cards.

You must remember: For the Excavation Method to work, you *must* continue to pay the same amount every month no matter how many cards you paid off and you cannot make any new charges on any credit cards. Use cash or your debit card instead.

Additional Payment Methods

In addition to using the Excavation Method, we suggest that you do the following in order to pay off your credit cards in less time and to decrease the amount of interest that you ultimately pay.

First, consider dividing the credit card minimum payments in half and paying that amount twice a month. Because interest is calculated based on the average daily balance of your account for the entire month, you are able to reduce your average balance during the month and therefore reduce the finance charges assessed.

Second, make *snowflake payments* to your credit cards. Snowflake payments are those you make toward your debts whenever you receive extra or unexpected money, such as money from gifts, garage sales, and earnings from overtime or part-time work. Putting these little extra amounts toward your credit card and other unsecured debts make a big dent in the overall amount.

Third, consider paying your credit cards and other unsecured debt directly from your paycheck or checking account so that you never control the money and are never tempted to spend it. This is a psychological trick that can make a big difference.

You can stop receiving prescreened credit card offers by notifying each of the three major credit bureaus: Equifax, Experian, and Trans Union (see Appendix A for more information).

Make Changes to Your Budget

The next step is to make changes to your budget. Very large outstanding balances on your credit card, medical, and other unsecured debts may call for major budget changes. In addition to the general overhaul of your budget, which we discussed in Chapter 2, you should consider the following changes in particular:

- Even the highest rate of investment returns can't compete with the interest payments due on credit cards. Cash in your savings or any investments.
- If you have a life insurance policy, you should think about borrowing against it. You can take your time paying back what you borrow but you must make sure you do pay the borrowed amount back. If you don't pay it back before you die, what you owed plus interest and potential penalties will be deducted from the settlement due to the beneficiary.
- Sell any extra and unnecessary items in a yard sale. You cannot expect to make big money through a yard sale, but every little bit helps. Plus, it will give you a good chance to clean out your house and to organize your life!

- Get a part-time or second job. We understand the last thing you want to do is spend more time away from your family, but the more you are able to put toward your debt now, the greater chance you will have time to do the things you enjoy doing in the future.

Know Your New Rights When Dealing with Credit Card Companies

The Credit CARD Act of 2009 restricts some of the more overbearing practices by credit card companies. Make sure your credit card companies follow these new rules:

- Wait until you're 60 days late in making the minimum payment before applying a penalty interest rate to your existing debt.
- Give 45 days' notice before raising interest rates.
- Send out your bill no later than 21 days before the due date. They cannot send a bill a week before its due date, making it difficult to make your payment on time.
- Give you at least until 5 P.M. on the payment due date for on-time payments. No more early-morning deadlines. Also, no more late fees if the due date is a Sunday or a holiday, and your payment doesn't arrive until a day later.
- Apply payments to the highest-interest debt first—whether it's your cash advance, balance transfer, or new purchase balance.
- Get your permission before allowing you the "privilege" of spending more than your credit limit and paying a $39 fee for that privilege per transaction. You should decline.
- For students: No one under 21 can have a credit card unless a parent, legal guardian, or spouse is the primary cardholder. Plus, parent or guardian permission is required to increase the credit limit. Students with their own income can submit proof and ask for an exception to the cosigner requirement.
- For gift cards: Sellers of gift cards will also have to inform the buyer of any dormancy fee, that is, fee for nonuse, and expiration dates must be at least five years.

Seek Professional Help

Credit counselors and debt management plans (DMPs) can be particularly effective for dealing with credit card, medical, and other unsecured debts. As we previously discussed, there are many good people who wish to help you with your debt problems. The problem is, however, there are many people out there who are looking to take advantage of you during a vulnerable time. The fifth step of getting out of unsecured debt is to seek professional help if you decide that you need extra help in dealing with your unsecured debts. (Please review Chapter 6). You are well advised to seek a counselor through the National Foundation for Credit Counseling (NFCC) and the Association of Independent Consumer Credit Counseling Agencies (AICCCA). Remember, just because a company calls itself "nonprofit," does not mean that it has your best interest in mind.

Remedies to Avoid with Unsecured Debt

A loan from your friends and family, borrowing from your 401(k) and pension plan, and taking out a home equity loan may all be considered to pay off credit card, medical, and other unsecured debts. However, we strongly recommend you avoid these remedies when dealing with unsecured debts if you are dealing with significant debt and financial issues.

Specifically, borrowing from your 401(k) or pension plan may make sense if you have only a cash flow problem and do not anticipate bankruptcy in your future. However, you must make sure to repay the money quickly so you continue to receive returns on that money. Repay the loan through payments taken directly from your pay check.

Do not use these remedies to pay off unsecured debt if you are teetering on the edge of bankruptcy unless you are certain that you can pay them back in full. We are adamant against using these remedies for unsecured debts when you are close to bankruptcy because credit card, medical, and other unsecured debts are dischargeable in bankruptcy, for the most part. This means that you will be able to get rid of these debts through bankruptcy. It's not worth the risk of losing a good relationship with a friend or family member, putting your retirement money at risk, or putting your house at risk to pay off unsecured debts. You are converting your credit card, medical, and other unsecured debts into more significant debts that are either treated differently through bankruptcy or may cause irreparable harm to your friendships, family relations, retirement, or home.

Consider Bankruptcy

Unless you are judgment proof because you have nothing that a creditor can collect from you, have no income or property a creditor could attach, and none of the suggested remedies was successful to drive away your financial woes, you should prepare to file bankruptcy to get rid of your credit card, medical, and other unsecured debt. In bankruptcy, you will likely be able to discharge, or extinguish, all of your credit card, medical, and other unsecured debt if you qualify for a chapter 7 bankruptcy case or you will likely have to pay a reduced amount of these debts over a three- to five-year period in a chapter 13 bankruptcy case.

Of course, you will need to consider your whole financial picture. If your credit card, medical, personal, and other unsecured debts are the roots of your financial problems and eliminating or reducing these debts will improve your life considerably, filing for bankruptcy may be right for you.

Points to Remember

- Negotiation tactics vary depending on the type of debt you wish to modify.
- You need only two credit cards.
- Use the Excavation Method to free yourself from all credit card and unsecured debt quicker.
- Credit card, medical, and other unsecured debt can be discharged, or reduced through bankruptcy. So do not put friendships, family relationships, your retirement, or your house at risk to pay off these debts.

Foreclosure Basics and Rescue Scams

I never wonder to see men wicked, but I often wonder to see them not ashamed.

—Jonathan Swift, "Thoughts on Various Subjects"

The information in Chapters 9 and 10 will show you how to fight foreclosure and save your home. But we think you should first know what your lender can do by understanding what foreclosure is and how it works. If you are in the midst of the foreclosure process, we present specific defenses you can use. We also discuss what you have to watch out for if you're near foreclosure. Instances of vultures and scam artists preying on homeowners are on the rise!

What Is Foreclosure?

Foreclosure is a state-regulated legal process that allows a lender to recover the amount owed on a defaulted loan by selling or taking ownership (repossession) of your real property (the house) securing the loan. Each state has variations in how it allows financial institutions to process foreclosures but foreclosure processes share the same basic steps.

Foreclosure proceedings can begin after a single missed payment, but most banks and lenders have a grace period for late payments, usually with a fee added on. After the second missed payment, however, you can expect to start getting phone calls. Many lenders will only accept both late payments to bring the loan current. They also may refuse any partial payments.

Once you fall three months behind, your lender will likely ramp up collection efforts and commonly will begin the foreclosure process. The foreclosure process will likely proceed in one of two ways depending on whether your state uses mortgages or deeds of trust for the purchase of real property. Generally, states that use mortgages conduct judicial foreclosures; states that use deeds of trust conduct nonjudicial foreclosures. Judicial foreclosure procedure requires that a court act in order to foreclose. Nonjudicial foreclosures can be completed without any court action at all.

Judicial Foreclosure Process

- Your mortgage lender will file suit with the court system.
- You will receive a letter from the court demanding payment.
- Typically, you will have 30 days to respond with payment to avoid foreclosure.
- At the end of the payment period, a judgment will be entered and your lender can request sale of the property by auction.
- The sheriff's office usually handles the foreclosure sale, although it may not occur until several months after the judgment.
- Once the property is sold, you could be served with an eviction notice by the sheriff's office, and you must vacate your home within the time periods established by state law. Depending on your state, the eviction could happen very quickly or it may take months.

Nonjudicial Foreclosure Process

- Your mortgage lender will serve you with papers demanding payment.
- After an established waiting period, a deed of trust is drawn up that temporarily conveys your house to a trustee.
- The trustee will sell the house at public auction for the lender.
- Many times, a court can review nonjudicial foreclosures to make sure everything was carried out legally.

- Most states require the lender to post a public notice of sale for the auction.
- Once the property is sold, you could be served with an eviction notice by the sheriff's office, and you must vacate your home within the time periods established by state law. Depending on your state, the eviction could happen very quickly or it may take months.

It's also important to consider your personal liability. Your lender can seek a "deficiency judgment" made against you if the sale of your property doesn't satisfy the amount of the loan. Some states allow the lender to seek the entire difference between what you owe and the price at foreclosure sale. In other states, you could be required to pay the lender the difference between the fair value of the property and the value of your loan.

Two states, Connecticut and Vermont, allow "strict foreclosure." In a strict foreclosure, once a court enters judgment for the lender lawsuit, the bank or lender automatically gets the property without a foreclosure sale or other sale process.

The foreclosure process ends in one of four ways:

- You reinstate the loan by paying off the default amount during a grace period determined by state law. The lender will then suspend or end foreclosure proceedings in this preforeclosure period.
- You sell or convey your house to a third party during the pre-foreclosure period as discussed later in this chapter. You then pay off the loan, extinguish your liability, and do not have a foreclosure on your credit report.
- A third party buys the house at a public foreclosure auction.
- The lender takes ownership of the property. Your lender can take ownership either through an agreement with you, such as a deed-in-lieu of foreclosure or by buying back the property at the public auction. Properties repossessed by the lender are known as bank-owned or real estate owned (REO) properties.

Some states give you the chance to redeem the house from the lender or the third-party purchaser for a limited number of days after the foreclosure sale if you can come up with full payment.

If your lender commences foreclosure, there are some very necessary actions to take, including:

- Do not ignore your mail. You cannot claim you never received something if your lender can show it was sent.
- Keep notes and keep everything in writing.
- Meet deadlines your loan servicer gives you.
- Do not move from your home during the foreclosure process. Moving out may disqualify you from some assistance programs and renting your house will change your house from your primary residence to an investment property. If it is characterized as an investment property, you may be disqualified from workouts, making deals with your lender or loan servicer, or other assistance.
- Demand that your lender produce the note. Your mortgage may have been sold repeatedly. Your lender or loan servicer is required by law to have your mortgage note in its possession before it can foreclose on your property. Writing a letter demanding that the lender produce the note will buy time and cause your lender to slow down or even back off. Contact a lawyer if they continue to foreclose without producing your note.
- Demand that your lender validate the debt. If your lender, the loan servicer, or an attorney sends you a letter threatening foreclosure, declaring a default, or for another similar reason, the letter should include a description of your right to dispute the mortgage debt. You should use this right, available under the Fair Debt Collection Practices Act (FDCPA), to dispute the debt in writing within 30 days of receiving the letter. This will delay lender activity because your lender will have stop collection efforts while your dispute is investigated.
- Seek out foreclosure mediation programs. From mid-2008 to mid-2009, fourteen different states launched twenty-five distinct foreclosure mediation programs. These programs help homeowners reach the people authorized to negotiate with them.
- If you are located in a designated natural disaster area, request your lender to stop or delay initiation of foreclosure for 90 days.

- Review your mortgage papers for violations of the Truth in Lending Act (TILA). If TILA violations are found on your mortgage, you may be entitled to significant monetary damages from your lender. Often, these damages can run in the tens of thousands of dollars. Violations often found in mortgage documents may include the following if not properly accounted:
  - Lender's failure to comply with TILA's "Notice of Right to Cancel" or the "3 Day Right to Cancel" provision that requires all lenders inform borrowers in writing that they can unwind or cancel the loan transaction should they be unable to consummate the loan transaction. This is the most common violation.
  - Lender charges excessive escrow deposits.
  - Lender includes junk charges such as yield spread premiums and service release fees.
  - Documents allow payment of compensation to mortgage brokers and originators by lenders.
  - Documents include unauthorized servicing charges, such as the imposition of payoff and recording charges.
  - Lender includes improper adjustments of interest on adjustable rate mortgages.
  - Documents permit upselling and referral fees to mortgage originators.
  - Documents fail to disclose the circumstances under which private mortgage insurance (PMI) may be terminated.

In 2007, approximately 405,000 homeowners lost their homes to foreclosure.
In 2008, 861,664 households lost their homes to foreclosure.
In 2009, more than 918,000 properties were repossessed by banks.
In 2009, one in every 45 U.S. households received a notice of default, auction sale, or bank repossession.

Source: http://money.cnn.com/2009/10/15/real_estate/foreclosure_crisis_deepens/.

Snatched from Under Her Feet

In 1997, Barbara and Mike Doyle purchased the home where they planned to spend their retirement years. Social Security and their savings easily covered the small mortgage payments. But then, the doctors found a tumor in Mike's stomach and he lost his battle with cancer in 2004. Mike's illness and uncovered medical expenses drained their savings so that, even working two jobs, Barbara could not manage the mortgage and the equity credit line she had obtained after Mike's death. In early 2007, Barbara faced foreclosure on her home. Her bank sent her a notice of default on her mortgage and filed its intent to foreclose at the registry of deeds.

In February 2007, Barbara received a call from Larry Bower. Larry and Barbara discussed the status of the mortgage on her house and the foreclosure proceedings against her house. Larry indicated to Barbara that he and his company could help Barbara sell her home prior to foreclosure and even make a profit on the sale. Larry assured Barbara that his company would repair, clean, and prepare her house for sale. In exchange for his company's services, his company sought to share in any profits Barbara obtained from the sale of her home.

Another man who said he worked with Larry met with Barbara at her home and presented her with numerous documents that he said granted permission to Larry to work on her house, prepare her house for sale, and place a "For Sale" sign in the front yard of her house.

He shuffled the stack of papers and Barbara dutifully signed. Barbara did not know it at the time, but one of the documents she signed was a deed to her house granting the home to Larry's company. Larry recorded the deed at the county's registry of deeds and became the owner of the house. Barbara had no idea.

Larry arranged for Barbara to move out of the house to an apartment while Larry made renovations to the house. He painted and sanded the floors. Larry promised to pay the rent until he gave her the proceeds from the sale of the house.

Three months after she moved out of her house, Barbara stopped by the house to see how the renovations were going. To her shock and dismay, a neighbor told her a new family had moved into the house. None of her personal belongings remained at the house. She called Larry to see where he stored her life-long possessions and when he planned on giving her the proceeds from the sale. He told her that his renovations cost over $150,000 so she had no money coming to her. In addition, he thought everything in the house was trash, so he threw it out.

The news completely devastated Barbara. She went to the police and a legal services agency who attempted to contact Larry. No one answered the only number Barbara had for Larry and his company. Barbara has lost most of her possessions, including her reminders of her deceased husband, and all the equity in her house. Larry absconded with $120,000 on the sale and could not be found by Barbara, her volunteer legal services agency, or the police.

Common Rescue Scams

As an increasing number of homeowners fall behind on their mortgages and toward foreclosure, predators are on the prowl. Predators will often learn of your mortgage debt problems through the published notices in the newspaper during the foreclosure process. In addition, private firms frequently compile and sell lists of distressed homeowners and the properties subject to foreclosure actions. Predators will target troubled homeowners because people often have thousands, tens of thousands, or even hundreds of thousands of dollars of equity in their houses.

The FBI reports that suspicious activity reports filed in 2008 involving mortgage fraud increased 36 percent to 63,713 from 2007. The FBI expects even greater numbers in the future.

Source: www.fbi.gov/publications/fraud/mortgage_fraud08.htm.

Predators will offer foreclosure relief services to homeowners struggling with their mortgages in a variety of ways. They will often advertise their services via television, radio, the Internet, newspapers, distributing flyers, or posting signs on telephone poles describing themselves as "foreclosure consultants" and "mortgage consultants" offering "foreclosure prevention" and "foreclosure rescue" services. They will promise to take care of your mortgage difficulties for you, but the underlying goal of these scams is the theft of your home or of the equity that you have in your home.

Even lawyers will scam you. Just because you've hired a lawyer, do not let your guard down and read all of the documents you sign. Virginia Gibson, a lawyer, would propose to her clients in chapter 13 bankruptcy cases that, for $15,000, he could save their homes from foreclosure. She would trick her clients into unknowingly signing a deed transferring ownership of the house to her or her company. She would then also dismiss the bankruptcy case without telling the client. When Virginia stopped paying the mortgages, some clients found themselves again facing eviction and foreclosure as well as being $15,000 poorer.

> The 10 states with the most mortgage fraud scams in 2008 were California, Illinois, Texas, Georgia, Ohio, Colorado, Maryland, Florida, Missouri, and New York.
>
> ———
>
> *Source:* www.usnews.com/money/blogs/the-home-front/2009/07/08.

In this section, we explain what to watch for if you are contacted about your mortgage difficulties. Most important, do not trust anyone who approaches you and offers help when you are having difficulties with your mortgage payments. We find that unsolicited "help" during hard times with your mortgage is most likely offered by a predator seeking to steal your home or equity. The following scams are some of the more common ones but new and different scams appear all the time.

Refinance Rescue Scams

In refinance rescue scams, predators will offer to act as your representative for dealings with your mortgage lender and promise to lower your payments by negotiating a repayment plan or modification of your mortgage. They may even "guarantee" to save your home from foreclosure. The predators will likely tell you to make payments to them directly and that they will forward payment to your lender for you. They will additionally tell you not to talk to anyone else because it could interfere with their negotiations.

The truth. You will pay a large up-front fee to the predators. You won't see this fee if you obtain legitimate help. You will then transfer your monthly payments to the predators who will not transfer any payments to your lender. Instead, the predators will likely pocket the

SURE SIGN OF A MORTAGE
FORECLOSURE RESCUE SCAM

up-front fee and all payments that were intended for the lender.
The predator will disappear with your money without having
paid the lender. You will end up with a larger debt, default, and
likely face imminent foreclosure while the scammer may pocket
your money and leave you in worse shape on your loan.

"Government" Modification Programs Scams

In "government" modification programs scams, the predator will
likely claim to be affiliated with or approved by the government and
claim that he or she can help you enter into a government mortgage modification or refinancing program such as HARP or HARM.
The predator will have a company or a Web site or both that sound
professional and related to the government, with words such as
TARP, *federal*, *treasury*, and *bailout* in their names.

The truth. The name and the alleged government affiliation
is bogus and designed to fool you into believing the predator is

approved by or affiliated with the government—which they are not. The predator will ask you to pay high up-front fees to qualify for government mortgage modification programs. The predator will take your money and make no effort to enroll you in any government program. Government mortgage relief programs are available through your lender and HUD-approved counselors. (See Chapter 10.) You should never need to pay to enroll in government programs.

Leaseback/Rent-to-Own Scams

In leaseback/rent-to-own scams, the predator will have you transfer the title to your home to the predator, his company, or his friend/affiliate so that the person who takes title can use a purported higher credit rating to obtain better financing on your home. You remain in the house as a renter and will have the opportunity to buy the house back when your finances improve.

The truth. The terms of this scam are usually so demanding and burdensome, including huge up-front fees, high monthly payments, or new mortgages on your home, that buying back your home is virtually impossible. You are evicted and your "rescuer" walks off with the house and most or all of the equity. The predator likely never had any intention of ever selling the home back to you. They simply want your home and your money.

Worse still, even if you are paying the rent as agreed, if the new owner defaults on the new loan, you will be evicted when his lender forecloses.

In a variation of this scam, the predator raises the rent to the point that it exceeds your former mortgage payments, and you cannot afford it. Then, after you miss some rent payments, the "rescuer" evicts you for failure to pay and sells your home.

Fake-Sale Scams

In fake-sale scams, the predator offers to find a buyer for your home, but only if you sign over the deed to your home and move out. The predator promises to pay you a major portion of the profit when the home sells.

The truth. Once you sign the deed of your house to the predator, the predator finds a renter to move into the house. The predator pockets the rent money while your lender continues with the foreclosure process. In the end, your home is foreclosed upon and you lose your home. Worse, you have paid rent at your new place while your mortgage debt increased and you still remain liable for the unpaid mortgage.

> Mortgage foreclosure rescue firms recruit staff through real estate seminars and late-night infomercials on television to work as "door knockers" who visit troubled homeowners at their houses or as "bird dogs" who play fake buyers.
>
> _____
>
> *Source:* www.businessweek.com/magazine/content/07_26/b4040041.htm.

Bankruptcy Scams

The predators promise to negotiate with your lender or loan servicer to reduce your mortgage or to refinance your mortgage if you pay an up-front fee. They claim that they will stop all foreclosure and collection activity through their negotiations. After the collection calls cease, the predators seek additional payments as "success fees."

The truth. Instead of contacting your lender or refinancing your loan, the predator files a bankruptcy case in your name without your knowledge. The bankruptcy stops the lender from continuing collection efforts or going through with a foreclosure. However, because you do not know about your bankruptcy, none of the bankruptcy requirements are completed and documents are not filed; therefore, the bankruptcy court will dismiss the case. Moreover, a bankruptcy will show on your credit report, and your lender will then resume collection efforts and/or initiate foreclosure. The predator pockets the fees.

Partial Interest Bankruptcy Scams

Partial interest bankruptcy scams are a variation of the bankruptcy scams already discussed. In this scam, you transfer a percentage of your ownership interest in your house to a third party for a fee. You are required to pay your mortgage payments to the predators who claim that they will pay your lender. The third party then files for bankruptcy and because the third party has a partial interest in your house the bankruptcy causes your lender to stop collection and foreclosure efforts against you. However, no payments are made to your lender, so after the third party's bankruptcy case closes, your lender will begin collection efforts against you again and you will owe a bigger balance because the predators have pocketed everything you sent to them.

Debt-Elimination Scams

In debt-elimination scams, the predators will claim that they can "eliminate" your mortgage debt based on "secret information" or "little-known laws" that they conveniently know. If you pay them a fee, they will negotiate with your mortgage lender using these secret legal arguments so that you will not have to pay back your mortgage.

The truth. These predators do not know any secret laws or secret arguments to eliminate your mortgage debt. They are telling you bogus and sham legal arguments. We have never heard of any secret laws that can be used to eliminate debt or prove that banks do not have the authority to lend money. They simply do not exist.

Bait-and-Switch Scams

In bait-and-switch scams, the predator charges you a fee to arrange a new mortgage loan for you and then claims that you're signing documents for this new loan and with this new loan you can pay off your existing mortgage or bring your existing loan current.

The truth. Instead, the paper you sign is actually the deed to your home. You sign the deed over to the predator and surrender the title of your home to him or her. In addition, you will probably have to pay an up-front fee or your monthly mortgage payments to the predator while the predator steals your home from you. You most likely won't even know you've lost the title to your home until you receive an eviction notice. The eviction notice could come months or even years later.

Red Flags of a Foreclosure Scam

The people behind mortgage foreclosure rescue scams are professionals who know exactly how to gain your trust. They know how to exploit the vulnerabilities of people who are down on their luck and they use techniques that have lasted for centuries and will continue to victimize people for years to come. Bernie Madoff,

Some homeowners have reported receiving as many as 20 calls and e-mails from "rescue" firms promising to help them keep their homes.

Source: www.businessweek.com/magazine/content/07_26/b4040041.htm.

architect of a $60 billion Ponzi scheme in which he fleeced thousands of sophisticated investors of their savings, used many of the same techniques.

The predators will lure you into their scam and build your trust by using the following techniques:

- They will tell you lies, exaggerations, and promises of results that exceed your expectations.
- They will exploit your belief that no one would lie to your face, especially someone who seems so nice.
- They will have you sign documents that conveniently run out of space for signatures on the pages containing text so that you sign a blank page that they can attach to an entirely different document.
- They will try to confuse you with facts and figures, so you have great difficulty figuring out how expensive their fees and the costs of the deals are.

Always be on your toes when a smooth-talking, likable person asks to talk to you about your mortgage or any other financial issue. Run away from any companies or people that make the following promises when you discuss avoiding foreclosure on your home. These statements and actions do not guarantee that you are dealing with a predator, but they're certainly red flags.

No contact. They tell you not to contact your lender, a lawyer, or friends because you will impair their negotiations. They just do not want you to catch onto their scam.

Up-front fee. They tell you to pay an up-front fee of more than $100 before they do any work.

Cashier's check. They tell you to pay by cashier's check or wire transfer. Legitimate businesses do not require payment in this manner.

Guarantee. They guarantee they can stop foreclosure and allow you to remain in your house.

Transfer of title. They offer to pay your mortgage and rent your home back to you after you transfer title to your home over to them. Signing over the deed to your home to another person gives that person the power to evict you, raise your rent, or sell the house. No legitimate business or person needs the title of your home to assist you. Plus, although you will no longer own your home, you still will be legally responsible for paying the mortgage on it.

Stop payment. They tell you to stop making payments to your lender or loan servicer, even if that person tells you that it will be done for you.

Secret information. They claim they know "secret laws or information" to eliminate your debt and have your mortgage contract declared invalid.

Fill-in-the-blanks. They tell you to sign now and that they'll fill in the blanks later. Take the time to read and understand *everything* you sign.

Backed by the government. They say they are affiliated with or are approved by the government or they tell you that you must pay them high fees to qualify for government loan modification programs. You do not have to pay to participate in legitimate government programs.

High pressure. They continually contact you and pressure you to work with them to stop foreclosure.

Direct payment. They tell you to make your mortgage payments directly to them rather than your lender.

Nothing in writing. They make promises they won't put in writing.

Protect Yourself

Unscrupulous people lurk everywhere and constantly seek a quick dollar by any means necessary. You should prepare, negotiate, and try to modify or refinance your loan yourself to resolve your mortgage troubles. If you need to speak to someone, contact a legitimate housing or financial counselor to help you work through your problems.

If you believe you are a victim of a mortgage foreclosure rescue scam, immediately contact the Federal Trade Commission (FTC), your state's attorney general, the Better Business Bureau, or a HUD-endorsed housing counselor (contact information is listed in Appendix A). You need to find a lawyer or a legal aide through your local volunteer lawyers referral service. You have to act fast to save your home or the equity in your home itself.

Points to Remember

- Learn how foreclosures work.
- Talk to your lender early in the foreclosure process.
- Never place your faith or your home at risk with an unsolicited mortgage foreclosure "rescuer."
- Never sign a blank piece of paper.
- Get a lawyer if you think you are in the midst of a mortgage foreclosure rescue scam.
- Immediately contact your state's attorney general or the FTC if you fear you are the victim of a mortgage foreclosure rescue scam.

Sizing Up Your Mortgage Debt

A house is made of walls and beams; a home is built with love and dreams.

—Unknown

Home ownership has long meant the fulfillment of the American dream, and over the last several years, more people than ever have realized that dream. At the same time, the lending standards of banks and mortgage companies loosened tremendously. It was easier than ever to get a mortgage with little or no money down. Millions of people overpaid for homes, believing the value would continue to rise and they'd get their money back. Many others tried to "play" the real estate market by buying a house and selling it for a quick profit. These factors brought about a gigantic housing bubble. That bubble, like any bubble floating in the air, burst. Now millions of people are having trouble making mortgage payments on homes whose values have plummeted.

Mortgage debt differs greatly from other debts because people have strong emotional ties to their homes. Moreover, when a person enters into a mortgage, the agreement is that the holder of a mortgage can foreclose, or take back, the house in the event of nonpayment. This can often happen in a matter of weeks without judicial process.

This chapter and the next chapter guide you along the road to handling mortgage debt and dealing with a potential foreclosure sale on your home. We suggest ways to reduce your mortgage payments and mortgage debts so you may stay in your home for as long as you choose. Most important, we discuss when it makes sense to give up your dream of staying in your home because the struggle to stay will not be worth the cost.

Taking the road out of mortgage debt, as with any debt, can seem daunting, but the key is persistence. Get behind the wheel and take the turns as they come. Eventually, the end will be in sight.

Don't Despair, Prepare

If your lender has scheduled your home for foreclosure, you may feel like your world is crumbling around you. If you are just starting to have difficulty in making your mortgage payments, you may feel desperate.

But our government and courts know that millions of Americans are struggling to meet their mortgage payments. Pressure is being put on lenders who have been inflexible with the terms of all those mortgages. As a result, you may have the ability to make changes to your mortgage and put yourself in a better financial position.

The first step in fighting back is having a basic understanding of your situation. Mortgages are confusing legal documents. However, like most of us, at the time you closed on your home, you probably signed your mortgage documents based on what your real estate agent or bank told you about the mortgage. If you didn't sign as directed, your sale may not have happened.

Now, in order to protect your home, you need to know as much as you can about your mortgage and your debt. Understanding your mortgage gives you power and leverage against your lender, whether you want to save your home from foreclosure or you need to reduce your mortgage payments.

When we say you need to know your mortgage, we do not mean that you have to memorize all of the small print. We mean you have to understand your mortgage's key provisions—know what you owe, the value of your property, and the key terms of your mortgage.

Know What You Owe

Remember that stack of papers you signed at the closing? One of them was called a promissory note or a note, and it's a legal document that represents your promise to repay the amount of money you borrowed plus interest. It sets forth the interest rate and the period of time over which you are borrowing the money. The term *mortgage* defines the legal document that pledges a person's property as security for payment of the note.

What you owe is the difference between what you borrowed plus the interest (and penalties, if applicable) and what you have paid. You may expect that finding out what you owe would be an easy task, but it can be difficult to learn the exact amount.

The best way to do this is by contacting the entity holding your note and mortgage, or your loan servicer. This may not be easy, but persist. You want to identify who actually holds your mortgage. Unless you took out your mortgage from a local bank, the same person or company that gave you your mortgage might no longer hold it because they sold it. Indeed, most mortgages are sold or reassigned several times; moreover, the billing collector, or "servicer," is usually another entity that can change as well.

You may find that actually talking to a live person at your loan servicer is a monumental task. You will have to deal with computerized voice mail systems that spin you in a seemingly endless loop with long waits. Be persistent. Your determined effort and perseverance will get you to a person who can help.

You can determine your current loan servicer by looking at your last payment statement or account balance statement and then can make your requests. If your loan servicer does not provide you with the information you request, you should send the loan servicer a more formal request called a Qualified Written Request, a part of the Real Estate Settlement Procedures Act (RESPA). The letter is a formal means to ensure that your loan servicer responds to you in a timely manner and corrects any errors (see "Example: Qualified Written Request Letter").

When you receive the information from your loan servicer, examine it carefully. Some of the billing irregularities that lenders or loan servicers make are as follows:

- Not recording every payment.
- Applying payments improperly, such as those for credit insurance.
- Charging late fees due to improper application of escrow balances.
- Charging higher late fees than what you agreed to under your mortgage contract.
- Charging fees for liability insurance when you have shown proof that you already have insurance.
- Refusing payments without a valid reason (such as not accepting your payment when your payment did not include a late fee).

Make sure you are satisfied with the information and that you understand how much you owe. If you suspect any significant errors, you may need to seek out a housing counselor or lawyer depending on the significance of the error.

Example: Qualified Written Request Letter

Under RESPA, your loan servicer must respond to a written request for information or investigate any claims of error concerning your account so long as you provide certain written information regarding your account. You must include your account number, name, address of the property, and a statement regarding your efforts to obtain your account balance or the reasons why you believe the account is in error, if that is the case.

Send this letter separate from your payment and request a return receipt so that you will have a record of when the servicer receives it. The loan servicer must acknowledge receipt of your letter within 20 days. The loan servicer then has up to 60 days after receiving your request to conduct an investigation if you claim an error on your account or to provide you the information you requested regarding the account balance. During the 60-day investigation, the loan servicer cannot give any information to credit reporting agencies. Here is an example of a Qualified Written Request Letter.

Dear Customer Service:

This is a qualified written request under Section 6 of the Real Estate Settlement Procedures Act (RESPA).

I am writing because:

[List your reasons for writing, including a description of the issues or questions you have, what action you believe the lender has taken in error, any conversations regarding the issue and to whom you spoke (if known) and the date, and any previous actions you have taken or attempts to resolve the issue. Also, state if you have been unsuccessful in obtaining your loan balance or account history.]

You may contact me at (XXX) XXX-XXXX for any questions or if you seek clarification. Nonetheless, I expect to receive written materials. I have attached the following supporting documents [attach documents].

I understand that under Section 6 of RESPA you are required to acknowledge my request within 20 business days and must try to resolve the issue within 60 business days.

Sincerely,
[Your name]

If you fail to receive a response to your qualified written request letter or find errors that the loan servicer or lender will not fix, you may consider filing a lawsuit. If you are successful in the lawsuit and have suffered damages because of the loan servicer's conduct, you may recover your actual damages, additional damages, costs, and attorneys' fees.

Source: For more information see: www.hud.gov/offices/hsg/ramh/res/respa_hm.cfm.

Appraise Your Home's Value

Now that you know how much you owe, we suggest that you determine the value of your home. In determining the value at this time, consider only its monetary value. To make the best decision on how to protect your home, you need to value it as a potential purchaser would and leave out the emotional value it has to you. That is, you have to make an estimate of its fair market value. How much will a willing buyer pay you as a willing seller?

Every house has its own strengths and its own weaknesses. Many factors go into the determination of value, including location, school district, overall condition of the home, number of bedrooms and bathrooms, square footage, and more. Plus, every buyer has his or her own tastes. In short, there is no way to know exactly what a sale price will be. You will never know the true value of your house until you actually put it on the market and sell it.

Several methods to determine the *approximate* value of your home are shown in Table 9.1.

Table 9.1   Appraising Your Home's Value

Method	Description	Pros	Cons
Hire an Appraiser	An appraiser views your house and compares it with the sales and listings in your area.	Most informative Most thorough Reliable Appraiser is familiar with housing market	High cost ($200–$1,000)
Real Estate Broker Evaluation (BPO)	A real estate agent or broker views your house and compares it with the sales and listings in your area.	Very reliable Agent's knowledge of market and real estate business	You may be obligated to hire the same real estate broker if you decide to sell Estimation may be higher than appropriate if the agent's only wish is to secure the listing
Do-It-Yourself Market Evaluation	Review recent sales of homes in your area and consult Web sites such as www.eppraisal.com or www.housevalue.com.	Inexpensive Can be effective if done correctly	Requires diligence in locating the recent sales Can't rely on Web site evaluation Must do your own research Not very reliable (no inspection) Difficult to ascertain similar and recent sales

Square Footage Estimate	Review recent sales of homes in your area and pick three listings most similar to your own house. Divide sales prices by square footage. Then multiply the average of the cost per-square-foot of each by the square footage of your house. *Note:* Number of bedrooms and bathrooms should be the same.	Effective Reliable Good ballpark figure	Difficult to ascertain similar and recent sales Prone to comparisons of houses that are not true comparable homes
Value Added Estimate	Multiply price paid and 50% improvements by the percentage growth/decline. Note: Check your local newspaper to determine the percentage growth/decline of your local housing market.	Rough estimate Simple technique	Not reliable More of a guess than true estimate

The evaluation and appraisal techniques in Table 9.1 can be combined to increase their reliability. Be sure to be honest with yourself and value your house objectively in order to get the most accurate assessment of your house's worth.

Know Your Mortgage Type

Over the past decade, lenders created many new and different mortgage products so that they could expand their business as much as possible. Originally, all mortgages had fixed terms and payment amounts. Now, lenders offer mortgages with interest rates that are fixed, interest rates that change (i.e., variable rates), and interest rates that start fixed but then turn variable. In addition, some mortgages contain clauses that call for a giant (balloon) payment at the end of the mortgage term to pay off a usually large balance. Mortgage types include:

- Traditional fixed-rate mortgages
- Adjustable rate mortgages (ARMs)
  - Simple
  - Hybrid

- ◆ Exploding
- ◆ Option or cash flow
- Balloon mortgages
- Interest-only mortgages

Before you take any more actions on your mortgage, you should understand what type of mortgage you have. See the Glossary for a full description of each mortgage type.

If you have an adjustable rate mortgage (ARM) or any other type of mortgage where your payments are not constant through the term of the loan, you want to set your goal to obtain the traditional fixed-rate mortgage. But before you can do that, you have to determine whether your current mortgage has a prepayment penalty. Many ARMs carry prepayment penalties that force borrowers to come up with thousands of dollars if they decide to refinance within the first few years of the loan. If you are having trouble figuring out what type of mortgage you hold or whether you will be hit with prepayment penalties, speak to a housing counselor.

Lenders developed most of these ARMs to have low initial payments, which caused people to gravitate toward a bigger mortgage loan. Suppose you could reasonably afford to pay only $2,000 a month on a mortgage, assuming a 6 percent interest rate. You would be able to secure a loan only on a traditional 30-year mortgage of about $334,000. But if you took an interest-only loan, you could get a mortgage of about $400,000 for the same monthly payment. Many people surmised, "Maybe I can stretch a little?" You are told if you can pay $2,500 a month, you can then get a $500,000 mortgage. So you start looking at houses that cost over $150,000 more than what you could afford with a straight-forward fixed-rate mortgage.

Interest-only loans can be misleading. Consider a 10-year, interest-only loan for $500,000 over a 30-year term at 6 percent costs approximately $2,500 monthly. A traditional 30-year fixed-rate loan would require you to pay about $2,997 each month for a loan of $500,000. You pay about $500 less a month on an interest-only mortgage. At the end of 10 years, however, you still owe $500,000 on an interest-only loan but with the traditional loan you would owe about $418,429. At the end of 10 years on an interest-only loan, you usually have to start paying principal. That means that

you now have 20 years to pay off the $500,000, which means that your payments will jump to about $3,582, or an additional $1,082 per month, and almost $600 more a month than the traditional fixed rate loan.

Knowing your mortgage type, what you owe on your mortgage, how much your house is likely worth, and whether your payments are due to increase are the cornerstones to help you determine what you should do with your house and mortgage.

Are You "Underwater"?

You have equity in your home if its value exceeds the total of your mortgage debts and other liens (such as municipal tax and water company liens). The opposite of that is being "underwater." You are underwater if your total mortgage debt balance exceeds the value of your house.

Approximately 23 percent, or nearly 10.7 million homeowners, owe more on their mortgages than their properties are worth. That means nearly 1 in 4 borrowers is "underwater"!

Source: "One in Four Borrowers Is Underwater" *Wall Street Journal*, November 24, 2009.

Quiz: Are You Facing Mortgage Meltdown?

Choose one or more of the following options that describes your situation:

A. You are "underwater."
B. You're having trouble making payments each month or make mortgage payments that exceed 30 percent of your monthly income.
C. You're having trouble making mortgage payments each month or make mortgage payments that exceed 30 percent of your monthly income. You have an exploding ARM mortgage and your monthly payment is increasing.
D. You have had a long-term reversal in fortune, such as a job loss or medical emergency.
E. You are having difficulty with mortgage payments. You expect that you will have more money soon, due to a new job, raise, or spouse going back to work, so that you will be able to pay your mortgage comfortably.
F. You are facing a foreclosure on your house.

What's Your Level?

F + any other letters = Deep Red Level: You are at great risk of losing your house at foreclosure.

A + B + D = Red Level: You are underwater, are having trouble making payments, and do not see your situation changing anytime soon.

A + C + D = Red Level: You are underwater, having trouble making payments, and you foresee more problems when the interest rate increases. You do not see your situation changing anytime soon.

A + C = Orange Level: You are underwater, and though you are able to make payments now, you realize you will have trouble when your payment amount increases because of an exploding ARM. You do not see your situation changing.

B or C = Orange Level: You have equity in your home, but you are having trouble making payments or will once the interest rate rises.

$A + B + E$ or $A + C + E$ = **Yellow Level:** You are underwater, and though you may need time, you will be able to pay your mortgage comfortably.

Your Level and Next Steps

Deep Red Level: Losing your house at foreclosure hurts, both emotionally and financially. Concentrate on slowing down or delaying the foreclosure process so you can dispose of your house on your terms or work things out with your lender. Speak to a counselor, sell or give up your home, or consider what bankruptcy can do for you. Also, see Chapter 10 for more information on foreclosure.

Red Level: Reduce your payments and/or reduce the principal on the mortgage. Otherwise, your best bet may be to get out of your mortgage and your house. You will own a house again but now you must concentrate on making sure that this house does not permanently impact you. We do not see many compelling reasons for you to continue to struggle with an asset that may now simply be a losing proposition.

Orange Level: Attempt to restructure your mortgage so that you can afford your payments and avoid the higher interest rate if you have an exploding ARM mortgage. If you're underwater, attempt to reduce the principal on your mortgage so that it is in line with the value of your house.

Yellow Level: Plan ahead before you lose your equity. Determine whether you have a traditional fixed-rate mortgage and, if you do, check to see whether the interest rate you are paying is higher than those being offered. By refinancing to a lower traditional fixed-rate mortgage, you may be able to lessen your payments. If you have an ARM, seek a traditional fixed-rate mortgage. Generally, work with your lender to make sure nothing adverse happens to you while you are period of low income. You should be able to keep your house and restructure payments at least for the short term. Concentrate on, as applicable, negotiating, loan modifications, or refinancing.

Brush Up on Your Negotiating Skills

The government and media have put pressure on lenders and provided them incentives to make changes to your mortgage. This does not necessarily mean that your lender will help you, so be ready to use the negotiation skills we discussed in Chapter 2 to make them listen.

You've done your research and know your situation and now it's time to contact your loan servicer. Have a hardship letter ready that you can refer to when you contact your loan servicer that explains your situation, why you are requesting a loan modification option, and what other steps you are taking to get your budget under control, such as bills and expenses you are cutting (see "Example: Hardship Letter").

Example: Hardship Letter

Dear Sir/Madam [if you have a contact name, use it]:

I/We am/are requesting that you review my/our financial state of affairs to see if I/we qualify for a loan modification.

I/We am/are having problems making my/our monthly payments because I/we have recently encountered financial difficulty.

[Provide your explanation: Divorce; Loss of job; Medical Bills; Excessive debt; Death of family member.]

I/We believe that I/we will be able to afford the mortgage if you enter me/us into a [loan modification option].

I/We am/are also taking the following actions to make sure I/we can satisfy my/our new obligations to you.

I/We would appreciate your consideration of this matter and ask that you will allow me/us to enter into [a new loan situation] so that I/we do not have to consider more drastic measures that would include looking at my/our bankruptcy options.

Signature,
[Your Name]

Seek Professional Help

You do not have to go through the foreclosure prevention process alone. A counselor with a housing counseling agency can assess your situation, answer your questions, go over your options, prioritize your debts, and help you prepare for discussions with your loan servicer. Housing counselors will also negotiate with the lender for you and will even help you work out a monthly budget plan. Counselors provide valuable services and charge little or nothing for their help. Just remember, legitimate housing counselors will not likely contact you. You have to take the first step. If someone calls you offering help, be very skeptical—they likely seek to scam you.

Call the local office of the U.S. Department of Housing and Urban Development (HUD) or the housing authority in your state, city, or county for help in finding a legitimate housing counseling agency nearby.

The National Consumer Law Center (NCLC) provides links to HUD-approved counselors as well as excellent information about all of your consumer rights. Additionally, you should consider contacting an attorney to guide you through your negotiations and advise you or assist you through a bankruptcy if one becomes necessary. The NCLC provides references for bankruptcy and other attorneys in your area.

The Federal Housing Authority (FHA) is also willing to help. If your loan is FHA-approved, you can get in touch with an FHA housing counselor who will walk you through possible solutions. Some FHA-approved and other agencies limit their counseling services to homeowners with FHA mortgages; many others offer free help to any homeowner who is having trouble making mortgage payments.

Last, consider contacting the Homeownership Preservation Foundation (HPF), which is a nonprofit organization that partners with mortgage companies, local governments, and other organizations to help consumers get loan modifications and prevent foreclosures.

Contact information for each of these agencies or programs is available in Appendix A.

Be wary of any housing counselors that charge large up-front fees or guarantee you a loan modification or other solution to stop foreclosure. They shouldn't be charging you high fees or making any guarantees. Take your business elsewhere. We discussed mortgage rescue fraud at length in Chapter 8.

Points to Remember

- Do your homework. Know your home's value, mortgage type, what you owe, and whether your interest and payments can or will change.
- The best housing counselors are HUD-approved, so be sure to do your research.

10

The Way Out of Mortgage Debt

I've got all the money I'll ever need, if I die by four o'clock.
—Henny Youngman, American comedian

Now that you've taken a good look at your mortgage debt situation it is time to develop a strategy. You should now contact your lender with the hope that they will agree to modify or refinance your loan. Beyond that, there are many federal and local programs available to help with loan modifications and refinancing. It's important to know what resources are available to you. Sometimes selling or leaving your home is the right decision, and we offer a few guidelines about that. If you need a refresher, look back to Chapter 8 to find out exactly what foreclosure is and some of the most common foreclosure rescue scams.

Modify Your Loan

Start with a call to your loan servicer so you have a contact name. The loan servicer's phone number and e-mail address is on your monthly mortgage bill or coupon book. You will have to be very persistent. People across the country continually complain about the difficulties they have with actually talking to a live person.

Remember to express your desire to stay with them but stress that the payments as they are currently structured make it impossible for you to remain with them. Also, be sure to talk to the right person at the right mortgage servicer—the servicer that actually holds your loan. Push for the modification that best fits your needs.

Mortgage lenders and loan servicers are historically poor at working with homeowners—they are getting lots of calls—so be patient and be persistent if you do not reach your loan servicer on the first try. If you cannot reach someone to discuss loan modifications, speak to a housing counselor or a local agency that can help. These are seasoned professionals who know the negotiation, modification, and refinancing landscape.

All of the modifications discussed in this section will allow you to keep your home, but make sure you pursue the one that best fits your short-term and long-term needs. Keep in mind that lenders exist to make money. In our experience, they are not willing to make major changes, especially if it means they will lose money. If you do secure a modification, examine it carefully to ensure that you are not taking on more debt in a different form or over a longer time period and to understand the consequences of missing mortgage payments or making late mortgage payments. The modifications we discuss are repayment plans, forebearance, and loan reinstatement, among others.

You enter a repayment plan when your loan servicer gives you a fixed amount of time to repay your debt by adding a portion of what is past due to your regular payment. This is a good option if you've missed a small number of payments and the difficulties that caused you to miss those payments have ended. Lenders will generally offer terms of 12 months for you to repay your past due amount. The lender will require that you make your regular monthly payment plus one-twelfth of the past due amount for 12 consecutive months.

For example, if the total past due is $6,000 and the regular monthly payment is $1,000, the monthly payment on a 12-month repayment plan will be $1,500. The major problem with a repayment plan is that the terms of your loan remain the same while you are making a higher monthly payment. These higher payments with the same mortgage terms could mean trouble and may be setting you up to fail.

Unless your lender agrees to accept less than your full mortgage payment and to apply that payment toward what you currently owe, do not make partial payments to your mortgage lender. Partial mortgage payments will not likely provide you with any benefit. Your lender will either send the payment back to you or not credit your account until it receives enough money to make a full payment. Either way, you will be hit with late fees and other penalties while you have lost the use of the money you've sent your lender.

Forbearance

Forbearance means your mortgage payments are reduced or suspended for a set period of time. At the end of the forbearance period, you resume making your regular payments as well as a lump sum or "balloon" payment or additional partial payments for a number of months to bring the loan current. Forbearance may be an option if you are experiencing a temporary financial hardship (e.g., you are on disability leave from a job). You should not seek loan forbearance if you are having chronic difficulties with your mortgage payments or are relying on winning the lottery to provide for your lump sum repayment. However, if you know you have a large amount of money coming your way soon, you may consider forbearance and the next option, reinstatement.

Loan Reinstatement

Reinstating your loan means that you will pay the loan servicer the entire past-due amount plus any late fees or penalties by a future date on which you both mutually agree. Reinstatement is similar to loan forbearance except that you are not requesting a period of non-payment because you have already missed payments. The loan servicer may require a lump sum payment or additional payments over a short period of time and will often expect you to find the money from a tax refund, loan from your 401(k), friend, or relative. Loan servicers often push this option because they find it easy and it carries little risk to them. You should consider this option if your problem paying your mortgage is temporary and you will have the ability to pay extra to your loan from your own resources without having to ask for loans from others.

Loan Restructuring

With loan restructuring, you and your loan servicer agree to permanently change one or more of the terms of your mortgage contract so that your payments become more manageable. Modifications may include reducing the interest rate, extending the term of the loan, and adding missed payments to the loan balance. A modification also may involve reducing the amount of money you owe on your primary residence by forgiving, or canceling, a portion of the mortgage debt. Under the Mortgage Forgiveness Debt Relief Act of 2007, the forgiven debt may be excluded from income when calculating the federal taxes you owe, but it still must be reported on your federal tax return. Your loan servicer may charge you a loan modification fee.

A loan modification may be necessary if you are facing a long-term reduction in your income or increased payments because of an interest rate change under an ARM. Remember, bigger loan principles and longer payment periods are helpful in the short term but will dramatically increase what you will pay over the entire term of the loan.

A $250,000 mortgage loan paid over 30 years with 6 percent interest:
    Monthly payment = $1,498.88
    Total payment = $539,595.47

A $250,000 mortgage loan paid over 40 years with 6 percent interest:
    Monthly payment = $1,375.43
    Total payment = $660,256.67

You pay $122 less a month in a 40-year mortgage but you end up paying more than $120,000 more on the loan!

Making Homes Affordable Program

The Federal Housing Administration (FHA), U.S. Department of Housing and Urban Development (HUD), and the Department of Veterans Affairs (VA) have their own workout programs for mortgages insured by them. Call your lender to ask whether your loan is insured by one of these agencies, and if it is, enter into a workout program.

In order to combat the mortgage loan crisis and the recession, the federal government established the Making Homes Affordable (MHA) Program, also known as the "Obama Mortgage Plan" or

"The Obama Plan." One component of MHA is the Home Affordable Modification Program (HAMP). HAMP helps borrowers who are struggling to keep their loans current or who are already behind on their mortgage payments.

> As of December 10, 2009, more than 728,000 HAMP temporary modifications were underway across the country. However, loan servicers had converted only 31,382 modifications to the permanent phase at that time— that's less than 5 percent!
>
> _____
>
> *Source:* http://makinghomeaffordable.gov/pr_12102009.html.

The government initially designed the program to help as many as 3 million to 4 million financially struggling homeowners avoid foreclosure by modifying loans to a level that the borrower can sustain over the long term. However, lender participation has not gone as anticipated. In March 2010, the government instituted changes so that more homeowners will be helped by this and other government programs. This program and all of the other government programs are changing (visit www.wiley.com/go/roadoutofdebt to stay on top of the changes).

You meet the minimum eligibility requirements for HAMP if:

- You are delinquent on your mortgage or you face imminent risk of defaulting on your mortgage.
- You are the owner-occupant of a one- to four-unit home and you occupy it as your primary residence.
- You entered into the first lien mortgage on or before January 1, 2009, and unpaid principal balance on the mortgage is not more than $729,750 if you own a one-unit property: two units: $934,200; three units: $1,129,250; four units: $1,403,400.
- You are employed.

If you are eligible, your loan servicer should take a series of steps to adjust your monthly mortgage payment to 31 percent of your total pretax monthly income. First, your loan servicer should reduce your interest rate to as low as 2 percent; second, if necessary, extend the loan term to 40 years; third, if necessary, forbear (defer) a portion of the principal until the loan is paid off and waive interest on the deferred amount. HAMP modifications begin with a three-month trial modification. If you are current on payments at the end of the three-month trial period and provide full supporting documentation, such as proof of income, then the modification becomes permanent. Another element that should cause lenders to reduce payments is if you are unemployed and seeking a job.

Be alert that some loan servicers violate HAMP guidelines by requiring borrowers to waive legal rights, requiring down payments or other prerequisites before they will enter into a HAMP review. Report these conditions to your state's attorney general's office so that your attorney general will prevent these loan servicers from continuing this practice in your state.

Do You Live in a Natural Disaster Area?

If the area where you live or work has been declared a natural disaster by the president, you may be eligible for a moratorium and assistance from your lender. Both the VA and the FHA provide relief plans to assist you. In many cases, you can get up to three months' relief from your monthly loan payments while you work out your home or work situation. Your loan servicer or HUD-approved housing counselor can provide you with more information.

Partial Claims and Insurance Funds

If you have a loan insured by the FHA and you can document temporary financial hardship, you may be eligible for an FHA partial claim. If you do not know whether you have an FHA-insured loan, look in your loan documents for an application, call your servicer, or talk to a HUD-approved housing counselor. An FHA partial claim, which can be obtained through you loan servicer, is an interest-free loan that will bring your account current. You then make your regular monthly payments and can delay payments on the FHA partial claim.

You may qualify for an FHA partial claim if:

- Your loan is between 4 and 12 months delinquent.
- You are able to begin making full mortgage payments again.
- The property is your primary residence.

You must sign a promissory note, and a lien will be placed on your property until the promissory note is paid in full. The promissory note is interest free and is due when you pay off the first mortgage or when you sell the property.

In addition, other, non-FHA mortgage insurance companies, including the Rural Development Services (RDS) and the Department of Veterans Affairs (VA), as well as some private mortgage insurers may have similar programs and will lend you the money to bring your loan current. If your loan has mortgage insurance, the insurance company stands to lose if you default. To help keep you in the house, the insurance company may help you get current on the loan.

Mortgage Debt Help for Servicemembers

The Servicemembers Civil Relief Act (SCRA), formerly known as The Soldiers' and Sailors' Civil Relief Act of 1940, provides military personnel important rights and protections as they enter active duty on issues that include mortgage interest rates, mortgage foreclosure, and credit card interest rates.

A major benefit of SCRA is the ability to reduce mortgage interest rates and consumer debt interest rates to a 6 percent limit under certain circumstances. The mortgage or debt must have been incurred before entry into active military service, and the servicemember must show that military service has had a "material effect" on the legal or financial matter involved. Mortgage lenders may also allow servicemembers to stop paying the principal amount due on their loan during the period of active duty service. Lenders may not foreclose or seize property for a failure to pay a mortgage debt while a servicemember is on active duty or within 90 days after the period of military service unless they have the approval of a court.

Source: www.militaryfamilynetwork.com/article.php?aid=13968.

Refinance Your Loan

You may want to consider refinancing if you have equity in your home and you want to deal with a bump up in your interest rate or you seek to bring down your monthly payments. You can shop around and find the lender of choice.

If you plan to refinance, understand the fees and accompanying costs that are incurred. As a rule of thumb, if you seek relief from

Refinancing
Menu

Fixed Rate Mortgage

erest Only Mortgage

Second Mortgage

Home Equity Line

Balloon Mortgage

Would you like that supersized to a jumbo mortgage?

Drive-Thru LOANS

Copyright © 2010 New Way Solutions, www.newwaysolutions.com.

burdensome mortgage payments, we suggest that you only consider a mortgage carrying an interest rate that is more than 1 percentage point less than the interest rate on your current mortgage that you can obtain with no points. *Points* are a percentage of the mortgage that lenders charge you up front but will often add to the principle of the loan. Look at the monthly payments (for principal and interest) on a 30-year fixed rate loan of $200,000 at 6.0 percent and 5.5 percent:

Monthly payment at 6.0 percent:	$1,199
Monthly payment at 5.5 percent:	$1,136
The difference each month is:	$ 63
But over a year's time, the difference adds up to:	$ 756
Over 10 years, you will have saved:	$7,560

Source: www.federalreserve.gov/pubs/refinancings/default.htm#consider.

Your monthly payment difference is only $63 dollars a month while you may have had to pay hundreds or thousands of dollars to enter into the new loan. You may have to pay fees at closing, such as an application fee (cost = $75 to $300); loan origination fee (cost = up to $4,500 on a $300,000 refinancing); appraisal fee (cost = $300 to $700); inspection fee (cost = $175 to $350); attorney review/closing fee (cost = $500 to $1,000); homeowner's insurance (cost = $300 to

$1,000); title search and title insurance (cost = $700 to $900); and others. Lenders will often offer to add these fees to the principle to lessen their impact in the short term, but it magnifies the effect over the long term. The fees and costs will far outweigh the benefit you receive from your reduced monthly payment unless you can reduce your rate by more than a point.

Watch out for prepayment penalties imposed by your current mortgage if you choose to refinance and be wary of anyone who contacts you about refinancing after you have missed payments on your current mortgage or have received a foreclosure notice. We have discussed that and similar scams in Chapter 8.

In this section, we'll explain the Home Affordable Refinance Program (HARP), FHA refinancing, and HOPE for Homeowners. For more information on any of these refinancing programs and others, visit http://makinghomeaffordable.gov/ and www.wiley.com/go/roadoutofdebt.

Home Affordable Refinance Program

In conjunction with the MHA program, the federal government has established the Home Affordable Refinance Program (HARP). The federal government designed HARP to help individuals who are making mortgage payments but cannot refinance because the value of their home has dropped and they're underwater. The federal government initially estimated that HARP would assist 4 million to 5 million homeowners.

You may be eligible to refinance your mortgage loan under HARP if:

- The loan on your property is owned or guaranteed by Fannie Mae or Freddie Mac.
- At the time you apply, you are current on your mortgage payments, you have not been more than 30 days late on your mortgage payment in the last 12 months, or if you have had the loan for less than 12 months, you have never missed a payment.
- You owe more than 80 percent of the home's value and the amount you owe on your first lien mortgage does not exceed 125 percent of the current market value of your property.

- You have a reasonable ability to pay the new mortgage payments.
- Refinancing improves the long-term affordability or stability of your loan.

Contact your loan servicer or HUD-approved counselor to determine your eligibility to enter into HARP.

Is Your Loan Owned or Guaranteed by Fannie Mae and Freddie Mac?

Having a loan guaranteed by Fannie Mae or Freddie Mac increases the options to deal with your mortgage as discussed throughout this chapter. You can call or e-mail them to determine if either agency owns or guaranteed your loan.

Fannie Mae
  1-800-7FANNIE (8 A.M. to 8 P.M. EST)
  www.fanniemae.com/loanlookup

Freddie Mac
  1-800-FREDDIE (8 A.M. to 8 P.M. EST)
  www.freddiemac.com/mymortgage

FHA Refinance

The federal government offers another program for refinancing called FHA Refinance. Even if you do not qualify for conventional refinancing because of your income level or credit rating, an FHA Refinance may still be an option for you because the standards are less strict. The eligibility requirements are:

- Your mortgage must ultimately be insured through the FHA.
- Your mortgage must be current and not delinquent.
- The results of the refinance must lower the monthly principle and interest payments for the borrower.
- No cash may be taken out on mortgages refinanced using the streamline refinance process.

Homeowners can determine if they are already eligible for mortgage assistance through the FHA's existing refinancing program

FHASecure. FHA has specialists who can talk to you about whether you qualify, refinancing, and other options.

HOPE for Homeowners

Prior to the Homeowner Affordability and Stabilization Plan (HASP) and HARP, the federal government commenced the HOPE for Homeowners (H4H) Program. H4H continues in conjunction with MHA. The program provides a new 30-year fixed-rate mortgage insured by the FHA if you and your lender or loan servicer agree to certain conditions. The government requires loan servicers to consider a borrower for refinancing into the H4H program when feasible. The qualification requirements are:

- Your existing loan must have been originated on or before January 1, 2008.
- Your existing mortgage payment (including all liens) must be greater than 31 percent of monthly income.
- Your new mortgage must be insured by FHA on or before September 30, 2011.

One problem that plagued H4H prior to its inclusion in MHA was that lenders had to voluntarily refinance delinquent mortgages by reducing the principal balance on loans to 90 percent of a home's current market value. The new 30-year fixed-rate loans would then be backed by the FHA. As a result, the program only helped one, yes one, homeowner avoid foreclosure in the first five months of the program's existence. Under the current plan, lenders would only have to write the home's value down to 93 percent. For example, if you owed $220,000 on a house valued at $200,000, lenders would have to forgive $34,000 of your loan to include you in the H4H program. The program is voluntary so lender participation is still a big question.

Sell or Give Up Your Home

Not every situation or mortgage problem can be resolved through your loan servicer's loan modification and foreclosure prevention programs. In our experience, most consumers are likewise not having great success with loan modifications. If you're not able to keep your home, if you're on the verge of a foreclosure sale, or if you simply no longer want to keep something where you are paying on a debt that exceeds what it is worth, consider selling or disposing of your house. The key is that you want to dispose of your house with the least amount of trauma to you, your family, and your finances. Your options are:

Sell. You can hire a broker or advertise your home for sale on your own. In addition, you may be able to persuade your loan servicer to postpone foreclosure proceedings if you have a pending sales contract or if you put your home on the market. Selling your house will work best for you if the proceeds from the sale can pay off the entire loan balance on all mortgages plus the expenses connected to selling the home (such as taxes and real estate agent fees). A sale that covers your balance means no late and legal fees or damage to your credit rating and it protects your equity in the house.

Short sale. A short sale is an agreement between you and your lender where your lender agrees to the sale of your house through a real estate agent for full satisfaction of your mortgage even if the sale price does not cover what you owe on the mortgage. A short sale benefits a lender because the lender will avoid costs and losses of a foreclosure sale. You benefit because you do not get a foreclosure notation on your credit report and you are not personally responsible for the deficiency between the sale price and what you owe. You have to make sure that any second or third mortgagors agree to the short sale and will release their claims. Also, do not enter into a short sale unless all lenders release you from personal liability.

　　If your loan servicer will not accept a short sale, stress to it that your next alternative is a bankruptcy filing where the loan servicer will receive even less.

Deed-in-lieu of foreclosure. A deed in lieu of foreclosure is a document in which you transfer all your interest in your house to your mortgage lender in order to satisfy your mortgage and avoid foreclosure. You benefit because you are immediately released from most or all of the personal indebtedness on the mortgage loan. You also avoid the foreclosure notation on your credit report and the ordeal of a foreclosure sale. Your lender benefits by avoiding the costs and time of a foreclosure sale and any vandalism or theft of the property. Do not enter into a deed-in-lieu transaction unless you receive forgiveness of your personal liability on the mortgage loan. Also, do not enter into the transaction if you have equity in your house; sell the house instead to capture the equity.

Also, you can try to negotiate a small payment from your lender to assist you in vacating the premises. A lender may enter these "cash for keys" transactions in order to avoid destruction to the house by the homeowner.

The Home Affordable Foreclosure Alternatives Program

The Home Affordable Foreclosure Alternatives (HAFA) Program is part of the MHA. HAFA provides incentives to lenders in connection with a short sale or a deed-in-lieu of foreclosure used to avoid foreclosure on a loan eligible for modification under the HAMP program. HAFA applies to loans not owned or guaranteed by Fannie Mae or Freddie Mac but these organizations have similar programs.

Walk Away

You can pack up your house and leave. Tell your lender what you are doing and then leave the house for your lender to pick up the pieces. This approach only makes sense if you are completely underwater, you see no chance of ever having equity back in the house, you're receiving no cooperation from your lender, you know that a foreclosure sale is inevitable, and you have no respect for your mortgage lender or servicer.

Even then, leaving your house and walking away is more vengeful than beneficial. Although some states have laws that prevent a lender from chasing you for the mortgage deficiency on your primary residence (such as California), in most states you can be held personally responsible and you may have an angry lender pursuing you. You can also lose 100 points or more on your credit score.

In January 2010, the owners of Stuyvesant Town and Peter Cooper Village apartment complex in New York City turned ownership over to the lenders and walked away from the property after defaulting on $4.4 billion of debt. The purchase of the 56-building, 11,232-unit apartment complex in 2006 was the biggest residential property purchase in U.S. history. The complex is now estimated to be worth around $1.8 billion.

Still, we understand the frustration of paying for something when its value is 75 percent or even 50 percent of the price you are paying. Nevertheless, we suggest you pursue any other alternatives, including filing bankruptcy.

Consider Bankruptcy

At a minimum, bankruptcy will provide you some breathing room and temporarily stall a foreclosure sale. We discuss in detail throughout the second half of the book the benefits and pitfalls of bankruptcy with regard to your home and mortgage. In general, you should know that when nothing is slowing the foreclosure of your home, bankruptcy provides the following:

- In a chapter 7 bankruptcy case, the automatic stay temporarily prevents a foreclosure process from continuing. Your mortgage lender can continue the foreclosure process with the permission of the court but that usually takes at least 60 days. You can use this time to work out a loan modification.
- In a chapter 13 bankruptcy case, the automatic stay likewise temporarily prevents your lender from continuing a foreclosure process so that you can regroup and work out a way to keep your home. In addition, you can cure a default or pay off the mortgage in installments over time through a chapter 13 plan.
- In all bankruptcy cases, you may be able to raise defenses to your mortgage lender's claims about how much you owe.
- Depending on the bankruptcy chapter and equity in your home above secured debt, you may be able to sell your house in chapter 11 and chapter 13 bankruptcy cases.

Points to Remember

- As a first option to avoid foreclosure, try modifying or refinancing your mortgage through your lender or a government program.
- Be persistent. You will encounter difficulties, so find the right person to discuss your issues with.
- Don't be afraid to sell your home or even turn it over to your lender.
- Bankruptcy may provide you with some breathing room to work out a deal regarding your mortgage.

CHAPTER 11

The Way Out of Auto Debt

*Another way to solve the traffic problems of this country is to pass a
law that only paid-for cars be allowed to use the highways.*

—Will Rogers

If you have obtained a loan to buy or refinance your vehicle, you
likely pledged the vehicle as security for the loan. In doing so, the
lender earned the legal right to repossess, or take back, the car if
you don't keep up with your payments. The lender can do this by
hiring a repossessor to break into the vehicle and remove it from
your control. Remember that automobile title loans, also known
as title pawn loans, are at the center of many predatory scams. As
we discussed in Chapter 5, falling prey to one of these scams never
ends well. You will pay exorbitant interest rates of several hundred
percent and risk losing your vehicle.

If you are behind in payments or in danger of getting behind,
the first step is to know your rights and your lender's rights to your
vehicle. To do this, read the document you signed at the time you
entered into the loan. If you cannot find that document, contact
the lender to get a copy. If the car is listed as security and your
lender's name is located on the car title or registration, then the
lender can repossess your car in the event of missed payments.

Your goal in handling your auto loan should be to avoid being at the mercy of your lender and the repossessors. Most people need a vehicle for everyday life—a way to get to work, school, health care appointments, children's activities, the grocery store, and many other places. You do not want to lose your car through repossession.

Repossession hurts. First, you lose your car. Second, you may still have to pay your lender for something you no longer own. Unless the sale of your vehicle by your lender exceeds the costs of repossession along with the outstanding balance of your loan, you still owe the part of the loan that the sale does not cover.

Most likely, the sale proceeds will not exceed what you owe on your loan. Lenders do not want to be in the car business, so they will dispose of your car by the easiest method: a dealer car auction. The prices on vehicles sold at auction never equal or even come close to what you could sell the car for yourself. Plus, the lender will add other charges to the amount you owe on your loan: the repossessor's fee, towing costs, late fees, storage costs, administrative costs, attorneys' fees, bank fees, sales fees, and anything else your contract allows.

"OF COURSE, NO ONE WILL FIND IT PARKED BEHIND THE HOUSE"

Repossessors work on commission, so you never know what they'll do to seize your vehicle and occasionally they take their job to extremes. Consider the example of the Simone brothers.

Ripped from Her Car

Tom and Jim Simone, two brothers only a few years out of high school, swung by Tara Mitchell's parents' house with two friends on their way out to the bars on a Friday night. To their pleasant surprise, they saw Tara's car idling in the driveway. They had searched for her car for the last seven days without luck.

They didn't seek her car because they knew she'd be home. No, they wanted her car because she had fallen behind on payments and her lender had contracted their father's repossession business to retrieve the car.

Tara checked on her five-year-old daughter in the backseat and then began to back the car out of the driveway. As she turned, Tommy reached through the window and started to pull her out of her seat. He punched her in the face and pulled at her so violently that he broke her necklace.

Tara's daughter implored her mother to drive away. Tara sped off but the brothers followed. Five miles down the road, Jimmy jumped on the hood of Tara's car and pounded on the windshield. Tara, horrified, drove with Jim on the hood to the police station where police quickly interviewed and arrested Jim. The police later found Tommy at his house and placed him under arrest as well. The police told Tara she was very fortunate that she kept her wits about her because they have seen situations like that end in tragedy.[1]

Tara Mitchell could sue the Simone brothers and the family business for damages. Their bad acts also give her a defense that she can raise in court to any personal liability on the auto loans. Even so, the lender could still repossess her car anytime in the future if she continues to miss payments.

How Repossession Works

If you are late or have missed a payment on your auto loan, your lender likely has the legal right under your loan contract to repossess your vehicle. Most auto loan contracts require that you put up your vehicle as collateral and that failure to pay, even one month, constitutes a default that gives the lender the ability to repossess the collateral.

Repossession stays on your credit report for seven years.

Most likely, one missed payment will not cause your lender to repossess your car, especially if your payment history does not suggest that the loan on the vehicle is in jeopardy. However, if you miss two or three payments, repossession of your vehicle is a distinct possibility.

Typically in most states, the time line of vehicle repossession will look something like this:

1. You miss a car payment or two.
2. You receive a letter or call from your lender.
3. You make no payments.
4. Your car disappears from where you parked it. You may report your car stolen.
5. You receive a notice that your car has been repossessed and that you have rights after repossession, including the ability to get it back. This ability, "a redemption right," allows you to get back the car if you pay off at least the back payments but may require paying off the whole loan plus fees and costs.
6. In some cases, you call the police to retract your stolen vehicle report.
7. You can get your car back if you work out a deal with your lender and will likely need to pay your back payments, repossession fees, towing charges, impound charges, storage fees, and other charges that you pay. Some states do not require all these costs.
8. If you don't pay, the lender sells your car, likely at auction and for a low price, well below the value of the car. Your lender will likely hold you responsible for the balance of the loan that the proceeds at auction don't cover (the "deficiency").

Last, in order to find your way out of auto debt, you will need to know the value of your vehicle. To learn what your vehicle is worth, we suggest that you consult Kelly Blue Book (www.kbb.com), N.A.D.A Guides (www.nadaguides.com, also sold at gas stations and convenient stores), Vehix.com, Autotrader.com, or various other automobile Web sites. You will be able to enter specific details about your car or truck and obtain prices that vary on how you sell it (private sale versus trade-in). You will not see a value for a foreclosure sale but as set forth in our example, you can expect an auction to obtain roughly 70 percent of the trade-in value, and the lender will add the repossession costs and fees to what you owe.

Knowing what can happen is often the first step in preventing the misfortune of losing your car. Your lender's ability to repossess your car is known as "self-help" because in most states your lender does not need court permission to repossess. Your lender can seize your car itself or hire a repossessor, commonly referred to as a repo man.

The laws of most states allow your lender to repossess your car at any hour of the day or night, without prior notice, and to send an agent to enter your property to do so. Lenders and their hired repossessors may even follow you around to learn your habits. They seek to discover where and when they will be able to repossess your car and encounter the least resistance. Many will come to your door and ask for your keys. But, others will have a spare key or a tow truck ready and will seize the car without your knowledge.

There are limits to self-help repossession, including:

- The car must be collateral for the loan or subject to a lease contract.
- The creditor must give you a chance to catch up on your late payments in these states ("right to cure"): CA, CO, CT, D.C., IA, KS, ME, MA, MI, NE, NH, PR, SC, SD, VA, WV, and WI. The state likely requires that the lender give you at least 20 days to cure.
- No self-help is generally allowed on Indian reservations. Louisiana, Wisconsin, and Maryland limit the extent and/or who has the right of self-help repossession.
- Some states must give you notice of your right to pay what you owe in back payments.
- A car cannot be repossessed from active duty military personnel if the debt was incurred before active duty.
- The lender cannot "breach the peace." We discuss what constitutes a breach of the peace in the next section.

No Breach of Peace

Lenders and repossessors prefer to have no one around when they seize your car because they are prohibited by law from "breaching the peace." A breach of the peace is basically an act that endangers or disturbs public peace and order. Repossessors breach the peace if they:

- Use bodily force or threaten you. The laws prohibit physical contact.
- Break open a locked garage to get your car. They can take it from your driveway or opened garage.
- Bring the police or other government official, unless they have a court order. They rarely have court orders. Don't be fooled if they say they do or even wave papers. Read them before you believe them.
- Use tricks to get your car. Most states outlaw tricks such as taking your car to make so-called free repairs or offering to perform a mandatory recall as a way to gain possession to repossess your car.
- In some states, taking the car against your protest or a close family member's protest.

Did the Simone brothers breach the peace when they attempted to repossess Tara Mitchell's car? Absolutely. They placed Tara, her child, and the general public in harm's way.

Should there be a breach of the peace in seizing your car, your creditor may be required to pay a penalty, or if you or your property is harmed, to compensate you for the damage. Also, because of a breach of the peace, your creditor may lose the right to collect the deficiency on its loan after the sale of the vehicle.

It's important to remember not to misplace your anger. While some repossessors step over the line to bend or break laws, most stay within the legal limits when they try to seize your car. Remember, they are agents for lenders and are acting on what the lender tells them. They have nothing personal against you. They make their living by seizing cars for lenders.

Your best course of action is to tell them to stop, and if they don't, call the police. Do not put yourself at risk for a lawsuit or arrest for assault.

Also, if you have missed a car payment, remove your personal property from the car. Although repossessors must legally return to you or store any personal property that you leave in the vehicle, personal property is commonly "lost" after repossession. If you cannot remove an item such as a spare tire or baby seat, make a list of all the items in your car—better yet, take pictures.

After Your Lender Repossesses

You have valuable rights after your lender repossesses your car. Your lender may come after you for the deficiency, which is the difference between what your lender receives after selling your car and what you owe on the loan. Under most auto loan contracts, the lender can hold you responsible for the deficiency on your loan. (See "Example: Repossession Hurts Twice.")

Also, you should ensure that your lender treats your car as the law requires. After your lender seizes your car, the lender decides whether to keep the car as compensation for your debt or to resell it in either a public or private sale. In either case, your lender should notify you about the decision.

Under most state laws, if your lender informs you that it wants to keep the car, you have the right to demand that the lender sell the car instead. You'll want to exercise this right if the car is worth more than what you owe on it. Most creditors will sell the car rather than keep it. If your creditor chooses to resell the car at public auction, state law usually requires the lender to notify you of the date so you have the option of participating in the bidding.

If your lender decides to sell the vehicle privately, your lender is usually required to send you a notice of the date after which it will be sold. The fees and costs of repossession usually chew up most of your equity in your vehicle. If your car's value exceeds what you owe, avoid repossession as best you can through the steps in this chapter.

No matter what your lender decides, in some states, you may be entitled to "redeem," or buy back, the vehicle by paying the full amount owed on it plus the expenses connected with its repossession, such as storage and preparation for sale. You must redeem your vehicle before your lender has disposed of or sold the property or signed an agreement to do so. In addition, some states have laws that do allow you to reinstate your loan. This means you can reclaim your car by paying the amount you are behind on your loan together with your creditor's repossession expenses.

Any resale of a repossessed car must be conducted in a commercially reasonable manner. Your lender has to make the sale according to standard custom for its business or in an established market. A commercially reasonable manner does not guarantee you a high price, or even a good price, for your car—it just means that the lender must sell your car in a way that it and others in its business commonly use to sell cars that they have repossessed. Should your lender not act in a commercially reasonable manner, you may have a claim against your lender for damages or a defense against your lender collecting a deficiency from you.

Example: Repossession Hurts Twice

Suppose that you bought a crossover vehicle for $25,000. To make the purchase, you took out a $20,000 loan for 5 years at 7 percent interest. Your monthly payment would be about $425 a month. One year later, the car is worth $20,000. You owe $16,500 on your loan.

If you sell the car to a private party, your profit would be:

Sale price:	$20,000
Balance of the loan:	$16,500
Profit to you:	**$ 3,500**

If you sell the car to a dealer, your profit would be:

Sale price:	$19,000
Balance of the loan:	$16,500
Profit to you:	**$ 2,500**

If you stop paying for the car, and your lender repossesses it, your profit would be:

Sale price:	$15,000
Balance of the loan:	$16,500
Repossession costs:	$ 1,000
Sales costs and fees:	$ 500
Storage/administrative fees:	$ 500
Profit to you:	**Negative $3,500**

If you allowed the vehicle to be repossessed, you would owe $3,500. Understand what a repossession would do to you. By selling the vehicle yourself, you may have been able to put $2,500 to $3,500 in your pocket. Instead, because of the repossession, you now owe your lender $3,500 for a car you no longer drive. By letting your lender repossess your vehicle, you lost at least $6,000.

Leased Vehicles

Since the 1980s, many consumers have opted to enter into lease agreements instead of purchasing vehicles. A consumer might lease a vehicle as a way to drive a nicer car than he would be able to buy. Unfortunately, lease terms can complicate the formula for figuring out the real cost of driving a car.

When you buy a car and take out a loan for the purchase, you typically own and hold title to the car. Your lender takes what is called a security interest in the car. However, when you lease a car, your lender typically owns and holds title to the car. You do not own the vehicle under a lease agreement; your leasing company does and you pay them to drive it for the contractual period. With most consumer leases, you return the vehicle at the end of the lease term and end the contract. You can also purchase the vehicle at a price that the lender determined at the time you first entered into the lease.

When you return the vehicle, you are responsible for paying end-of-lease charges, such as excess mileage, wear and tear, and disposition costs. These charges are known as buy-out or back-end costs. If you return your leased vehicle before the end of the lease term, the lender still holds you liable for the back-end costs and you will likely be charged an early termination fee. Because you are obligated to pay these contractual fees in addition to any recovery or repossession costs and fees, you must do what you can to avoid repossession.

In addition to the steps discussed that follow, you should consider renegotiating your lease terms with your leasing company, including extending the lease term, to avoid repossession. If your contract does not prohibit transferring your lease, consider transferring it to a third party. Web sites such as leasetrader.com provide a forum to transfer leases. Watch out for leases that require you to guarantee the payments of whoever takes over your lease. If the lease requires your guaranty, you must pay if the new lessee stops paying.

The cost to just walk away from your lease by surrendering your vehicle to the dealership is high. You will have to pay the early-termination costs plus the costs and fees to sell your vehicle that you incurred after repossession. Your car can be sold at auction and the leasing company can hold you responsible for the difference between the sales price at auction and the value it places on the car, repossession costs, and fees, plus the early-termination fees.

Special rules and laws cover repossessed vehicles subject to auto leases. When your leased car is repossessed, the contract terms govern how much you owe in addition to all of the other repossession costs and fees. The amount the lender will assert that you owe after a repossession of your leased vehicle could range from $5,000 to $10,000 or more. You may want to consider contacting a lawyer to challenge the amount because state and federal laws offer strong protections to consumers under lease agreements.

The rest of this chapter discusses steps for dealing with auto debt and avoiding repossession of your vehicle.

Bring Your Loan Current

The first step to dealing with your auto debt should be the most obvious, but it may be the hardest for you to accomplish: Do your best to bring your payments current. If you do not have enough to pay all your bills, pay your auto loans before your credit cards, doctor bills, and other unsecured debts. If you miss two or three months of payments, you face the real possibility of losing your vehicle. You can miss several months of payments on your credit cards, medical bills, and other personal loans before you are in danger of losing property. Moreover, you should have advance warning and a chance to go to court before you lose any property on account of unsecured debts.

Many states allow you to make up your back payments and late charges to prevent repossession. This right of second chance, known as the right to cure, requires that creditors send you a notice of your ability to bring your loan current and information on how much you need to pay. In other states, however, making up the back payments may not be enough to stop repossession unless your lender agrees in writing. Nevertheless, even if you have the right to cure by law, you should contact your lender, which is the second step to avoiding repossession.

> Keep your insurance current. If your insurance is canceled, your lender can repossess your car or bill you for more expensive insurance.

Contact Your Lender and Negotiate

If you cannot bring your loan current, are afraid that your lender may contemplate repossession, want to cure defaults, or otherwise want to make different payment arrangements, you should contact your lender. Your goal in contacting your lender should be to negotiate a workout with affordable monthly payments. You should explain your situation and your prospects for future payments. Any workout should lower your monthly payments and contain a guaranty that the lender will not seize the car. You may also ask for a brief respite from payments if you have legitimate reasons and an explanation of why you need the respite and present how your money will come back. If you do enter into a modification, make sure that the new loan lowers your payment without extending the repayment period for an excessive amount of time, and get it in writing.

In negotiating a workout arrangement, use any past issues with the vehicle that would give you grounds to sue as leverage, such as the argument that you were sold a lemon or the lender attempted an illegal repossession. These issues will give you a better ability to work out a good deal. If you decide that you need some assistance in your negotiations with your lenders, you can always contact a credit counselor. Most reputable credit counselors possess great skills in negotiating with lenders. See the discussion on credit counselors in Chapter 7.

If you get your lender to agree to any modifications in your loan or to delay repossession, make sure you get the changes or new agreement in writing. You should insist that your lender signs a new agreement or sends a letter specifying the new terms.

Sell Your Car

Your trouble with your auto loan may stem from buying a car that is more expensive than you can afford. The downturn in the economy, unwise credit decisions, and certain government initiatives may have facilitated placing many millions of people with a monthly payment that exceeds their ability to pay.

Your best move may be to sell the car yourself. A personal sale will most likely obtain a much higher price than an auction sale after repossession. Plus, you avoid all the costs that your lender adds on if it does repossess your car, such as towing, storage, auction cost, and other fees. Make sure you own the car and you are not under a lease agreement. You do not have the right to sell a car that you are leasing, unless the leasing company agrees in advance.

When you sell, either make sure that your sale price will exceed what you owe on the vehicle or that your lender agrees in writing that the sale price will pay off the loan in full even if it is less than the current balance. Most lenders will not let a new owner assume your loan, making you personally responsible for the whole loan. Ideally, you can sell your car and have some money left over so that you can buy a used car with low to no monthly payments, or you can live a few months without a car so you can save money. If your lender won't agree to the sale price you are offered, save a written copy of the offer so that if the lender seizes the car, you can argue that your responsibility for the deficit ends at the bid price.

Surrender Your Car on Your Terms

Many car dealers arrive at their lots on Monday morning to find vehicles parked with notes that read, "I surrender this vehicle." Many consumers believe by returning their cars in this manner they will be free of any responsibility for the balance of their loans. Unfortunately for these consumers, lenders do not necessarily free people from their obligations on their auto loans in this way.

Surrendering your vehicle to your lender is simply a voluntary repossession. Your lender will hold you personally liable for the cost of the loan that the lender's sale of the vehicle does not cover. By surrendering the vehicle, you reduce your liability somewhat because your lender will not add any repossession costs to your loan. However, the lender will likely still sell your car at auction, which means that it will likely result in an inadequate sale price. Moreover, the costs of the fees and costs of the auction are added into your debt on the loan. The lender can still collect any deficiency on the loan from you. In addition, you may also waive some claims and defenses to the contract.

> Because in Dubai you can be thrown in jail for excessive debt, the Dubai airport resembles a used-car lot. People fleeing the country will park their cars and abandon them in the airport parking lot. Many will eventually call or write their auto lenders to tell them where the car can be found.

Should you attempt to surrender or turn in your car to your lender, follow the same guidelines as we discussed in the section "Sell Your Car." Discuss the terms of the surrender with your lender. Make sure the lender will accept the vehicle as full payment for the loan and that your lender does not report the surrender to the credit agencies. Make sure that the agreement of surrender is in writing.

You should make the surrender option as attractive to your lender as possible by emphasizing any problems with the loan or the car when it was sold to you, your inclination to fight repossession to increase the lender's expense, your financial situation would prevent your lender from getting any of the deficiency from you personally, and you are contemplating a chapter 7 or chapter 13 bankruptcy filing.

Resist Repossession Reasonably

We do not recommend resisting repossession as a method of dealing with your auto loan because it will likely work only temporarily and will increase what you owe. Nevertheless, because a repossessor cannot breach the peace, you can resist repossession and give yourself extra time with your vehicle.

Vehicle finance companies lose on average in excess of $8,000 on each vehicle they repossess. While the lender may attempt to hold the car owner responsible for the deficiency, the potential loss gives lenders a reason to work out a deal with you.

Source: Greg Garland, "For the Repo Man, Business Zooms; Gas Cost, Economy Mean More People Can't Meet Payments," *Baltimore Sun,* May 31, 2008.

However, most states have laws making it a criminal offense to hide collateral, such as your vehicle, or to take the vehicle out of state. We ultimately see resisting repossession as a losing battle because it is impractical and it may increase your costs in the long run. However, if you do decide to resist, we suggest keeping these tips in mind:

- In most states, a polite objection to the repossession when the repossessor arrives should stop the repossession.
- Locking your car in a garage should likewise prevent a repossessor from getting your vehicle.
- Never resort to force or violence.
- Check credentials if someone claims to be a government official.
- Watch out for tricks, such as waving papers that they claim to be court orders to get your car; offering to fix a problem for free or conducting an inspection; or enticing you to drive to the lender's office to discuss a workout.

Repossessors use online databases to track down owners of vehicles they seek. They will also make calls and knock on doors of friends and neighbors—an estranged spouse or angry girlfriend looking for revenge can be a good source of information.

Consider Bankruptcy

Because of the automatic stay, filing bankruptcy stops your lender from seizing your vehicle. Bankruptcy halts all attempts to take any of your property, even property on which your lenders have liens. Moreover, if your car has been repossessed but not sold, bankruptcy may help you get your car back. Bankruptcy also provides ways to keep your car for the long term.

At the beginning of your chapter 7 bankruptcy case, you must file a document called a Statement of Intention. In this statement, you must tell the court what you plan to do with any secured collateral such as your car. In a chapter 7 bankruptcy case, you can redeem your vehicle, reaffirm your debt, or surrender the vehicle. A fourth option—to do nothing and keep paying the loan—may also exist but it is questionable and depends on obtaining the consent of the lender. If you do not act in accordance with the Statement of Intention, the lender who holds the security interest on that collateral will not be barred by the automatic stay of picking up that collateral 30 days after the Section 341 creditors meeting.

Moreover, bankruptcy also provides you the ability to challenge your auto debt or a repossession to ensure that they were lawful in form and execution.

Redemption

To redeem your car in bankruptcy, you pay your lender only what the car is worth, not what you owe on your loan. Redemption in bankruptcy can save you considerable amounts from redemption outside of bankruptcy. Outside of bankruptcy, to redeem you have to pay your entire loan, including all costs and fees. In bankruptcy, you redeem at the replacement value without deducting for the costs of sale. If your car is worth $10,000 but you still owe $15,000 on your loan, you only have to pay $10,000 to redeem the car in bankruptcy.

The problem for most people, however, is that you must pay the entire redemption amount in cash. Most people cannot come up with the cash. Some creditors let you redeem in installment payments but

Example: Vehicle Redemption

If you owned a 2007 Jeep Grand Cherokee, the vehicle redemption might be as follows:

Kelly Blue Book value in January 2010:	$12,000
Outstanding balance on loan:	$18,000
You pay to redeem outside of bankruptcy:	$18,000
You pay in full to redeem during bankruptcy:	$12,000

the bankruptcy court cannot require a lender to accept installment payments. Also, some lenders may offer you a loan for the present value of your car, so you can redeem in your bankruptcy case. These are called "redemption" loans. You may find this new loan with a much lower principal than what you owe very appealing, especially if you can value your car at a very depressed level and may be able to refinance again in the future.

However, beware of interest rate and fees. We have seen redemption loans with interest rates that exceed 25 percent. That's worse than buying a car with your credit card (and we do not recommend buying a car on your credit card either!). Rather, you may consider a loan from your 401(k), pension plan, or other retirement plan, but only if you can and will pay it back in full over a period of five years or less.

Reaffirmation

When you enter into a reaffirmation agreement, you agree to repay a debt that would otherwise be discharged in your bankruptcy case. Your personal liability on your auto loan would normally be discharged in bankruptcy, but your lender would continue to have the right to repossess. You would reaffirm an auto loan in order to keep a car in which a lender has a security interest.

You must meet certain requirements to enter into a reaffirmation agreement. First, your reaffirmation must be effective under non-bankruptcy law and the creditor must make numerous disclosures of the costs of reaffirmation. Second, you must enter into the reaffirmation agreement before you receive a discharge in your bankruptcy case. In addition, the bankruptcy court will often approve your reaffirmation only if you appear before the bankruptcy court for a hearing and you prove that reaffirmation is not a hardship. At this time, you will be told that dischargeable debts, such as your auto loan, do not have to be reaffirmed. In addition, the bankruptcy judge will tell you the consequences of entering into a reaffirmation agreement, including repossession and a deficiency judgment if you default.

Because bankruptcy law protects lenders from pressuring debtors into a reaffirmation of an auto loan, reaffirmation requirements include that:

- An agreement be executed before discharge
- The debtor has a right to rescind for 60 days
- Lenders provide specific disclosures
- An agreement be filed with the bankruptcy court
- The debtor appears at a hearing in front of a bankruptcy judge if not represented by a lawyer
- A lawyer provides the debtor's signature if represented by a lawyer

If you have an attorney, he or she must file an affidavit stating that your reaffirmation is voluntary and does not impose an undue hardship on you. You must disclose your income and expenses reflecting your ability to pay the reaffirmed debt, except if the lender is a credit union. If you are without an attorney, the bankruptcy court must evaluate whether the agreement will impose undue hardship on you and that the agreement is in your best interests. The court will not approve the agreement if it will not improve your situation.

Bankruptcy courts are generally reluctant to allow you to enter into a reaffirmation agreement when you want to reaffirm in order to keep driving a luxury car. Also they hesitate to allow you to enter into a reaffirmation agreement if you seek to protect the guarantee of a friend or relative. Even if you meet all the requirements of a reaffirmation agreement, you get a 60-day cooling-off period in which you are free to rescind the reaffirmation.

We believe that unless you are in payment default, you should never reaffirm your car loan in bankruptcy. Many creditors will send the debtor a letter with an executed reaffirmation agreement and instruct the debtor to complete the form, sign it, and file it with the court. You would make a big mistake to sign as instructed by the lender without conducting an analysis of your abilities and interests. You should never reaffirm an auto loan simply because you want to keep the car.

Consider all alternatives before reaffirming a debt such as an auto loan. Most important, make sure that you can make the monthly payments because if you breach an approved reaffirmation agreement, you will still owe the entire debt, including any deficiency after the sale of the vehicle, notwithstanding the bankruptcy discharge.

First, contact your lender and ask if the lender will continue to keep accepting regular payments without a reaffirmation agreement. This is referred to as a "voluntary retain and pay agreement" and must be obtained in writing.

If your lender will not agree to this option, seriously consider selling your car and replacing it with a less expensive used car before you enter into a reaffirmation agreement.

We think that you have no need to reaffirm because you will not likely be in danger of losing your car through repossession. Lenders will not likely take a car on which you are current in your payments so do not legally bind yourself to a debt that your bankruptcy will discharge. Moreover, in some states, lenders cannot repossess unless you've had a payment or other default on your auto contract because filing for bankruptcy does not give the lender the default grounds for repossession.

Do not consider reaffirmation if the debt is completely unsecured, you have no interest in the property, you cannot afford the loan, or you can never keep up with the payments. You may want to consider reaffirming if your lender makes big concessions that make the loan worthwhile for you to keep and the payments are at a level where you can easily make them going forward.

Treatment of Vehicle Loans in Chapter 13

In a chapter 13 case, your best bet is to pay off your car in monthly payments in three to five years through your chapter 13 plan. You may be able to reduce your interest rate in the plan and potentially reduce what you owe to the current value of the car if your loan is not a purchase money security interest on a car purchased within 910 days before the bankruptcy.

For purchase money security interest on vehicle purchases less than 910 days before bankruptcy, the vehicle loan must be paid in full either over the life of the plan or according to the terms of the loan agreement. You should determine which option presents the most affordable method to pay your vehicle debt and draft the chapter 13 plan accordingly.

Vehicle Leases in Bankruptcy

Before you take any actions in bankruptcy regarding your vehicle lease, you must make sure that you have a true lease rather than a rent-to-own transaction. The difference between a true lease and a rent-to-own transaction is considerable in your bankruptcy case. In a rent-to-own transaction, you give a security interest rather than an ownership interest in the vehicle to your lender.

You may have difficulty determining whether you entered into a vehicle lease that is a true lease rather than a credit transaction. You have likely entered into a true lease if your financing entity actually owns the vehicle and at the end of the term, you have nothing: You have to return the vehicle and you cannot sell the vehicle. Under a true lease agreement, the terms of the lease contract govern the rights and obligations between you and the lender. Typically, your vehicle lessor has the right to repossess the car for any default, such as nonpayment of an installment or lack of insurance, in the same manner as a secured party would.

In a bankruptcy case, you can assume the vehicle lease—meaning you can agree to continue with the lease and cure defaults—or reject the lease—meaning that you can surrender the vehicle and have no further obligation to pay lease installments. If you do not expressly assume or reject your vehicle lease within 60 days of filing a chapter 7 bankruptcy case, the lease is rejected by operation of law. Your vehicle lessor is entitled to repossess the vehicle without seeking relief from the automatic stay. In all "chapters" or types of bankruptcy cases, you must indicate in your initial bankruptcy documents your intent to assume your vehicle lease.

Points to Remember

- Review your loan or lease documents to determine what your and your lender's obligations are.
- Contractual termination fees make repossession of leased vehicles especially expensive.
- Contact your lender no matter how you plan to deal with your auto debt.
- Sell your car if you can pay off the loan through the sale.
- Work out a deal to wipe out the deficiency if you surrender the vehicle.
- Bankruptcy offers several options that can allow you to keep your car.

The Way Out of Tax Debt

But in this world nothing can be said to be certain, except death and taxes.

—Benjamin Franklin

The Internal Revenue Service (IRS) is responsible for collecting the money to keep the U.S. government running. This very serious and determined agency possesses numerous powers that allow it to fulfill its duties to the United States.

Anyone would experience a moment of fear if they received a letter from the IRS claiming they owed money on their taxes. After all, the IRS usually has its facts and figures right. When other law enforcement agencies couldn't touch the notorious Chicago gangster Al Capone, the IRS gathered evidence that convicted him of tax evasion and he went to prison for 11 years. The list of celebrities and businessmen prosecuted for tax evasion is endless.

Still, like everyone, the IRS makes mistakes and you may have the grounds to challenge the IRS's claims. Lori Singleton-Clarke, a Maryland nurse, accomplished a rare feat when she stood up against the IRS in tax court and won.[1] Lori believed she had properly deducted her business school tuition from an online business school. The IRS disagreed, audited her tax return, and denied the deduction. Lori took her fight to tax court without a lawyer. The IRS brought a legal team. Lori impressed the court with her presentation, preparation, and meticulous record keeping. A year after her hearing, the tax court found that she was right in taking the deduction.

Lori's case demonstrates that you need favorable facts, obsessive organization, and fearlessness to prevail against the IRS. Disputing a claim that the IRS makes against you can be intimidating. This chapter offers steps you can take to avoid ever being in the position of challenging the IRS in tax court. Your best options for finding your way out of your tax debt include paying in installments, paying reduced penalties and interest, or even negotiating for a lesser debt. This chapter will explain each option and how to determine which one is right for you (see Appendix A or www.wiley.com/go/roadoutofdebt for more information on specific forms and resources). But first and foremost, always file your tax return.

Always File a Tax Return

No matter who you are, what you do, or how much money you owe, it doesn't make sense not to file a tax return. The only exception is if you earn less than a certain amount. For example, in 2009, a single individual with gross income of less than $9,350 did not need to file a federal tax return.

Taxes do not go away. If you ignore your taxes, the situation only gets worse. Unpaid taxes, whether state or federal, incur fines, penalties, and interest that substantially increase what you owe. Failure to comply with the IRS's demands for payment can result in garnishment of your paycheck and seizure of your bank accounts, personal and business property, and real estate.

Simply put, don't mess with the IRS. You must deal with the IRS on their playing field and by their rules. The IRS will not forget about you if you do not file your tax return. They have one of the most advanced computer systems in the world and if you have

Though the IRS does not have a tax amnesty program that can free you from paying penalties and interest, it's worth checking to see if your state taxing authority does.

a Social Security number or have ever held a job, the IRS will track you down.

Once the IRS discovers that you've not filed a tax return, it will send you up to four notices requesting that you file your delinquent return. You must file your overdue return or provide the IRS with proof that you did file as soon as possible after receiving the first notice. Failure to respond to the request can result in a criminal investigation for assessment of substantial criminal penalties.

Always file a tax return on time even if you cannot pay the tax that you owe. If you owe several years of back returns but owe little or no taxes, you could file the back returns separately, for example, one week apart. Filing in a staggered manner may prevent an investigation for fraud by the criminal investigation division of the IRS. If you owe more than two years of back returns and a substantial amount of taxes, you must be careful and should probably consult a tax attorney. If you need more time to file, consider seeking an extension.

Filing an Extension

An extension allows you to file your taxes by October 15th rather than the usual April 15th deadline. You can request this six-month extension to file your taxes, which the IRS will grant automatically. However, the extension does not extend your time to pay what you owe, but only extends the time you have to file your tax return. If you don't pay what you will likely owe, the IRS will charge you interest and likely assess a late payment fee. You are better off filing your return on time and paying what you can. If you cannot pay all your taxes immediately, pay as much as you can because by paying now, you will reduce the amount of interest and penalty you will owe.

Do not fabricate information, guess, or include incorrect information on your tax return to file it on time. If you do not include enough information to figure out the correct tax or put down information that clearly shows that the tax you reported is substantially incorrect, you have filed a frivolous return. You may have to pay a penalty of $5,000 if you file a frivolous tax return or other frivolous submission. Outright lies constitute fraud. If you underpay what you owe based on fraud, the IRS will charge a penalty of 75 percent of the underpayment due to fraud.

For members of the military serving in Iraq, Afghanistan, or other combat zones, the filing and payment deadlines for federal taxes are normally postponed 180 days from the time they leave the combat zone.

Criminal Penalties

The IRS may criminally prosecute you if it suspects that you have committed any of the following actions: tax evasion; willful failure to file a return, supply accurate information, or pay any tax due; fraud and false statements; or preparing and filing a fraudulent return. The two most common infractions are failure to file and failure to pay.

By willfully failing to file your return, you commit a misdemeanor punishable by fine of not more than $25,000 and imprisonment for not more than a year. But in order for the IRS to successfully prosecute you for criminal offenses, the IRS must demonstrate that you were required by law to file a return, you failed to file the return by the deadline, and your failure to file was willful. Because of the difficulty proving the willful prong, the IRS rarely pursues criminal actions unless you are a celebrity, a high-profile person, or you owe a large amount of taxes. An examination of your personal tax return for accuracy by the IRS is known as an audit.

Even though you will likely avoid jail, the IRS will assess fees, penalties, and interest. These costs grow from the date you were required to file the return regardless of whether you filed your return.

The combined penalty and late payment fees are 5 percent of your taxes owed for each month or part of the month you are late after the date upon which you were supposed to file your return, up to a maximum of 25 percent. When you file more than 60 days late, the minimum penalty you will pay is the smaller of $100 or 100 percent of the taxes owed.

Plus, by not filing a return, you also run the risk that the IRS will file your return for you. The IRS could summon you to their local office, require you to bring all your financial records for the year, and then complete your return as you sit there. You do not want the IRS to complete your return.

However, if you file your tax return but don't pay what you owe, you have not committed a crime. You simply have not paid a debt. The fees and penalties reflect the lower severity in failing to pay. The penalty is 0.5 percent for each month the tax is not paid in full. There is no maximum limit to the failure-to-pay penalty. The penalty is calculated from the original payment deadline until the balance due is paid in full. Interest continues to accrue from the original payment date.

What were your chances of being audited by the IRS in 2009?

If your income exceeded $1 million, you had a 6.42 percent chance of being audited.

If your income exceeded $200,000, you had a 2.89 percent chance of being audited.

If your income was less than $200,000, you had a 0.96 percent chance of being audited.

Source: www.irs.gov/newsroom/article/0,,id217442,00.html.

Talk to the IRS

When you realize you need to address your IRS tax problems, immediately call, write, or visit the nearest IRS office to explain your situation. Find one particular agent so you can keep in easy contact. You want to keep the IRS on your side and communication goes a long way toward that goal. Your IRS representative will likely ask you to fill out forms detailing your monthly income and expenses in order to better advise you on ways to pay your tax. By making the first contact, you may be able to keep your case out of the automated collection branch of the IRS, which does not offer you as many options.

In addition, the Taxpayer Advocate Service, an independent organization within the IRS, can assist you with general guidance and help resolve tax problems that have not been resolved through normal channels. See Appendix A for contact information.

You can also go to a low-income taxpayer clinic. These clinics provide representation in federal tax controversies with the IRS for free or for nominal charge if you qualify as low-income. The clinics also provide tax education and outreach if you or a family member has limited English proficiency or speaks English as a second language. You can learn more about low-income taxpayer clinics at www.irs.gov or by calling your local IRS office.

IRS Enforcement Action

The IRS has the right to collect outstanding federal taxes for 10 years from the date your tax liability was assessed. The collection period could be suspended for the time that:

- The IRS considers an installment agreement or compromise
- The IRS considers a request for innocent spouse relief
- You are in bankruptcy, plus an additional six months
- You live outside the United States for a continuous period of six months or more

These suspensions are discussed in detail in the next section, but it's important to know that the IRS has formidable powers to enforce the collection of taxes. Before taking enforcement action, the IRS will give you a chance to voluntarily pay what you owe by sending a Notice of Tax Due and Demand for Payment, which tells you how much you owe in taxes. After the notice, if you do not pay your taxes in full or at least contact the IRS to explain why you cannot pay, how you plan to pay, or why you disagree with the reasons the IRS believes it has the right to take enforcement action, the IRS will take action. In addition to bringing criminal and other actions in court, the IRS can do the following:

- File a Notice of Federal Tax Lien that notifies the public that you owe the government money.
- Serve a Notice of Levy that allows the IRS to seize and sell your property, including your house, to satisfy the tax debt.
- Offset a refund to which you are entitled. If you have overpaid your taxes for one tax period but owe taxes for another, the IRS can apply your refund to reduce the unpaid tax.
- Serve a summons to secure information, records, or testimony.

In 2009, the IRS made 581 seizures, enforced 965,618 liens, and imposed 3,478,181 levies for a total of over 4.4 million enforcement actions. In addition, the IRS conducted 1.4 million audits in 2009.

Source: www.irs.gov, "Internal Revenue Service, Fiscal Year 2009 Enforcement Results."

Liens

Liens give the IRS a legal claim to your property as security for payment of your tax debt. After the IRS has assessed your tax liability, you have 10 days after the IRS sends you a Notice and Demand for Payment to fully pay your debt.

If you refuse or neglect to pay and do not have any productive conversations, the IRS may then file a Notice of Federal Tax Lien in the public records. By filing a Notice of Federal Tax Lien, your creditors are publicly notified that the IRS has a claim against all your property, including property you acquire after the lien was filed. The lien attaches to all your property, including your house and car, and to all your rights to your property. You likely will not be able to sell your property until you satisfy the lien. The lien applies only to the state where the IRS files the lien. You can sell property free and clear if you own the property in another state. Once a lien is filed, your credit rating may be harmed. A lien may affect your ability to get a loan, buy a house or a car, get a new credit card, and sign a lease.

The Long Arm of the IRS Extends to the Rich and Famous

While it's not likely to make the cover story of a magazine or entertainment news program, countless celebrities and politicians have struggled with tax debt. Here's a list of some of them:

- Comedian and actor Sinbad: sued for $8.1 million for seven years of unpaid taxes.
- Governor Arnold Schwarzenegger: had a lien on his properties for $79,000.
- Richard Hatch, first winner of the game show *Survivor*: prosecuted for failure to pay taxes on his *Survivor* winnings of $1 million. Sentenced to four years and three months in prison.
- Singer Willie Nelson: fined $16.7 million for unpaid taxes and fines. (To help pay his debt, Nelson released an album, "The IRS Tapes: Who'll Buy My Memories.")
- Billionaire hotel operator and real estate investor Leona Helmsley: prosecuted for tax evasion. She served 19 months of a 16-year sentence and is reputed to have said, "We don't pay taxes. Only little people pay taxes."

(Continued)

- Actor Nicholas Cage: had two liens on real estate totaling $12.9 million.
- Actor Wesley Snipes: convicted of three misdemeanor counts of not filing tax returns. Sentenced to three years in prison and may have to pay $13 million in taxes and fines. He has appealed the decision.
- Actor and singer Marc Anthony: charged with failure to file tax returns from 2000 to 2004. He believed his accountant had filed, and he avoided prosecution by paying a $2.5 million fine.

Levies

Levies are legal seizures of property to satisfy tax debts. Levies differ from liens because a levy actually takes property to satisfy IRS debts while liens are claims used as security for the tax debt.

If you do not pay your taxes or make arrangements with the IRS to satisfy your debt, the IRS can seize and sell your property (such as your car, boat, and house). Additionally, the IRS can levy property that belongs to you but someone else holds, such as your wages, retirement accounts, dividends, bank accounts, rental income, Social Security benefits under Title II of the Social Security Act (OASDI), state tax refund, the cash value of your life insurance, and commissions.

After the IRS has assessed your tax and sent you a Notice and Demand for Payment that you neglected or refused to pay, the IRS will send you a Final Notice of Intent to Levy and Notice of Your Right to a Hearing. The IRS will send this notice at least 30 days before it commences the levy.

The IRS gives you at least 30 days before it will seize your property and also tells you of your right to appeal. At the appeal hearing, you can challenge the amount or assert defenses, such as your status as an innocent spouse.

The IRS prefers to levy your wages and your bank accounts before it seizes your property. The IRS does not need a court order to take such action. It need only file a notice with your employer or with your bank that directs it to turn over your assets to the IRS.

A levy on your paycheck will remain in effect until your tax bill is paid in full. The IRS allows you to exempt a small portion in the paycheck for yourself as well as an amount for dependents.

Levies on your wages, salary, commissions, and other payments for personal services are continuous and apply to each paycheck. A levy on your bank account applies to the money in the account at the time of the levy. A bank will normally wait to transfer the money in your account for at least 21 days. The 21-day holding period allows you time to resolve any dispute about account ownership.

The IRS will only take property in which you have substantial equity so that the IRS can make a meaningful gain by selling it. The IRS will not take any property in which you have very little equity. In addition, the IRS may not levy your property on the day you attend a collection interview in response to a summons.

In addition, laws prohibit the IRS from levying certain property, including:

- School books and certain clothing
- Fuel, provisions, furniture, and personal effects for a household
- Books and tools you use in your trade, business, or profession
- Unemployment benefits
- Certain annuity and pension benefits
- Certain disability payments
- Workers' compensation
- Salary, wages, or income included in a judgment for court-ordered child support payments
- Certain public assistance payments
- A minimum weekly exemption for wages, salary, and other income

Summonses

A summons, like a subpoena, legally compels you or a third party to provide information, documents, or testimony to the IRS that will be used to determine or collect your tax liability. The IRS can serve a summons on you to compel testimony, bring in books and records to prepare a tax return, or bring in documents and records to assist you in preparing a Form 433, Collection Information Statement. The IRS can summons third parties such as financial institutions, accountants, and other people with information relevant to your case for testimony, records, and documents. To avoid these enforcement actions, you have to work your way out of tax debt as set out next.

Find a Way to Pay

If at all possible, you should seek a way to pay off your debt to the IRS with a lump sum payment. Due to the interest and fees that grow considerably on your debt combined with the difficulty of resolving your debt with the IRS, we suggest that you do what you can to pay off your tax debt as quickly as possible. For tax debt, specifically, we loosen our rules on debt solutions to avoid. You may take a loan from your family or friends, charge it on your credit card, borrow or withdraw from your 401(k), or tap equity from your home to pay off your IRS debt. You could also consider borrowing or cashing in life insurance or even an additional mortgage or home equity line of credit on your house to pay the bill. A mortgage provides you the added benefit of deductible interest.

We normally do not recommend these sources to pay your debts but because of the severe repercussions that can result from failure to pay your taxes, we open up these avenues. The fees and fines that you can incur from nonpayment of your tax debt sometimes may not exceed the fees for an advance on your credit cards. Nevertheless, we still recommend using your credit card if possible because you have more options to deal with credit card debt should your financial situation deteriorate more, although the credit card debt is nondischargeable.

Paying off the IRS provides you with benefits because you stop any additional interest and fees on your tax debt, you get the IRS off your back, and you minimize any fees for professionals assisting you. It may be difficult to come up with the money, but the result of making the full payment benefits you in the long term.

Enter into an Installment Agreement

If you cannot find a way to pay off your IRS debt in a lump sum, you should consider an installment agreement. The IRS offers installment agreements so that you can make a series of smaller, more manageable payments on your debt over a period of time. The IRS offers four different types of installment agreements: guaranteed, streamlined, partial payment, and nonstreamlined.

Guaranteed Agreement This installment agreement type is guaranteed because the IRS must allow you to enter into an installment plan if you meet its requirements:

- Your tax debt is less than $10,000
- You have paid your taxes on time in each of the last five years
- You filed all your tax returns and filed on time in each of the last five years
- You can pay off your balance in 36 months
- You have not entered into an installment agreement in the last five years
- You agree to file and pay on time in the future

Finally, you must offer to pay a minimum monthly payment that is not less than your entire debt, including interest and fees, divided by 30. For example, if you owe $9,300 in taxes, interest, and fees, you should propose a minimum monthly payment of $310 ($9,300÷30) or greater.

Streamlined Agreement If the balance on your tax debt, including interest, fees, and penalties, does not exceed $25,000, you can apply for a streamlined installment plan. You must plan to pay off your debt under the installment plan within 60 months or less. However, if the 10-year statute of limitations in which the IRS can collect your debt will expire during the 60-month term, you must propose a plan that pays off your debt before the expiration of the statute of limitations.

The IRS will likely accept a proposed installment plan that does not exhaust the remaining time on the statute of limitations if your minimum payment is greater than your total debt divided by 50, all of your tax returns are filed, and you agree to pay all of your taxes and file on your returns on time. If you owe $20,000, your proposed minimum monthly should be $400 ($20,000 ÷ 50) over a 60-month term. If only 36 months remain on the statute of limitations, you should then propose at least $555.56 ($20,000 ÷ 36).

Partial Payment Agreement If you cannot fully pay your tax debt during the 10-year collection statute of limitations but can pay a portion, the IRS may consider you for a partial payment installment agreement (PPIA). Instead of set formulas, your monthly payment under a PPIA will depend on what you can actually afford. You cannot apply for a PPIA but instead the IRS must make the determination.

The IRS completes a financial analysis to determine the best method of resolving your tax matter. If the IRS determines that your best method is an installment agreement but understands that you cannot make payments to fully pay the debt within the statutory period for collection, then the IRS will consider you for a PPIA.

Under a PPIA, you make installment payments over the length of time remaining on the statue of limitations for collection of your debt. You have to fully disclose your financial information, including all income, assets, and liabilities, through the use of IRS Form 433-A. You should pursue a PPIA if you can prove financially that you cannot pay back your taxes in full. You must make a good faith effort to use any assets you have to make payments to the IRS. If a Notice of Federal Tax Lien has been filed, it will remain in place until you have paid off the debt through the agreement. Your full debt remains on your account until completion. The IRS will review your financial situation every two years and can adjust payments based on any changes to your finances.

> In fiscal year 2008, the IRS entered into 22,555 partial payment installment agreements (PPIAs). One out of every 115 taxpayers with a delinquent account received a PPIA.
>
> _____
>
> *Source:* IRS Small Business/Self-Employed Division, Collection Activity Report NO-5000-6, *Installment Agreement Cumulative Report* (FY 2008).

Nonstreamlined Agreement If you don't meet the requirements for the other installment agreements, owe more than $25,000 to the IRS, or need a repayment term greater than five years, you will need to negotiate your own installment agreement. This type of installment agreement is often called a nonstreamlined installment agreement because there are no standard guidelines to follow.

As with a PPIA, the IRS will ask that you provide a financial statement as Form 433-A. The IRS will analyze what they believe is the maximum you can afford to pay each month toward your balance. The IRS will then examine whether you can sell any assets,

Table 12.1   When Do You Need Professional Help?

Amount Owed to the IRS	Do You Need Professional Help?
Less than $10,000	Probably not. You can likely work it out on your own.
$10,000–$25,000	Maybe. Help can make sure tax returns were accurate and you can afford payments.
More than $25,000	Yes. Risk is too great to manage on your own. To negotiate a tax debt effectively, consider hiring an attorney.

get a bank loan, or get a home equity loan to pay off your tax debt without an installment agreement.

If your debt exceeds $25,000 or you otherwise need to negotiate a nonstreamlined installment agreement, contact the IRS Taxpayer Advocate Service and seek the advice of a licensed tax professional. Tax professionals can analyze your financial situation, talk to the IRS on your behalf, and help you manage the process. However, make sure that you go to a reputable professional by checking with your state's attorney general and the Better Business Bureau. Avoid the services that make grand promises on reducing your tax liability without seeing your financials. (See Table 12.1.)

How to Apply for an Installment Agreement   You should take the first step to apply for an installment agreement. We recommend being as proactive with the IRS as possible. Hopefully, you have found one person to speak to who knows your situation. Start by calling your contact. If you do not have a contact, you can ask for assistance with the Taxpayer Advocate Service as we discussed earlier in the chapter or follow these instructions:

1. Call the IRS at 1-800-829-1040, fill out an application online at www.irs.gov/businesses/small/article/0,,id=108347,00.html, or fill out Form 9465. For PPIAs and nonstreamlined installment agreements, you will have to fill out additional forms, including a financial statement, IRS Form 433-A.
2. Figure out your total debt, including interests and fees. Then figure out your minimum monthly payment as described earlier.
3. Determine how you would like to pay monthly (i.e., direct deposit, check, credit card over the phone, or Internet).
4. Pay the user fee of $52 for direct deposit, $105 without direct deposit or $43 for low-income taxpayers (those with income

less than 250 percent of the Department of Health and Human Services poverty guidelines). For direct deposit, you will have to provide checking account information.

5. Choose the date and the amount you want to pay. We recommend that you set the minimum payment as your payment amount. You can always pay more. Also, make sure that you can pay by that date every month.

6. The IRS can normally process an installment agreement request within 60 days. However, during the peak filing season it may take up to 90 days. The IRS issues a letter to these taxpayers after 45 days to inform them that their proposal is under consideration.

Generally, IRS collection actions, such as levies against personal and real property, are not made while an installment agreement request is being considered, while an agreement is in effect, for 30 days after a request for an agreement has been rejected, and for any period while a timely appeal of the rejection or termination is being evaluated by the IRS. However, if you default on your installment agreement, the IRS may quickly respond by filing of a Notice of Federal Tax Lien or commencing an IRS levy action.

Qualify for an Offer in Compromise

An offer in compromise settles a debt to the IRS for less than the full amount of what you owe. The IRS accepts offers in compromise when it believes that collection of the full tax amount from you will never occur and what you offer them now is what the IRS reasonably believes it could collect from you. Your goal in making an offer in compromise should match the IRS's goal in accepting an offer in compromise. The offer in compromise should provide payment to the IRS at the earliest time for the least cost to the IRS.

In 2008, the IRS entered into 10,677 offers in compromise. One out of every 244 taxpayers with a delinquent account received an offer in compromise.

Source: IRS Small Business/Self-Employed Division, *Collection Activity Report* NO-5000-108, Monthly Report of Offer in Compromise Activity FY 2008 Cumulative Through September—National Total.

The IRS will not likely accept your offer in compromise unless you make a reasonable offer based on your particular circumstances. To make this reasonable offer, you should determine what you can live on as a bare minimum and what you can obtain if you were to sell nonessential possessions. The amount you offer should be based on the maximum amount you can afford to pay when you have sold your assets and reduced your spending to a bare minimum. You must offer your maximum amount because the IRS rarely accepts less. The IRS will make the same determination on what your maximum offer should be after viewing all your financial documentation and requires you to answer questions about your finances.

An offer in compromise is the only way that you have a chance of settling your debt to the IRS for a significant amount less than what you owe or for "pennies on the dollar." However, the IRS's requirements for an offer in compromise are based on each individual's finances. If you have no assets, no ability to ever pay, and no way to get a loan, then you may be a candidate for settlement for pennies on the dollar. Otherwise, you must make a reasonable offer based on your particular circumstances.

Stay away from anyone or any company that promises to settle your debts for pennies on the dollar without thoroughly reviewing finances. No person or company has magic abilities to resolve your tax debt by any means other than those discussed in this chapter. As we have discussed throughout this chapter, resolving IRS debt is difficult and done on the IRS's terms. (See Table 12.2.)

Table 12.2   Comparing Offer in Compromise with a Partial Payment Installment Agreement

Offer in Compromise	Partial Payment Installment Agreement
What you owe to the IRS is removed from your IRS record if your offer is accepted.	What you owe remains on your IRS record until the 10-year statute for collection expires.
Notice of Federal Tax Lien is released relating to the account being considered fully paid.	Notice of Federal Tax Lien remains in place until the 10-year statute for collection expires.
Payment equivalent to what you own free of liens in your assets must be made.	What you own free of liens in your assets must be considered but PPIA may be granted without this equity being utilized.
IRS cannot seek collection from future increases in ability to pay.	Changes in ability to pay can result in changes to amount you must pay the IRS.

Source: www.irs.gov.

Types of Offers in Compromise   The IRS may accept an offer in compromise based on three grounds:

1. *Doubt as to collectability.* Doubt exists that you could ever pay the full amount of tax liability owed within the remainder of the 10-year statutory time period for collection. The IRS considers a "doubt as to collectability" offer when it determines you could not make full payment by liquidating assets or through an installment agreement. Most often, the taxpayer does not have monthly income to meet necessary living expenses, no real property or equity in real property, and no ability to fully pay the debt now or through monthly installment payments.

2. *Doubt as to liability.* A legitimate doubt exists that you owe part or all of the assessed tax liability. Doubt may exist if the IRS agent did not correctly interpret the law or did not consider all of your evidence regarding your obligation to pay the tax, for example.

3. *Effective tax administration.* You do not challenge that the tax is correct or that you have the potential to pay your debt in full or in installments, but an exceptional circumstance exists that would allow the IRS to consider an offer in compromise. To be eligible for a compromise on this basis, you must demonstrate that the collection of the tax would create an economic hardship or would be unfair and inequitable. For example, the IRS may consider your offer in compromise when you recognize that you owe a tax and can pay it now, but if you do pay, you will not have enough money to provide for the basic needs and necessities of a dependant child diagnosed with a serious long-term illness.

People most often submit an offer in compromise on the basis of "doubt as to collectability." If you believe you qualify, you should apply and pay careful attention to the application and the other requirements.

How Do You Apply?   To apply for an offer in compromise, you will need the workbook and application available at www.irs .gov/businesses/small/article/0,,id=210594,00.html. You can also call the IRS and ask for Forms 656 and 656-B. Determining your eligibility and completing the application requires great detail and attention, so seek help from a reputable tax professional or the IRS's Taxpayer Advocate Service if you are uncomfortable with your answers.

We cannot stress enough how important it is to complete the application diligently and completely. In almost half of the cases, the IRS cannot grant an offer in compromise because they do not have enough information or the process was not followed properly. In fiscal year 2008, 29 percent of offers were returned, 10 percent

> ## "Settle Your Tax Debt for Pennies on the Dollar!"
>
> No doubt you've heard this claim advertised. Don't believe it. All these services can do is help you apply for an offer in compromise. They will not likely review your eligibility but still charge significant fees to help you apply. You are better off applying on your own or with the assistance of a tax professional who will look at your individual situation and provide you true guidance.

were determined to be not processable, and 10 percent were withdrawn or terminated.[2]

You start the process to obtain an offer in compromise by filling out IRS Form 656 (Offer in Compromise) and submitting it to the IRS with the $150 application fee. In addition to Form 656, you need to submit a collection information statement and Form 433-A. In some states, you may have to also submit data on your spouse. After you submit the application, the IRS will ask you for various financial documentation including pay stubs, bank records, and vehicle registrations.

What's the Right Amount for an Offer in Compromise?   Though there are ways of estimating what the acceptable offer in compromise might be, only the IRS can say what it will accept. This is another reason you should not trust anyone who offers to settle your tax debt for pennies on the dollar.

The IRS will assess your offer based on your assets and earning potential. Consider how much money you would have left if you sold all your assets and paid off any loans on them (your value of assets) and how much extra money you have each month from your monthly income after paying for living expenses (your disposable income).

Adding your value of assets and disposable income should give you a good estimate of the amount you should offer in compromise.

You then have three payment options: lump sum cash offer, short-term periodic payment, and deferred periodic payment. With the exception of Doubt as to Liability offers, you will need to fill out a collection information statement (Form 433-A or Form 433-B) to get the process started. All payment offers require a $150 application

Table 12.3   Payment Options for an Offer in Compromise

Payment Option	Terms	Calculating Your Offer
Lump Sum Cash Offer	Must pay 20 percent of the offered amount when Form 656 is submitted. Balance must be paid in five or fewer installments.	*If paying in 5 months or less:* Value of assets + Disposable income over 48 months of payments or remaining time on the 10-year period to collect, whichever is shorter. *If paying in more than 5 months and within 24 months:* Value of assets + Disposable income over 60 months of payments or remaining time on the 10-year period to collect, whichever is shorter. *If paying in more than 24 months:* Value of assets + Disposable income over remaining time on the 10-year period to collect.
Short-Term Periodic Payment	Must include an initial offer payment. Regular payments must continue while the offer is being investigated. Offer must be paid in full within 24 months from offer date.	Value of assets + Disposable income over 60 months of payments or remaining time on the 10-year period to collect, whichever is shorter.
Deferred Periodic Payment	Must include initial offer payment. Regular payments must continue while the offer is being investigated. Offer must be paid in full in 25 or more months but within the time remaining on the statutory period for collection.	Value of assets + Disposable income over remaining time on the 10-year period to collect.

Source: www.irs.gov.

fee. Details of each payment option and our suggestions for your offers are shown in Table 12.3.

Taxpayers qualifying for a low-income waiver and taxpayers submitting doubt as to liability offers are exempt from the required 20 percent payment on a lump sum cash offer and all payments required during the investigation of a short-term periodic payment or deferred periodic payment offer. All required payments are not refundable and are applied to your tax debt whether or not the IRS accepts your offer in compromise.

Qualify as a Hardship Case

The IRS may consider you as a hardship case or "currently not collectible" if you have no ability to pay your taxes. Being currently not collectible does not mean that your debt goes away. Instead, it means that the IRS has determined you cannot afford and have no ability to pay the debt *at this time*.

To be considered "currently not collectible," you must provide the IRS with financial information on IRS Form 433-A, and supply supporting documentation. The IRS will look at your entire financial situation, including whether your monthly income exceeds your monthly allowable expense for necessities. The IRS additionally considers extraordinary circumstances, such as impending medical expenses for you or a loved one.

If you qualify for this, you still owe the debt to the IRS. Penalties and interest will continue to be added to the debt. However, the IRS will suspend all collection activities against you. The IRS will monitor your financial situation to see if it improves so they can demand payment. The IRS usually reviews your situation once a year and will seek information from you regarding your situation.

While in the currently not collectible status, the 10-year statute of limitations on tax debt collection continues to run. If your status does not change and the IRS cannot collect the tax within the 10-year statutory period, your tax debts will expire.

Consider Bankruptcy

Because of the strict requirements to enter payment arrangements with the IRS, you may consider filing bankruptcy to resolve your debts to the IRS. Bankruptcy does not as effectively deal with debts to the IRS as it does with other debts. Not all tax debts can be discharged in bankruptcy.

All tax debts, however, reap the benefit of the automatic stay. The IRS, and all creditors, must stop all collection actions against you once you have filed for bankruptcy. The automatic stay remains in place while your bankruptcy case is pending unless the bankruptcy court grants the IRS relief from the automatic stay to continue collection actions. The IRS does not normally seek relief from the automatic stay. While the automatic stay is in place, you can negotiate with the IRS to work out payment terms.

You can discharge or extinguish your income tax debt to the IRS if you meet the following five criteria:

1. Due date for filing your tax return was at least three years prior to the filing of your bankruptcy case.
2. You filed your tax return at least more than two years prior to the filing of your bankruptcy case.
3. The IRS assessed the tax debt at least 240 days prior to the filing of your bankruptcy case. If you filed for an offer in compromise that the IRS disapproved, then the time period from filing to when the IRS disapproved it needs to be added to the 240-day rule plus 30 days.
4. Your tax return was not fraudulent.
5. You are not guilty of tax evasion.

In a chapter 7 bankruptcy case, you eliminate all debts that are dischargeable and you would not therefore have to pay any tax debts regardless of whether they satisfy the requirements set forth here. Certain tax debts that do not fit the requirements we've discussed are called nondischargeable debts. Your chapter 7 case will not extinguish nondischargeable debts and you will have to pay them in full.

In a chapter 13 bankruptcy case, nondischargeable tax debts are considered priority debts and must be paid in full during the three- to five-year term of the chapter 13 plan without interest. Dischargeable tax debts that meet the previous requirements are treated as general, unsecured claims. These claims are likewise paid over the term of the chapter 13 plan but, unlike nondischargeable debts, do not have to be paid in full.

The secured IRS tax liens are:

- A tax lien filed by the IRS on your property prior to your bankruptcy filing. Your bankruptcy filing will not remove the lien. Even exempt property cannot be sold or transferred without payment of the secured IRS tax lien.
- In a chapter 7 bankruptcy case, secured tax liens cannot be discharged.
- In a chapter 13 bankruptcy case, the secured portion of tax liability must be paid by the plan, in full and with interest, but without further penalty.

You must also provide your tax returns for the four years prior to your bankruptcy filing. See Appendix A for ways to obtain your federal tax return transcript, which is an acceptable substitution for your tax return. You may not have had to file a tax return if your income was below the level set by the IRS for that year. For example, in 2009, a single individual with gross income of less than $9,350 did not need to file a tax return.

Tax debts that arise from failure to file tax returns are not dischargeable. As discussed, you incur tax debt whether or not you file your return. The IRS will tax you even when you do not file your tax returns and you cannot discharge this debt. This is why it is always wise to file your tax returns.

Points to Remember

- Don't mess with the IRS.
- Read and respond quickly to all correspondences from the IRS.
- Always file your tax returns, even if you cannot pay all or any of the tax debt you owe—penalties are much more severe for not filing rather than for failure to pay.
- If at all possible, find a way to pay your debt to the IRS in full.
- Reducing your debt through a partial payment installment plan or an offer in compromise is very difficult. See if you qualify for and can enter into an installment agreement first.
- Bankruptcy may provide you with some benefits on your taxes to the IRS.

PART

III

WHEN TO TAKE THE BANKRUPTCY ROUTE

CHAPTER

Is Bankruptcy Right for You?

*Even if you're on the right track, you'll get run over if
you just sit there.*

—Will Rogers

Bankruptcy can do some great things for some people. Just
ask Connie. Connie Hartwell was an 83-year-old, desperate woman
when bankruptcy relief gave her a new lease on life. Bankruptcy was
her last chance before her financial life completely unraveled.

In 1977, Connie purchased her home for $30,000. She originally
had a 30-year fixed-rate mortgage loan with monthly payments of
$207.63. In 1988, Connie was approached by a door-to-door salesman
who suggested that she make a variety of home repairs, including the
installation of new vinyl siding and windows. In order to make
the repairs, the salesman referred Connie and her granddaughter
to another lender to finance the repairs and consolidate other
outstanding loans.

The salesman and the new lender gave Connie, who had limited
financial resources, a loan that nearly doubled her current interest
rate in the principal amount of $137,611.01. After Connie informed
the lender that she was having trouble with the monthly payment, the
lender refinanced her loan twice in 1991. Eventually, Connie entered

into a new loan with a principal amount of $149,150.00 that included a balloon payment at the end of the loan term that was greater than the principal amount. The monthly payment of $2,005.71 equaled 98.5 percent of Connie's and her granddaughter's combined incomes.

It was not long before Connie and her granddaughter realized that they could not make the monthly payments. Afraid of losing her home, Connie contacted the lender who agreed to lower the monthly payments to $800. The lender failed to explain to Connie and her granddaughter that these reduced payments would result in an increased amount of the balloon payment at the end of the loan. In 2001, a new lender who claimed to own the loan started foreclosure proceedings against Connie and her granddaughter. The new lender claimed that Connie owed approximately $363,000.

Connie filed for chapter 13 bankruptcy relief. Bankruptcy stopped the foreclosure proceedings. Then, with the generous and very able help of a nonprofit legal services agency, Connie was able to bring legal action against the lenders claiming violations of the Truth-in-Lending Act, Fair Debt Collection Practices Act, and other consumer protection acts.

The bankruptcy court ruled that the lenders had acted unconscionably, engaged in predatory lending, and violated Connie's legal rights. The bankruptcy court allowed Connie to rescind the mortgage. Following the bankruptcy court decision, the case was resolved favorably for Connie in an out-of-court settlement. Connie kept her home, the mortgage was discharged, and she received additional damages and attorneys' fees.

Bankruptcy rescued Connie. It saved her home and her way of life. Bankruptcy stopped Connie's world from crumbling down around her. Connie's case is exceptional but to some extent, bankruptcy has this power because of the fresh start and the new beginning from financial problems that it offers.

Bankruptcy Basics

Bankruptcy is a system of federal laws and rules of procedure enacted by the U.S. Congress pursuant to its powers under the Constitution of the United States. These laws are administered through the U.S. bankruptcy courts in the 94 jurisdictions where there is a federal court. Bankruptcy is a federal system. Bankruptcy cases cannot be commenced in state courts but must be commenced by filing a bankruptcy petition with the clerk of the bankruptcy court. Bankruptcy is a legal procedure that allows individuals and businesses, large or small, to obtain relief from debts to obtain a fresh start in their finances and, as in the case of Connie Hartwell, remedy financial injustices. Any individual who lives in or has property in the United States can file a bankruptcy petition.

> The Supreme Court has described the "fresh start" of bankruptcy as a remedy for the "honest but unfortunate debtor" that gives a "new opportunity in life and a clear field for future effort, unhampered by the pressure and discouragement of preexisting debt."
>
> _____
>
> *Source: Local Loan Co. v. Hunt*, 292 U.S. 234, 244 (1934).

Bankruptcy also makes sure that creditors obtain their fair share of a debtor's available assets. Once a bankruptcy case is commenced (done by the filing of a petition with the bankruptcy court), a debtor has breathing room from efforts by creditors to collect debts. When the bankruptcy court enters a discharge order upon successful completion of the bankruptcy case, a debtor will be released from his obligation to repay debts. The discharge order has exceptions and restrictions that are covered in Chapter 15.

There are many factors to evaluate when you are considering whether to file for bankruptcy protection. In this chapter, we discuss the factors in reaching that decision, the scope of bankruptcy protection, and the extent to which the law can help you. We will also discuss less drastic strategies that you can adopt rather than file for bankruptcy. In the chapters that follow, we discuss what type of bankruptcy relief may be right for you.

There are six types of bankruptcy relief and each type is called a *chapter* for its section in the bankruptcy legislation. The types of bankruptcy are chapter 7, chapter 9, chapter 11, chapter 12, chapter 13, and chapter 15.

Should You File?

When deciding whether to file bankruptcy, you must make an analysis based on the facts, circumstances, and laws applicable to your particular case. Often when there is an emergency and you are in the Red Level we discussed in Chapter 1, such as with an impending foreclosure or wage garnishment, then the decision to file is easy. Absent such an emergency, you need to evaluate your other options and decide exactly what bankruptcy can do for you before you file.

Advantages

Many advantages greet a debtor in a bankruptcy case. The most important advantage is the fresh start that bankruptcy gives you. Again, just ask Connie Hartwell. As soon as you file a petition, the bankruptcy court will issue a notice of the automatic stay of creditors' actions against you. The automatic stay means that any actions that your creditors have started or have threatened to start, including foreclosures, repossessions, wage garnishments, and collection actions on credit cards and other personal loans, must stop. Creditors must stop calling, sending demand letters, filing lawsuits, and seizing assets. Immediately after filing for bankruptcy, all the stress from the harassment of aggressive creditors will be lifted from you.

Unless the court orders otherwise, you will obtain a discharge of unsecured debts, such as obligations resulting from credit cards, personal loans, past due rent owed to landlords, and utilities. The discharge is a release of liability on debts and a permanent injunction against a creditor from collecting the debt. When you are granted a discharge in bankruptcy, you will not have to pay back any debts that are included in the discharge. Moreover, in every bankruptcy case, you are entitled to claim exemptions of property, which, if allowed, means that you, the debtor, will be able to retain the exempt property free of the claims of creditors.

If you are reorganizing your debt rather than liquidating it, you may be able to cure defaults in payments on secured debt and modify certain types of secured debts. By curing or modifying your debts on your secured property, such as your house and car, you will be able to keep this property throughout and after your bankruptcy. Finally, bankruptcy court is a forum where debtors can challenge debts of creditors and bring lawsuits against creditors who have violated collection and other laws, causing the debtor financial harm.

Disadvantages

Despite its many advantages, bankruptcy is not a cure for all financial ills. You may not obtain relief from many types of debts, including most home mortgages, alimony, child support, taxes, as well as debts determined to result from fraud. Student loans have special protection in bankruptcy and are not dischargeable unless you can show undue hardship in repayment, which courts have interpreted to mean a permanent inability to pay. Although in a bankruptcy case past due rent can be discharged, you cannot obtain reinstatement of a terminated lease unless state law so permits and eviction may be inevitable notwithstanding bankruptcy. You may retain your exempt property but the bankruptcy case will generally not impact your secured debts because as a general rule, subject to certain exceptions, secured liens pass through bankruptcy unaffected. In other words, bankruptcy may not aid in the retention of collateral subject to your mortgages and car loans if you have past due payments after the bankruptcy case is filed.

In addition, if a bankruptcy court finds that you have not complied with the duties of a debtor, such as the duty to disclose all of your assets, the bankruptcy court may not grant you a discharge. Moreover, the discharge affects only debts existing as of the date of bankruptcy and does not affect future debts. You will not be able to obtain another discharge for eight years after filing a typical chapter 7 bankruptcy case in which you received a discharge. Therefore, if you encounter further financial problems, you will not have the bankruptcy option to address those problems for the ensuing eight years. Finally, you could lose some property in the bankruptcy case as a bankruptcy court may order that your nonexempt property be sold.

The negative impact of a bankruptcy filing could be significant. First, your credit rating will suffer. But, then again, if you are considering bankruptcy, your credit rating may not be very good anyway. Still, once a bankruptcy is filed, a debtor will be considered a Class D borrower by most institutional lenders. Under federal law, credit reporting agencies are allowed to reflect a bankruptcy filing on a credit report for 10 years after a chapter 7 bankruptcy case is commenced and for 7 years after a chapter 13 case is filed. Although the decision to extend credit is up to an individual lender and many debtors can get credit after bankruptcy, most creditors do hold a bankruptcy against a debtor for at least three to five years. Still, others are ready to lend, especially credit card companies.

Stigma

You must additionally keep in mind that a stigma of bankruptcy still exists, as many people consider financial failure embarrassing. In some areas, bankruptcy filings are reported in local newspapers and journals. Because bankruptcy court records are public, they can be easily checked by anyone who wishes to obtain information about a filing and a case.

However, as we discussed in the Introduction, many successful people have used bankruptcy as a vehicle to solve their financial problems. Moreover, the U.S. government has recently supported the bankruptcy cases of Chrysler and General Motors to help solve major financial difficulties in the automobile industry. Thus, the public's perception of bankruptcy is shifting away from viewing bankruptcy as a sign of failure to seeing it as a vehicle for change and rehabilitation.

> For the 12-month period ending September 2009, 1.34 million nonbusiness debtors filed for bankruptcy, which is 34 percent more than the previous period. This means a filing occurred more frequently than once every 30 seconds.

Consider the Alternatives

For many reasons, bankruptcy should be considered as a last resort. As we discussed in the prior chapters, you should carefully consider the alternatives to filing for bankruptcy. Before you file, revisit the following alternatives: doing nothing, obtaining credit counseling, negotiating directly with creditors, mortgage loan modifications, and refinancing. One alternative we do not recommend is foreclosure rescue, and we discuss the reasons in this section.

Doing Nothing

Doing nothing sounds counterintuitive, but it is often the least expensive and easiest option for someone in financial trouble.

If you have no assets that creditors can get, you are referred to as judgment proof. If you are judgment proof, you should consider not filing bankruptcy at all but instead write letters to your creditors stating that you are judgment proof. Although only a bankruptcy will stop collection efforts as a matter of law, many creditors can be persuaded with a letter that they should abandon the effort to collect assets from a judgment-proof individual. The letter should tell your creditor to stop contacting you, that you may file for bankruptcy, in which event your case will be closed as a no-asset case, and that it is futile for the creditor to continue its collection efforts. Failure of a creditor to cease collection efforts after your letter may subject the creditor to liability for violating FDCPA, as explained in Chapter 3.

Credit Counseling

There are many good credit counselors who will do their best to help you avoid filing for bankruptcy. Some credit counselors are bad and will just collect money from you without providing any valuable services. Tread carefully and review Chapter 6 if you wish to reconsider hiring a credit counselor before you file for bankruptcy.

Workouts

Direct workouts, negotiations directly with creditors, may be a way to resolve your financial problems. There are numerous types of workouts that often depend on a creditor's policies. You may be able to work out a repayment plan for some or all of the debt over time with a reduced interest rate that could include forgiveness of some or all of your debt. Read more about this in Chapter 3.

Mortgage Loan Modifications

As a homeowner, you can try various measures to avoid foreclosure outside of bankruptcy; however, all measures require some type of concession by the home mortgage company. With increasing frequency in tough economic times, lenders are entering into loan modifications as an alternative to foreclosure or bankruptcy. Loan modifications are specific to each homeowner and lender and involve a negotiation of workout terms. If you wish to review your personal situation, see Chapter 9.

Refinancing

Refinancing debts through the equity in your home (such as through a second mortgage, reverse mortgage, or home equity line) is also an alternative to bankruptcy. Be aware of the risks, and review Chapter 8.

Foreclosure Rescue

You should never pursue a foreclosure rescue transaction to avoid bankruptcy. Never transfer your house to another individual or company that promises to refinance it and pay your mortgage. These deals are always scams. Transferring the title to your home or property is permanent and fraught with danger. Read more in Chapter 8.

Seek Professional Help

When anyone is plagued by financial troubles, he or she is not always in the state of mind to make the best decisions about their financial condition. Even before deciding to file for bankruptcy, seek advice from a competent professional about whether to file for bankruptcy. Consumer bankruptcy lawyers will often provide a consultation to prospective clients for little or no fee. We urge you to seek a consultation before you embark on the road of bankruptcy to try and see if there are less drastic alternatives that could work for you. There are many reasons to stay out of a bankruptcy case and there are reasons to choose to file. If the choice to file is made, there are further issues as to the appropriate chapter for relief, the timing of a bankruptcy filing, as well as technical requirements affecting a debtor's rights. These decisions are extremely complicated and require an evaluation of the facts of a particular case and an assessment of the applicable law. Good representation by a qualified professional is critical.

Points to Remember

- Know the basics of the bankruptcy system.
- Understand the advantages and disadvantages of bankruptcy so that you can decide whether it is right for you.
- Understand the alternatives to bankruptcy so that you can choose the best strategy for debt relief.
- Consider seeking the assistance of a professional who specializes in debt relief.

21 Bankruptcy Myths

The great enemy of the truth is very often not the lie—deliberate, contrived and dishonest—but the myth—persistent, persuasive and unrealistic.

—John F. Kennedy

With all matters unknown or unfamiliar, people find it much easier to make up stories and myths rather than to understand and learn the truths. People naturally believe that which fits best with their preconceived notions.

Myths about bankruptcy are no different. Myths about bankruptcy arise from extraordinary incidents that most debtors never encounter. Yet, these are the stories that persist and influence what most people think about bankruptcy.

By this point in the book, you now know ways to solve your financial problems without the need for bankruptcy. If you have decided that filing for bankruptcy is your best alternative and will most benefit you in your unique circumstances, do not let myths about bankruptcy hold you back and prevent you from gaining the fresh start that bankruptcy offers. We address twenty-one bankruptcy myths here.

Myth #1: Bankruptcy Is Expensive

For most people on the brink of bankruptcy, avoiding bankruptcy may be much more expensive and more difficult than filing for bankruptcy.

Filing fees for chapter 7 and chapter 13 bankruptcies cost less than $300. When you hire a lawyer, the average cost of a chapter 7 case is approximately $1,500. For a chapter 13 bankruptcy case, you should expect to spend between $2,500 and $3,500 if you hire a lawyer. While not cheap, the amounts you will pay are minimal when compared to your costs of not filing. The interest alone on your outstanding debts will likely far exceed the costs to file. If you factor in the peace of mind that you will receive once you have put your debts to rest, the expense is well worth it. You will now be able to go forward refreshed and move forward with your life.

Myth #2: Saying "I Declare Bankruptcy" in a Public Place Is the Same as Filing for Bankruptcy

You may have seen this approach on television (e.g., Michael Scott on *The Office*), but a simple declaration does not file a bankruptcy. To file bankruptcy, you have to submit a petition, a list of creditors (a matrix), and other documents, usually electronically, in the clerk's office at your bankruptcy court. See Chapter 16.

Myth #3: Proceedings Can Last for Years

In most bankruptcy cases, the debtor never appears before the bankruptcy judge. Debtors only appear in public at the "meeting of creditors" where each debtor is asked questions about his or her finances by the bankruptcy trustee for about five or ten minutes.

In most chapter 7 cases, the case is complete and debts discharged in about four months without an appearance before the bankruptcy judge. In chapter 13 cases and the other reorganization chapters, the proceedings will last four to six months. The payments the debtor makes during the reorganization plan will continue for three to five years but the debtor will most likely have nothing to do with the bankruptcy court unless he or she defaults in making plan or home mortgage payments.

Copyright © 2010 New Way Solutions, www.newwaysolutions.com.

Myth #4: You Can File Only Once

Do not avoid bankruptcy filing because you fear that you may run into future financial troubles and will have used up your chance to file for bankruptcy. You may never intend to file again, but a job loss coupled with a crippling medical emergency down the road may necessitate it. The law takes future necessities into consideration.

You can file more than one bankruptcy case and have your debts discharged. You can receive a discharge from a chapter 7 bankruptcy case once every eight years. You can receive a discharge from a chapter 13 bankruptcy case every two years. If you obtain a discharge in a chapter 7 case, you have to wait six years before getting a discharge in chapter 13. If you get a chapter 13 discharge, then you need to wait four years to obtain a discharge from a chapter 7.

Myth #5: Another Person Will Make All of Your Financial Decisions

Although the bankruptcy court appoints a trustee to oversee your bankruptcy case in both a chapter 7 and chapter 13 bankruptcy case, you are the person responsible for making your own financial decisions. Only nonexempt assets are subject to inclusion in a chapter 7 case and fall under the power of the chapter 7 trustee. The chapter 7 debtor keeps and controls his or her exempt assets. In a chapter 13 or other reorganization case, the debtor retains all assets unless he or she decides to sell them. We explain the different bankruptcy chapters in Chapters 13 through 20.

Myth #6: It's the Most Trying and Heart-Wrenching Experience

No one can deny the potential difficulty and trauma in admitting to a dire financial situation. However, at the time you seriously contemplate bankruptcy, you are already in the midst of a most trying and heart-wrenching experience.

You do have to complete a good deal of paperwork in order to file your bankruptcy case. The paperwork primarily concerns your income, expenses, debts, and assets. Many of the forms you need can be obtained from the bankruptcy courts' websites and through www.wiley.com/go/roadoutofdebt and www.roadoutofdebt.com. If you have been working on a budget, you are well on your way to completing many of the necessary bankruptcy forms. A skilled lawyer is very helpful in this process.

Bankruptcy may put an end to the stress, aggravation, and harassment that you are feeling. After you complete your bankruptcy, you will likely be much relieved and feel better about your finances than you have in a long time. You will embark on the road to financial peace and success with a fresh start.

Myth #7: You're a Failure and a Bad Person

Most bankruptcy filings result from events in people's lives beyond their control: job loss, medical bills, divorce. Bankruptcy was set up as a safety net for such people. You, as have most people, have worked hard to pay your bills. And like most people, your inability to continue to pay has directly resulted from a life-changing situation, such as divorce or job loss combined with the severe economic recession that has affected the world.

You must keep in mind that millions of businesses and individuals file for bankruptcy each year. These companies and people complete the bankruptcy process and again become productive members of society. Bankruptcy filers are not bad people or irresponsible companies. In many ways, bankruptcy filers are responsible and conscientious because they seek to confront their financial problems rather than running away and avoiding creditors. Filing for bankruptcy can be a responsible decision.

Myth #8: Bankruptcy Hurts America

We've all heard of the automaker Chrysler. In 1979, Chrysler planned to go into bankruptcy. Its President, Lee Iacocca, turned to the government and borrowed $1.5 billion. Chrysler was important to America so the U.S. government saved it. Thirty years later, automobile makers Chrysler and General Motors, along with automobile parts dealers, filed for bankruptcy backed by the blessing of the government. Other important companies, including the great brokerage house Lehman Brothers Holdings Inc. and the country's largest mall operator, General Growth Properties, have done the same. These filings did not hurt America but made it stronger because the reorganization of their finances allowed them to emerge as stronger companies.

You know by now that our Founding Fathers bestowed upon every American a federal right to go into bankruptcy. The Founding Fathers also recognized the need for bankruptcy and forgiveness of debts because at the same time in England, people who could not pay their debts were sent to prison. Even some American states had debtors' prisons at the end of the eighteenth century. Our Founding

Fathers believed that a person in prison is neither producing nor is capable of helping himself, his family, or his country. Our Founding Fathers concluded that bankruptcy benefited America and its future.

Myth #9: Avoid Bankruptcy at All Costs

If you can work out your debts and maneuver past the hurdles erected by the credit and lending industries without bankruptcy, of course you should avoid it. But never consider avoiding bankruptcy "at all costs."

Some costs are just too much to bear. Remember, bankruptcy allows you to make a fresh start and discharges many of your debts to creditors. The longer you remain out of bankruptcy, the longer banks and creditors will pursue you for payments on their debts and the larger the amount you owe them will grow due to interest accrual. Creditors will fight hard to persuade you that bankruptcy is a remedy you should never pursue. They'll tell you this because they don't want you to be in bankruptcy where they lose their power over you.

No one knows your unique circumstances. Only you can decide whether bankruptcy is right for you. You have to weigh the positive and negative factors of your own bankruptcy for yourself.

Myth #10: Your Spouse Must Also File for Bankruptcy

A bankruptcy filing by one spouse does not affect the other and does not require the other spouse to file. If one spouse has a significant amount of debt in his/her name, that spouse can file without the other spouse. However, if spouses have significant debts for which they are both liable and they want discharges, we recommend that spouses file together.

Otherwise, if only one spouse files bankruptcy on joint debt obligations, the creditors will simply demand payment for the entire amount from the nonfiling spouse. The worst thing that married couples do, however, is attempt to transfer their joint assets in one spouse's name and extinguish their debts through a bankruptcy case of the other spouse. Debtors who commit fraudulent transfers will be denied the discharge of their debts and may suffer criminal prosecution and penalties.

Myth #11: It Often Causes Family Strife and Divorce

Constant anxiety about burdensome debt, creditors, calls, the influx of bills, attempts to make do with little money, and the inability to do simple things your family once enjoyed cause family strife and problems. Overwhelming debt and the stress it produces can erode family relationships.

Bankruptcy helps eliminate financial stresses. Eliminate the financial stress and much of the household friction is likely to disappear. Bankruptcy closes the door on many types of debt. It is the new beginning that allows a family to move on without the weight of their debts growing larger in their minds on a daily basis. The relief from the financial stress bankruptcy provides restores peace in the home and gives relationships that may have frayed the fighting chance they need to become loving again.

Filing bankruptcy may be the wisest decision you can make for you and your family so that you can resolve your debt issues and make a fresh start in your life, rather than continuing to ignore or avoid your creditors.

Myth #12: Everyone Will Know

Few people will ever know you commenced a bankruptcy unless you decide to tell them—unless you are a prominent person in the community, a celebrity, or executive of a well-known corporation about whom or which the media decides to publish a story. Most people are busy with their lives and aren't concerned with following bankruptcy cases.

If you have borrowed money from your neighbors or relatives, which we advise against, then they—as your creditors—will know and will be sent notice of your bankruptcy filings. Except for that, the chances are very good that the only people who will know about your bankruptcy will be you and your creditors.

Bankruptcy is a public legal proceeding with a public record. Thousands of people file bankruptcy each day. Most people do not keep track of the filers and very few publications have the space, resources, or desire to publish bankruptcy filings.

Unless you have a nosy neighbor, it is unlikely that anyone will know about your bankruptcy. But even if it's made publicly known, you should maintain that bankruptcy is the right thing to do. So what if everyone knows? With so many people being forced to file for bankruptcy, few give it a second thought. After having seen the trillions of dollars the United States has given to companies in financial trouble in recent years, most people see bankruptcy court as an appropriate place for people to resolve their financial problems.

Myth #13: You Could Lose Your Job

Some people who have filed for bankruptcy have lost their jobs. As far as we can determine, many issues caused their termination, not just the bankruptcy filing. A far greater number of employees have filed for bankruptcy and their jobs were never affected.

If you are an at-will employee, you can be fired for any reason. This can be done despite the Bankruptcy Code's prohibition of discrimination against a person who is a debtor in a bankruptcy case. Unless your employer tells you that it is firing you because of your bankruptcy case, it is very difficult to prove that you were discriminated against solely on the fact that you filed for bankruptcy. However, your present employer will not likely learn of your bankruptcy unless a creditor of yours or you decide to tell someone there of your bankruptcy case. Next, as a valued employee, your employer will not use your bankruptcy filing as an excuse to interfere with the relationship. A wise employer would consider you a more valued employee because you will not be distracted by all of the worries and concerns that overwhelming debt brought you previously.

Myth #14: You Must Report Your Bankruptcy on Job Applications

The Bankruptcy Code prohibits private employers from discrimination based on bankruptcy. Nevertheless, whether you filed for bankruptcy may be a question on a job application. A question about a bankruptcy filing on an application is most relevant for jobs that involve handling other people's money or such other financial responsibilities. Your job prospects could be hindered in these industries.

If a potential employer is interested in your candidacy, it will interview you and ask you about the bankruptcy filing. Be up-front about your case if the question is raised. If you've made your decision to file for bankruptcy responsibly and reasonably, a potential employer should not view the bankruptcy filing as a negative.

A potential employer can only look at your credit report with your permission. If an employer requests such permission, be prepared for questions about your bankruptcy. Don't be ashamed of your bankruptcy.

Myth #15: You'll Lose Everything . . . So Say Good-bye to Your House and Car

Many people believe that after bankruptcy they will be forced to live in their car or in a cardboard box under a bridge. This simply isn't true. Every state has exemptions that protect certain assets and typically allow every individual to keep at least some, if not all, of their personal property and many states have opted to allow bankruptcy filers to choose federal exemptions. The property that you will be able to claim as exempt may include household goods, jewelry, clothing, and much more. If you have a mortgage and a car loan, you can usually keep these assets as long as you keep making the regular payments. In fact, most people complete their bankruptcy cases without losing any assets at all. Moreover, Congress has made a policy decision that certain types of property are not reachable in a bankruptcy case, such as Employee Retirement Income Security Act (ERISA) qualified pension plans, and thus bankruptcy will not affect these types of assets at all.

In addition, as a debtor, you make the final decisions on what happens to your valuable assets. Whether you lose your house or your car will depend on what you decide to do in your bankruptcy case. You may decide that it's not in your best interest to retain your house or car and therefore you may relinquish that asset in bankruptcy to the lien holder.

However, if you decide that you want to keep your house and your car, you will be able to do so in your bankruptcy case if you reaffirm or redeem the asset from the secured creditor. In a chapter 13 bankruptcy case, you are able to pay the amount that you are behind on your loan over a three- to five-year term of a plan, while making regular monthly payments.

Myth #16: Only U.S. Citizens Can File for Bankruptcy

If you own substantial property in the United States, you can file for bankruptcy in the United States. You do not need United States citizenship.

Myth #17: You'll Never Be Able to Buy a House or a Car

As your credit improves after bankruptcy, so does your ability to make major purchases on credit. Although the overall lending environment and the economy will always impact your ability to obtain credit to make big purchases, you should soon be able to purchase a house or a car if you are timely and conscientious in paying your debts after bankruptcy. Although it may take some time until you are offered the best interest rates, you should be a good credit risk once you emerge from bankruptcy.

Occasionally, we hear of debtors who have found themselves eligible for mortgage loans on terms equal to someone who has not gone through bankruptcy in as little as two years after a chapter 7 bankruptcy case. Some creditors decide to rely on your ability to pay more after they weigh the fact that you filed for bankruptcy. In the end, the individual creditor decides whether to extend you credit.

Myth #18: You Won't Be Able to Get a Credit Card

You may begin to receive credit card offers within weeks of your discharge in bankruptcy, even from creditors whose debts you discharged. Some credit card companies actually consider you a better risk after filing for bankruptcy, as you have little or no debt and can pay on your new credit purchases. Although your interest rates may initially be higher than those you received prior to bankruptcy, you will be able to reestablish your credit rating and lower the interest rates within a couple years of your bankruptcy discharge. (See Myth #19.)

Although federal law allows a bankruptcy to stay on your credit report for up to 10 years, if you are considering bankruptcy, you already likely have a poor credit score and credit report. Defaults and late payments you have already incurred stay on your credit report for up to seven years.

The reality is that what ruins credit is the inability to pay. Bankruptcy wipes out debts that would otherwise linger in your life and on your credit report. Once you wipe out your prepetition debts, you can start rebuilding your credit by making current, full payments on the debts that you decide to retain throughout your bankruptcy or those that you acquire after your discharge. Timely payments during and/or after your bankruptcy case create a record that will lead to better credit. You should be able to obtain credit on a secured basis without any problem and timely payments on a secured credit card will improve your credit dramatically.

Many people actually obtain a higher credit score in the years following a bankruptcy than they ever had if they improve their spending habits. But remember to keep credit card use to a minimum.

Myth #19: Your Interest Rates Will Always Be High after Bankruptcy

Initially, after bankruptcy, you will find that your interest rates drift higher as credit offers will likely come from subprime lenders. However, as you reestablish your credit through timely payments and because your debt load has diminished greatly, you will find that the interest rates you are offered will become lower and lower. The more payments you make on time and the more you establish your credit after bankruptcy, the more desirable you become to creditors. Then, in order to get your business, creditors will lower the rates that they charge you.

Myth #20: Creditors Will Harass You Even after You File for Bankruptcy

Filing for bankruptcy provides an automatic stay against any harassment from creditors. Creditors are not allowed to contact you for any reason, which includes calling or even billing you. If they continue to harass you, you are entitled to seek damages in bankruptcy court and punitive damages and attorneys' fees may be awarded.

Myth #21: It Doesn't Affect Your Medical Debts

You will be able to extinguish your unsecured medical debts. In fact, debts from medical bills and medical problems were the leading cause for filing in more than half of the bankruptcy cases in the last ten years. Medical debts are unsecured debts. Like almost all unsecured debts, including credit cards and personal loans, your bankruptcy case will discharge ordinary medical debts.

Finding a Fresh Start

Finally, do not believe the myth that bankruptcy can cure all your problems. Some problems go beyond your resolution of your financial problem.

Still, bankruptcy gives the honest person a fresh start. Bankruptcy can put your life back on track. It is a safety net. Bankruptcy stops you from tumbling further out of control and deeper into debt. You can regain control of your life. Bankruptcy allows you to come to a stop, wipe the slate clean, and start again. Think about the feeling when you left a bad job for a new start. You leave the old problems behind as a new day starts in your life. As long as you don't let the myths that surround bankruptcy deter you, it can do the same for you.

Point to Remember

Don't let a myth about bankruptcy prevent you from filing if bankruptcy will help you resolve your financial problems.

Overview of Bankruptcy Types

Bankruptcy is a remarkable phenomenon. It is financial death and financial rebirth. Bankruptcy laws literally make debts vanish.

—Sullivan, Theresa A., Elizabeth Warren, and Jay Lawrence Westbrook (Beard Books, Washington, D.C. 1999).

Bankruptcy cases are all over the news these days as more and more companies and people are filing for bankruptcy protection. You've probably heard bankruptcy cases described as chapter 7, chapter 11, or chapter 13, but what does that mean? Understanding the types, or chapters, of bankruptcy is an important step in deciding whether bankruptcy is right for you. Chapter 7 bankruptcy is the most common but that does not necessarily mean you should file a chapter 7 bankruptcy.

This chapter is an overview of the different types of bankruptcy relief you can choose to fit your particular circumstances. But first, take the "Do You Know the Bankruptcy Basics?" quiz to test your knowledge.

Quiz: Do You Know the Bankruptcy Basics?

1. What types of debt make you the best candidate for chapter 7 bankruptcy?
   A. Credit card debt
   B. Medical bills
   C. Mortgage loans
   D. Student loans
   E. All of the above
      Answer: A and B
      Chapter 7 bankruptcy, as you will learn in this chapter, allows you to extinguish (discharge) certain debts, such as high credit card debt and legal or medical debt that you don't think you'll ever be able to pay back. Other types of debt, such as mortgage debt, student loans, and alimony, are not discharged in the typical chapter 7 bankruptcy.

2. What can filing a chapter 13 bankruptcy do for me?
   A. Stop the repossession of my car.
   B. Stop the foreclosure sale on my home.
   C. Stop the garnishment of my wages.
   D. All of the above
      Answer: D
      In chapter 13 bankruptcy you have the ability to stop all actions by creditors. You will also have the chance to make up all the payments you missed so that you can choose whether you wish to continue living in your house or driving your same car.

3. A person is not allowed to file a chapter 13 bankruptcy when?
   A. She does not have a regular income.
   B. She owes $1.2 million on her mortgage.
   C. She has medical debts of $500,000.
   D. All of the above
      Answer: D
      Individuals can file a chapter 13 bankruptcy when they have a regular income, their unsecured debt, including credit cards, medical, and other personal debts, does not exceed $360,475 and their secured debt, including mortgages, does not exceed $1,081,400. In this question, the person does not have a regular income, medical bills exceed the unsecured limit, and mortgage debt exceeds the secured limit. Three strikes on chapter 13 bankruptcy. The person would instead have to file a chapter 11 bankruptcy to reorganize her debts or a chapter 7 bankruptcy to liquidate her assets.

While the Bankruptcy Code provides for six different types or chapters of bankruptcy cases, four chapters are available to individual debtors:

- Chapter 7: Liquidation
- Chapter 11: Reorganization
- Chapter 12: Family farmer or family fisherman debt adjustment
- Chapter 13: Individual debt adjustment

Chapter 7 is a liquidation of your non-exempt assets that extinguishes debts that are discharged so that you no longer have to pay them. Chapter 13, chapter 11, and chapter 12 are reorganization chapters that require you to make payments on your debts after your bankruptcy case.

While most people file chapter 7 bankruptcy cases, chapter 13 is most often the choice among the reorganization chapters of bankruptcy.

This chapter of the book offers an overview of bankruptcy types, each of which is the focus of a later chapter. It's important to understand all of the options to choose the one that makes the most sense for you.

Chapter 7 Bankruptcy

A chapter 7 bankruptcy case is a liquidation of both your debts and your assets. Chapter 7 cases are, more often than not, routine, and the vast majority of them are discharged or released and administratively closed without the trustee liquidating any assets or distributing any assets to creditors. In a majority of chapter 7 cases, you never appear in front of the bankruptcy judge but only attend a meeting of creditors conducted by a trustee.

When you file a chapter 7 case, your bankruptcy case is controlled by a trustee appointed by the U.S. Trustee's Office (a division of the Department of Justice). In a chapter 7 case, the trustee investigates a debtor's assets, determines whether to object to the debtor's exemptions, and has the ability to sell any assets that are not exempt and distribute the proceeds of the sales to creditors. The trustee also has the ability to object to creditors' claims against the debtor. Debtors who choose chapter 7 must qualify for relief.

To qualify for relief in chapter 7, a debtor must satisfy criteria by obtaining prepetition credit counseling briefing and completing a means test to determine whether the debtor's income and expenses are above or below the median income as compared to other individuals in the state. The debtor must file a schedule of assets, including claims of his or her exemptions and liabilities, and must pay the filing fee unless excused by the bankruptcy court. Unless an objection is filed, the court will enter a discharge. The discharge of a debtor in a chapter 7 case may not affect secured debt like a house and car, however.

Many debtors in chapter 7 bankruptcy cases enter into reaffirmation agreements for the purpose of retaining secured collateral. Reaffirmation means that the debtor continues payment on a loan as if bankruptcy had not occurred usually in order to retain the collateral.

A chapter 7 debtor will not receive a discharge of debts excepted from the discharge under the Code, or if the court carves out a particular debt from the debtor's discharge after litigation. Moreover, a debtor can be denied a discharge if found to have lied to the trustee or court, fraudulently transferred property, or destroyed records. In addition, the discharge can be revoked if it was obtained through fraud by the debtor.

Approximately 66.5 percent of personal bankruptcy filings were chapter 7 bankruptcy cases in 2008.

Reorganization Chapters

In chapters 11, 12, and 13—the reorganization chapters—you have many of the same duties and file many of the same documents as in a chapter 7 case. The main difference between chapter 7 and the reorganization chapters is that shortly after the commencement of the reorganization case, the debtor proposes a plan to repay some percentage of or all of the debt over a certain period of time, usually three to five years. As a general rule, the debtor's reorganization plan must pay creditors the amount they would receive in a chapter

7 liquidation case, and must devote the debtor's disposable income toward payment of creditors. The plan may provide different legal treatment of secured and unsecured debts.

Creditors will have an opportunity to object to the debtor's plan, and the bankruptcy court will decide whether to approve it at a confirmation hearing. During the duration of the plan, the debtor remains under the jurisdiction of the bankruptcy court and the automatic stay remains in place unless lifted by the court. Upon completion of a chapter 13 plan, the debtor will be granted a discharge; in chapter 11 and chapter 12 cases, an individual debtor will not be granted a discharge until confirmation of the plan. Chapters 12 and 13 have limits to the amount of debts that a debtor can owe and we will discuss those limits further in later chapters. Finally, in reorganization cases, the debtor is required to file all outstanding tax returns early in the case.

Before commencing a case by the filing of a petition, a debtor must make the decision of which chapter of bankruptcy relief to choose. Each case is unique, and a debtor must consider the personal goals of the bankruptcy before deciding under which chapter to seek relief. Choice of chapter is often a complicated question, and the best legal strategy requires an analysis of many factors. However, the following guidelines will assist you in evaluating your situation and deciding which chapter is the appropriate choice.

Evaluate Your Situation

Now that you are acquainted with the four bankruptcy chapters available to individuals, review the lists that follow to see if one might be the best choice for you.

Chapter 7 may be the best choice for you if:

- You have primarily unsecured debts, those debts are dischargeable, and you have not committed fraud.
- You have no nonexempt property that will be lost.
- You do not have disposable income that could be required to fund a reorganization plan.
- You do not need to cure any defaults to retain property secured by mortgages and security interests.

Chapter 13 may be the best choice for you if:

- You wish to avoid foreclosure of your home or repossession of your car, cure a default with respect to a mortgage or security interest, and have not been able to reach an agreement with the secured party.
- You wish to retain nonexempt assets.
- You have net disposable income every month that warrants a finding that filing a chapter 7 case would be considered an abuse of bankruptcy laws.
- You wish to protect a cosigner or guarantor of your consumer debts from collection action.
- You have nondischargeable debts, such as taxes, alimony, and child support, that are in arrears, and you need time to pay the amounts in default.
- You meet the debt limitation requirements of chapter 13.

Chapter 11 may be the best choice for you if:

- You wish to retain nonexempt assets and cure defaults with respect to secured debt but exceed the debt limitations of chapters 12 or 13. However, it should be noted that the filing, administrative, and legal fees in chapter 11 cases are much more expensive than such fees in chapter 7, 12, and 13 cases.

Chapter 12 may be the best choice for you if:

- You are an eligible family farmer or fisherman with regular annual income who meets the debt limitation requirements of chapter 12 and wish to retain assets and restructure secured debts.

Timing It Right

In addition to choosing the appropriate kind of bankruptcy chapter, we advise that you consider the timing of the filing of the bankruptcy petition. There are reasons to file quickly and there are reasons to wait. For example, you may wish to delay the filing of your petition if your exemptions or the discharge of particular debts, such as taxes, may be affected by the timing of the filing. On the other hand, you may have to immediately file to deal with a Red Level emergency, such as a foreclosure or repossession.

Points to Remember

- Understand the different chapters of bankruptcy relief and how each chapter assists in dealing with various types of debts. This will help you decide which chapter may best suit you.
  - Chapter 7: Liquidation
  - Chapter 13: Reorganization with debt limits
  - Chapter 11: Reorganization without debt limits
  - Chapter 12: Farmer or fisherman
- Evaluate when you should file your bankruptcy case to maximize the benefits of bankruptcy law and to minimize risks and traps.

CHAPTER

Understanding the Bankruptcy Process

Fear makes the wolf bigger than he is.

—German proverb

Some years are better than others. The year 2008 was especially bad for Ron Jacobs. When the year began, Ron was enjoying a flourishing career in medical sales that supported his caring family and a fairly modest house. But then, unexpectedly, Ron became a casualty of the economic downturn that hit medical sales hard and he lost his job. Soon after, one of Ron's daughters broke her leg. Ron still had insurance but it didn't cover all of the hospital bills or any of the rehabilitation.

After a few months, Ron's wife, Sally, started working part-time. But Ron's unemployment benefits, their savings, and Sally's income could not cover the mortgage, medical bills, and the rest of their monthly bills. They decided to work together to keep their lives as normal as possible. The family set a budget that covered the bare necessities and Ron called all their lenders. Even after a couple of lenders made arrangements, they could not pay their mortgage.

Despite the couple's pleas, the mortgage lender was proceeding with a foreclosure on the family home.

As the day of the auction approached, Ron and Sally were growing desperate and depressed at the thought of being forced to move from the house where their children were so comfortable. They feared the worst. But after talking to a lawyer and learning how bankruptcy could help them, they decided to fight a little more. On the eve of the foreclosure auction, they filed for chapter 13 bankruptcy. The bankruptcy filing stopped the collection of the bills and halted the foreclosure. They now had some more time to see if they could work out their financial issues. The year 2009 turned out to be much better for Ron and Sally. Ron was able to find a new job and, through the bankruptcy, they rehabilitated their financial affairs and saved the house.

You may have heard other stories like that of Ron and Sally about how bankruptcy rescued someone from the brink of financial disaster. But you have little or no idea about how bankruptcy works. Most people who don't know much about bankruptcy tend to react to the idea of it with fear. This chapter will lessen your fears and explain generally how bankruptcy works. It provides an overview of the personal bankruptcy process and explains the basics of bankruptcy law applicable to all chapters of bankruptcy available to you as an individual. We also discuss generally how to navigate the complex waters of the federal bankruptcy laws and rules of procedure.

The Code, the Rules, and the Forms

Congress has enacted bankruptcy laws commonly referred to as the Bankruptcy Code and Federal Rules of Bankruptcy Procedure with Official Forms (U.S. Constitution, Article 1, Section 8). We will refer to these laws, which provide the substance and procedure for all bankruptcy cases, as the Code, the Rules, and the Forms. This section introduces the procedure for filing for personal bankruptcy and what will happen when you do.

Since you cannot file for bankruptcy in state court, you must turn to the federal court system. Each of the 94 federal judicial districts of the United States has a bankruptcy court, and some jurisdictions have several bankruptcy court locations. To obtain bankruptcy protection, an individual must file a petition with the bankruptcy court. Each bankruptcy court has a clerk who accepts documents for filing and maintains the public records in bankruptcy cases. The primary way to file bankruptcy documents is by computer through the court's electronic filing system, although some bankruptcy courts will accept the filing of documents by hand, mail, or facsimile transmission. Furthermore, most bankruptcy courts have local rules and forms that supplement the federal rules and forms.

Each bankruptcy case is assigned to a U.S bankruptcy judge, who has the power under the Bankruptcy Code to make decisions with respect to any matter in the cases assigned to him or her, including whether a person is eligible to file and whether a discharge should be granted. Bankruptcy judges decide disputes in bankruptcy cases; they are not often involved in the administration of the case. An agency of the U.S. Department of Justice, the U.S. Trustee program, is charged with the oversight and administration of bankruptcy cases in every jurisdiction except North Carolina and Alabama, where a bankruptcy administrator performs similar administrative functions. Through these programs, a trustee is assigned to every individual bankruptcy case. The trustee examines the debtor under oath, reviews the documents filed by the debtor, and recommends action about the case to the court. Many bankruptcy cases are closed, and the debtor is granted a discharge without the debtor ever having to go to the bankruptcy court and appear before a judge.

Overview of the Process

Bankruptcy provides numerous protections and benefits to you but follows well-established rules and laws that dictate what happens to you and your property. If these rules and laws are not followed, a bankruptcy case may be dismissed by the court.

The Automatic Stay

The moment you commence your bankruptcy case, the *automatic stay* goes into effect without a court order, but it has the effect of a court order. The automatic stay requires cessation of *all* collection actions, lawsuits in which the debtor is a defendant, foreclosures, wage garnishments, evictions, demands for repayment of debts, and phone calls to collect debts. If a creditor takes action in violation of the stay, the debtor may recover actual and punitive damages as well as attorneys' fees from the creditor.

The automatic stay is not unlimited. Congress has declared 28 exceptions to the automatic stay, including fines from the prosecution

of criminal actions and the collection from the debtor of alimony and child support. The bankruptcy court may grant a creditor relief from the automatic stay upon the filing of a motion in which the creditor gives the bankruptcy court good cause to lift the automatic stay as to its debt. Other limitations on the automatic stay can arise, especially when the debtor has had one or more prior bankruptcy cases that were dismissed within a year of the current filing. There are special provisions that apply to eviction cases that give landlords and debtors specific rights and obligations.

Acts undertaken in violation of the automatic stay are not only void but may expose the violator to monetary sanctions.[1]

Property of the Estate and Exemptions

When you commence your bankruptcy case, all your "legal and equitable" interests, including interests in real and personal property, become property of the bankruptcy estate. All "legal and equitable" interests basically covers everything you own or have the ability to receive or possess. The trustee of the bankruptcy case will then administer all of the nonexempt property for the benefit of the debtor's creditors, although you are ultimately responsible for your financial decisions and control exempt assets. As a matter of policy, Congress has excluded certain categories of assets from property of the estate, such as retirement plans and spendthrift trusts. The property included in the bankruptcy estate depends on the chapter of relief the debtor chooses. In a chapter 7 case, property acquired after the bankruptcy petition is filed, such as salary of the debtor, generally is not included in property of the estate. In a chapter 13 case, the definition of property of the estate is more expansive and includes postpetition assets, such as salary, obtained during the term of the chapter 13 plan.

Bankruptcy law entitles an individual debtor to claim certain property as exempt. Exempt property can be kept by the debtor and stays out of the hands of his or her creditors. Depending on where you live and in the jurisdiction where you file, you may be required to claim only state law exemptions or you may be required to claim federal bankruptcy exemptions or state law exemptions. Some state law exemptions have been the law for hundreds of years and are outdated, such as exemptions for church pews, the family Bible, two swine, and four tons of hay.

You are typically allowed to exempt the following property:

- Some or all of the equity in your home
- Some or all of the value in a vehicle
- A debtor's tools of the trade
- Household goods
- Jewelry
- Life insurance
- Personal injury claims

The list of exemptions available under the federal exemption laws is more current and provides categories of exempt property with values that are adjusted for the cost of living every three years. See www.wiley.com/go/roadoutofdebt for a link to the current federal exemptions. Remember that bankruptcy protects exempt property from creditors. In the event a creditor has a court-ordered lien on your property that impairs your ability to file an exemption, you may request that the creditor's lien be avoided, and if so ordered, this judicial lien will be released.

The Discharge

The U.S. Supreme Court has emphasized that bankruptcy "gives to the honest but unfortunate debtor . . . a new opportunity in life and a clear field for future effort, unhampered by the pressure and discouragement of preexisting debt."[2]

The discharge order of the bankruptcy court releases a debtor from personal liability for the debts specified on the order. The discharge provides a permanent injunction preventing collection of all of the debts to which it applies. After a discharge, a debtor enjoys his or her property (other than property of the estate) free from the claims of creditors. The best example of property that is free from the creditors after discharge is the chapter 7 debtor's future earnings after the commencement of the case. Contrast the chapter 7 debtor with a debtor in a chapter 13 case whose earnings after the commencement of the case and during the plan term are property of the estate. The chapter 13 debtor is not entitled to discharge until the completion of the plan.

However, the discharge does not apply to all debts. There are automatic exceptions set forth in the Code, such as most taxes, alimony, spousal and child support, criminal restitution and fines, and student loans, unless the debtor can prove that repayment is an undue hardship. Moreover, a creditor can bring a proceeding within a bankruptcy case (known as an *adversary proceeding*) to determine that a debt should not be discharged if the debt was incurred by fraud, willful, and malicious injury, and other like causes. The bankruptcy court may determine after litigation that a debt will not be discharged or is nondischaregable. If the debtor commits certain offenses, such as not disclosing all of his or her assets, or making a false oath in the bankruptcy case, the bankruptcy court may deny the debtor a discharge of all debts.

Filing Requirements

In addition to legal principles applicable to personal bankruptcy cases, all individuals are required to perform certain duties, such as undergoing credit counseling and filing particular forms and documents. These duties are discussed in this section.

Credit Counseling Briefing

Before filing a bankruptcy petition under any chapter, an individual must obtain a briefing by a credit counseling agency approved by the U.S. trustee or the bankruptcy administrator. The briefing must be obtained within 180 days before commencement of the case, and a certificate of proof of completion must be filed with the court. The cost of the briefing is about $50, and it can be completed over the Internet, by telephone, or in person. The court can excuse the debtor from the requirement if the debtor is physically or mentally disabled or is in active military duty. Also, the court can approve a delay in obtaining the briefing if there are exigent circumstances preventing the debtor from obtaining the counseling before filing the petition and if the debtor has at least requested the briefing within seven days prior to the filing of the bankruptcy petition. These extensions are difficult to obtain.

Filing Fees

Bankruptcy petitions must be accompanied by a filing and administrative fee payable to the court. Currently, the fees for bankruptcy cases are $299 for chapter 7 cases, $279 for chapter 13 and 12 cases, and $1,039 for chapter 11 cases.

> In the six months leading up to and including the beginning of the General Motors' bankruptcy filing, General Motors paid $80 million in legal fees to three law firms.

Filing and administrative fees are in addition to attorneys' fees and counseling fees. A debtor may file an application to pay the filing fees in installments, and courts usually allow payment over time in four to five segments. In a chapter 7 case, the court may approve a waiver of the filing fee upon application by the debtor that conforms to Official Form 3B and proof that the debtor's income is less than 150 percent of the official poverty line based on the size of the debtor's family. These figures are available on most courts' Web sites.

Filing Documents

Several documents must be filed with the court by all individual debtors in personal bankruptcy cases soon after the case is commenced.

If these required documents are not filed, the court will dismiss the case and the debtor will lose the benefits of bankruptcy protection.

To commence a case, the debtor must file the following documents:

- Official Form 1: Voluntary petition
- Official Form 21: Statement of Social Security number
- A list of creditors' names and addresses, known as the Matrix.
- A certificate from an approved credit counseling agency that the debtor had the required briefing

The list of creditors, often known as the *mailing matrix or Matrix*, is not an official form but is often the subject of a local form. The Social Security statement must contain the debtor's full number. Pursuant to the privacy policy of the U.S. Courts, the full Social Security number does not become a public record, and only creditors will receive the full number to enable them to identify the debtor in their records.

At the same time or shortly after a case begins, the debtor must file:

- Official Form 7: Schedules of assets, liabilities, income, and expenses
- Official Form 7 (cont'd): Statement of financial affairs
- Official Form 22-A, B, or C: Means test calculation
- Form B 203: Attorney's disclosure of compensation
- Chapter 7 case only, Official Form 8: a statement of intention with respect to secured debts
- Chapter 13 case only, chapter 13 plan: No official form exists for the chapter 13 plan, but many jurisdictions have a local model form of the chapter 13 plan that is required or suggested.

Many of the required documents must be signed by the debtor under the penalty of perjury. If a debtor makes false statements on the forms or omits information that makes the forms misleading, the consequences may be severe, including denial of discharge or criminal prosecution. A debtor must make sure that all forms are accurate and complete and if mistakes are discovered, the documents should be promptly amended. These documents are usually due within 14 days after the petition date. If these documents are not filed, the court will issue an order to file the documents. The debtor may obtain an extension of time for filing the documents, but this must be requested before the deadline. Courts will dismiss the case if the debtor does not file the documents on time and this may have consequences in future cases with respect to the automatic stay and will in any new case filed within a year. See Appendix A for more information on forms and other resources.

Payment Advices or Proof of Income

An individual debtor must file copies of all payment advices with the court or submit them to the trustee. *Payment advices* are evidence of salary or income earned within 60 days before the commencement of the case. Some courts require that the documents be filed with the court, whereas others require that they be submitted to the trustee before the meeting of creditors. If a debtor does not have payment advices, it is advisable to file a declaration that the debtor did not receive "payment advices."

Tax Returns

An individual debtor must produce tax returns to the trustee, and to creditors upon request. The federal income tax return or an IRS tax transcript for the most recent tax year before the filing of the petition must be given to the trustee within a week before the meeting of creditors. However, if the debtor was not required to file a return, for example because he or she had insufficient gross income under the IRS rules, a return need not be provided. In 2009, an individual with gross income of less than $9,350 need not file a tax return. If a debtor does not have a tax return, a transcript can be obtained from the IRS and submitted to the trustee instead of a return. If the debtor fails to provide a tax return or transcript to the trustee, the court may dismiss the bankruptcy case.

Don't have your most recent tax return? You can easily get your federal tax return transcript for free by calling 1-800-829-1040, or by mailing or faxing IRS Form 4506T to the IRS. Transcripts are available for the current and three prior calendar years. See www .irs.gov for more information.

Meeting of the Creditors

After the case is commenced, the debtor will receive notice of the meeting of creditors, which is commonly referred to as the Section 341 meeting, after the Bankruptcy Code section requiring the meeting. The debtor must attend this meeting in person. The trustee will administer an oath to the debtor and the trustee will ask the debtor questions about his or her assets, liabilities, income, and expenses. The proceedings are recorded. The purpose of the trustee's questions is to ascertain whether the debtor has made a complete and accurate list of assets and liabilities and whether there are any assets that can be liquidated for distribution to creditors. Most debtors never see the inside of a bankruptcy courtroom, and the Section 341 meeting is often the only event that a debtor must attend in person.

The Section 341 meeting is recorded and is held in a public place, usually with other debtors present. Creditors of each debtor may attend the meeting. However, creditors are not required to attend and usually do not attend. The trustee will usually examine the debtor for 5 to 10 minutes, but may continue the meeting on another date if there is insufficient time and the examination is not concluded. The debtor is required to bring to the meeting a picture form of identification, proof of their Social Security number, recent bank account statements, and proof of current income, such as a pay stub. Some trustees will send the debtor a letter requesting that additional documents be brought to the Section 341 meeting. Because the debtor has the duty to cooperate with the trustee, it is in the debtor's best interest to satisfy all of the trustee's requests to the best of his or her ability. If the debtor does not speak English, the debtor can provide an interpreter for the Section 341 meeting or the trustee can call an interpreter by telephone to interpret for the debtor.

Personal Financial Management Course

All individual debtors must complete a personal financial management course after the commencement of a bankruptcy case. In order to obtain the discharge order in the case, debtors must file with the court a certificate of completion of the course. The course must be given by an instructor approved by the U.S. trustee program. In a chapter 7 case, the certificate must be filed within 45 days after the Section 341 meeting, and in a chapter 13 case by the last plan payment. The cost of the instruction varies but it generally does not cost more than $100. A debtor may ask the court for a waiver of the course requirement on the ground that the debtor is mentally or physically disabled or is in active military duty.

Once the debtor has performed his or her required duties, the discharge will routinely enter unless a creditor or the trustee files an adversary proceeding against the debtor seeking an exception to discharge or denial of the discharge.

Seeking Legal Advice

By now, you may be asking whether you should file the bankruptcy case with or without an attorney. The rules and standards you must adhere to are the same whether you have a lawyer or not. You will have to comply with the requirements of the Code and the Rules. You must properly file your bankruptcy case and handle it properly throughout the case.

Bankruptcy is a specialty in the law. Based on our combined 40 years of experience in this field, we strongly recommend that you either consult or hire a lawyer to represent you in your bankruptcy case. The federal laws, the procedural rules and forms, the state laws applicable to an individual's bankruptcy case, plus the particular customs and practices of the trustee and judge assigned to an individual's bankruptcy case present a web of problems and issues. In addition, bankruptcy laws change periodically. Understanding bankruptcy laws and rules is often beyond the ability of a person not educated in the law, and even many lawyers who do not regularly practice bankruptcy law. The legal rights available to you under your personal situation will vary. The consequences of making mistakes in a bankruptcy case can be drastic.

Seek the advice of a competent attorney who specializes in consumer bankruptcy law before you seek bankruptcy protection. The lawyer will likely discuss your situation and give you his or her opinion at an initial consultation, even if you choose not to retain his or her services.

It's important to do your own research so you understand the process, know how to prepare, and get the most benefit from the bankruptcy process. The more knowledge you have, the more successful your bankruptcy case will be. Our advice to hire a bankruptcy attorney triggers two very practical questions: First, how can I afford an attorney? Second, if I decide to hire an attorney, how do I find a competent and trustworthy lawyer?

How Can I Afford an Attorney?

Ironically, most debtors need to save money to go bankrupt. Attorneys generally charge an up-front cash fee or a combination of an up-front fee with the balance to be paid over time. Remember that all debtors must also pay a filing fee with the bankruptcy petition unless the court waives the fee or allows it to be paid in installments as discussed earlier in this chapter. If you are truly destitute, there are pro bono programs and agencies that provide free legal services to debtors. Lawyers have a professional obligation to provide legal services to those who are unable to pay. Often bar associations have resources for referring people with financial problems to legal services agencies or attorneys who will appear pro bono or for a discounted fee.

How Do I Find a Competent Lawyer?

Should you go to just any lawyer? The answer to that question is no. Do not attempt to find a lawyer by simply looking in the phone book or on the Internet. The lawyer with the biggest advertisement or glitziest website may not be the best lawyer. Bankruptcy laws and procedures are so complicated that many lawyers in general practice or in other specialties do not understand the intricacies of the system. Even sophisticated business lawyers from large law firms often do not understand the requirements of representation of consumer debtors in a personal bankruptcy case. There are many ways to obtain a good referral and you should employ all of them until you find the best lawyer whom you trust and can work with. Ask an attorney you know or friends and relatives if they know of a good consumer bankruptcy lawyer. The best attorneys may be obtained by word of mouth.

Warning: You will see advertisements for bankruptcy petition preparers. Be careful in seeking the services of these companies. They are not lawyers and cannot provide you with legal advice. Unfortunately, many will give legal advice, often bad legal advice, and then charge a high fee (fees should be less than $250 for a petition preparer). If you run into an unscrupulous bankruptcy preparer, contact your state's attorney general or your local U.S. trustee's office.

If you cannot obtain a referral from someone with actual experience, contact your local bar association and ask if it has a consumer bankruptcy section or committee and obtain the contact information for the chair. Contact the chairperson and ask for the names of three competent consumer bankruptcy lawyers who are active in the association, have good reputations for competence and ethics, and frequently appear in the bankruptcy court of your jurisdiction. If the local bar association does not have a bankruptcy section, contact the association's lawyer referral service and ask for the names of consumer bankruptcy lawyers. Be clear that you seek the services of a consumer, not a business, bankruptcy lawyer. Finally, contact the clerk of the bankruptcy court, the U.S. trustee's office, or the office of the bankruptcy administrator in your area and ask for several names of competent consumer bankruptcy lawyers.

Points to Remember

- Bankruptcy comes with many benefits: most creditor actions are stayed (i.e., stopped), including debt collection and lawsuits; certain assets are retained; and many debts are discharged.
- Bankruptcy contains a complex set of laws. In exchange for the many benefits of bankruptcy, debtors must perform specific duties.
- Duties of a debtor include filing many documents and appearing for an examination by a trustee.
- Failure to comply with the requirements of the Code, the Rules, and the Forms will result in the loss of the benefits of bankruptcy as the case may be dismissed.
- Seek a competent bankruptcy lawyer to make your trip through bankruptcy less mysterious, less stressful, and more successful.

PART IV

ROAD TRIPS: SIX CASE STUDIES IN BANKRUPTCY

17

Two Trips through Chapter 7 Bankruptcy

Unless you're Bill Gates, you're just one serious illness away from bankruptcy.
—Dr. David Himmelstein, MD, Associate Professor of Medicine, Harvard Medical School

To help you understand what you will encounter in your bankruptcy case, we present the stories of two debtors who owe consumer debts and file for bankruptcy under chapter 7 of the Bankruptcy Code: the Henris and the Robinsons. The presentation of realistic cases will help you understand the bankruptcy process, the legal concepts of bankruptcy law, the remedies available to consumer debtors, and what actually happens in a bankruptcy case. Sometimes debtors encounter "bumps in the road" during their bankruptcy cases, so we've included those as alternative scenarios along the way.

All of the bankruptcy forms mentioned in this chapter are available at www.uscourts.gov (see Appendix A or www.wiley.com/go/roadoutofdebt for more information).

Chapter 7 Basics

Chapter 7 of the Bankruptcy Code is entitled Liquidation. We find the name somewhat deceptive because in the vast majority of individual cases, debtors do not lose their property. Bankruptcy laws ensure that you do not end up living in a cardboard box after bankruptcy and make some assets exempt and outside the creditors' reach. Your property may be subject to liens and mortgages so that you have no equity in that property, meaning that creditors have a claim to every penny of that property and you have none. If the chapter 7 trustee finds that you have no equity in property, the trustee will take no action against or abandon this property. Because of these exemptions and the mortgages and loans that encumber a debtor's property, most chapter 7 debtors retain all their property subject to the liens.

A chapter 7 bankruptcy case does not involve the filing of a plan to repay creditors as a debtor must in a chapter 13 bankruptcy. In chapter 7 bankruptcy, as in all chapters, you must file the schedules and other documents disclosing assets, liabilities, income, and expenses. A chapter 7 trustee then reviews the documents for accuracy and questions you under oath for the purposes of determining whether the disclosures are truthful and whether you have nonexempt assets that the trustee can liquidate and distribute to creditors. In the unusual chapter 7 case in which a trustee finds nonexempt, unencumbered property, the trustee will sell these assets to generate proceeds to pay creditors in accordance with the priorities of payment set forth in the Bankruptcy Code. Generally, the chapter 7 trustee finds no assets and closes the case as a no-asset case.

Most chapter 7 cases breeze through bankruptcy court without the need for the debtor's appearance before a judge because they are no-asset cases and the debtor is entitled to a discharge. One of the primary purposes of bankruptcy is for the debtor to obtain a discharge so that the honest individual debtor can receive a fresh start. The debtor has no liability for and will not have to pay debts discharged through his bankruptcy case.

The right to a discharge, however, is not absolute. If you commit bad acts, the bankruptcy court can deny your discharge. Also, the Bankruptcy Code excepts certain debts from discharge, such as child support and criminal fines. Moreover, if you commit fraud during the chapter 7 case, such as omitting assets you own or giving false testimony, the bankruptcy judge will not allow a discharge of any debts. In addition, a bankruptcy discharge does not extinguish a lien or security interest such as a mortgage on property. These secured liens will continue on the property or ride through after the bankruptcy case unless you negotiate with the lender during the course of the bankruptcy case.

Eligibility Requirements

To be eligible for chapter 7 relief, you can be an individual, a partnership, a corporation, or other business entity. You are not eligible for chapter 7 (or any other chapter) if during the preceding 180 days the bankruptcy court dismissed your prior bankruptcy petition due to your willful failure to appear before the court or comply with orders of the court, or you voluntarily dismissed your previous case after a creditor filed a motion for relief from the automatic stay.

In addition, under chapter 7 (or indeed any chapter of the Code) you must, within 180 days before commencement of the case, have received a credit counseling briefing from a credit counseling agency approved by the U.S. trustee's office. You may request a deferral of this credit counseling briefing in an emergency or may request a waiver of the requirement if you are physically or mentally disabled, or on active military duty or for exigent circumstances if you requested counseling but were declined within seven days of your request. Otherwise, you must file a certificate during the first days of the case stating that you received the counseling within 180 days prior to filing your case or the bankruptcy judge will dismiss your case.

The Procedure

You usually commence a chapter 7 case by filing a voluntary petition in the bankruptcy court where you live. You and your spouse may file a joint petition or individual petitions. Upon filing, a chapter 7 trustee is assigned to oversee your case. In addition to the petition, you must file with the court the documents we discussed in Chapter 16.

As an individual with primarily consumer debts, you have additional document-filing requirements. You must file a certificate of credit counseling and a copy of any debt repayment plan developed through credit counseling; evidence of payment from employers, if any, received 60 days before filing; a statement of monthly net income and any anticipated increase in income or expenses after filing; and a record of any interest you have in federal or state qualified education or tuition accounts.

Pay Your Fees

Filing fees for a chapter 7 case, unless otherwise ordered by the court, are $299, including a $245 case filing fee, a $39 miscellaneous administrative fee, and a $15 trustee surcharge. You pay these fees to the clerk of the bankruptcy court with the petition. If a joint petition is filed, only one filing fee, one administrative fee, and one trustee surcharge are charged. With the bankruptcy court's permission, however, you may pay the filing in installments, usually over four months. However, you must make the final installment no later than 120 days after filing the petition.

The court may extend the time to make any installment, provided that you pay the last installment no later than 180 days after filing the petition. If your income is less than 150 percent of the poverty level (as determined by the Department of Health and Human Services; you can find the amount on bankruptcy courts' Web sites), and you are unable to pay the chapter 7 fees even in installments, the bankruptcy court may waive the fee requirements. If you do not pay the fees and the bankruptcy court does not waive them, the court will dismiss the chapter 7 case.

Then, within two weeks after case commencement, unless the time is extended by the bankruptcy court, you must provide the following information for the court: a list of all creditors and the amount and nature of their claims; the source, amount, and frequency of your income; a list of all of your property; and a detailed statement of your monthly living expenses, that is, food, clothing, shelter, utilities, taxes, transportation, medicine, and all costs of living.

If you are married and live in one household with your spouse, you must include the financial information for both you and your spouse even when your spouse does not file. The court requires both spouses' information so that the court, the trustee, and creditors can evaluate the household's financial position.

Understand Your Exemptions

One of the most important schedules that an individual debtor must file is Schedule C—Exempt Property. The Bankruptcy Code allows you to protect certain property that the law recognizes as necessary for a fresh start. Exempt property is protected from the claims of creditors either under federal bankruptcy law or under the laws of your home state. Many states have opted out of the federal bankruptcy exemptions and have adopted their own exemption laws instead of the federal bankruptcy exemptions.

In some jurisdictions, though, you have the option of choosing between the federal exemptions or state exemptions. You can choose the exemptions that best fit your particular needs and property. Because of the complexities of exemptions and the different laws in each jurisdiction, you should consult an attorney to determine the exemptions available in the state where you reside.

The Automatic Stay

The filing of a chapter 7 petition results in an automatic stay stopping most collection efforts by creditors against you and your property except certain actions listed under 11 U.S.C. § 362(b) such as criminal actions. Moreover, the automatic stay may last only for a short time or may not be effective at all if the debtor is a repeat filer. The stay arises automatically as soon as you file your petition without judicial action. As long as the stay is in effect, creditors generally are not allowed to file or continue with lawsuits, wage garnishments, or even make telephone calls to you demanding payments. The bankruptcy clerk sends notice of the bankruptcy case to all creditors whose names and addresses are provided by you. If a creditor willfully violates the automatic stay by pursuing your debts after bankruptcy, you may be entitled to actual or punitive damages and attorneys' fees.

Role of the Trustee

At the commencement of a chapter 7 case, the bankruptcy court appoints a trustee to take charge of the administration of the case. Typically, within the month after the commencement of the chapter 7 case, the trustee holds the Section 341 meeting, also known as the meeting of creditors. At the meeting, which usually lasts for no more than 10 minutes, the trustee administers an oath to you, and the trustee asks you, or both you and your spouse in the case of a joint petition, questions about your assets and liabilities. You must attend the meeting and answer questions regarding your financial affairs and property. Failure to attend will likely result in dismissal of your case without a discharge. In addition, you have an overriding duty to cooperate with the trustee and to provide any financial documents that the trustee requests.

Shortly after the meeting, the trustee or the U.S. trustee makes a decision as to whether the trustee believes the case should be presumed to be an abuse under the means test, in which event the trustee or U.S. trustee will ask the court to dismiss it. The means test enables the court to determine whether a debtor should have filed his or her case under chapter 13. To determine whether a presumption of abuse arises, all individual debtors in a chapter 7 case with primarily consumer debts must complete a questionnaire that resembles a tax return, often referred to as the means test on Official Form B 22A. The bottom line indicates whether you are above or below the median income for your state.

Through this form, the court decides if you are abusing bankruptcy law by proceeding in chapter 7. Absent such a finding, the bankruptcy court will allow your case to proceed. Contrary to popular belief, how much you owe, own, or make does not preclude you from a chapter 7 filing. However, your goal in filing a chapter 7 should be to obtain a discharge and retain all of your assets. Therefore, if you have assets that would be available for liquidation, you may want to consider another chapter, especially chapter 13. Instead of dismissal, a chapter 7 debtor may convert a chapter 7 case under chapter 11, 12, or 13 if the debtor is eligible to be a debtor under the other chapter.

If the trustee concludes that all of your assets are exempt or subject to valid liens, the trustee will file a no-asset report with the court, and there will be no distribution to unsecured creditors. Most chapter 7 cases involving individual debtors are no-asset cases. But if the case appears to be an asset case at the outset, unsecured creditors must file proofs of claim with the bankruptcy court by a deadline, usually within 90 days after the first date set for the meeting of creditors for regular creditors, and 180 days for governmental creditors.

In the typical no-asset chapter 7 case, creditors do not need to file proofs of claim because the case will have no distribution. If the trustee later recovers assets for distribution to unsecured creditors, creditors will receive a notice that they have time to file a proof of claim. A secured creditor does not need to file a proof of claim in a chapter 7 case to preserve its security interest or lien because the lien "rides through" or passes through a chapter 7 case unaffected, unless the court enters an order avoiding it for impairing or interfering with one of your exemptions.

The Discharge

Your primary goals in a chapter 7 case should be to retain exempt property and to receive a discharge of as many debts as possible. As previously discussed, a *discharge* is an order of the bankruptcy court that releases individual debtors from personal liability on most debts, subject to the exceptions discussed below so that you are no longer obligated or liable to pay. The discharge prevents the creditors who are owed the discharged debts from taking any actions to collect the debts from you or your property. Generally speaking, the overwhelming majority of individual chapter 7 debtors receive a discharge and the bankruptcy court will enter the discharge approximately four to six months after the filing.

As mentioned earlier in this chapter, if you commit certain bad acts or fail to act in accordance with court orders, your discharge may be denied by the bankruptcy court. The bankruptcy court may deny discharge of all your debts if the court finds that you made a false oath in the bankruptcy case, such as omitting assets on the schedules; failed to keep or produce financial records; failed to explain satisfactorily any loss of assets; committed a bankruptcy crime such as perjury or hiding assets; failed to obey a lawful order of the bankruptcy court; fraudulently transferred, concealed, or destroyed property that would have become property of the estate; or failed to complete the required financial management course.

You cannot discharge certain categories of debts as a matter of bankruptcy law. Debts automatically excepted from the discharge include debts that are domestic support obligations, such as alimony and child support, certain taxes, and student loans. Creditors may bring complaints to prevent certain other debts from discharge, including debts arising out of a debtor's fraud, debts based on a debtor's false financial statement, debts for willful and malicious injury by the debtor to another entity or to the property of another entity, debts for death or personal injury caused by the debtor's operation of a motor vehicle while the debtor was intoxicated from alcohol or other substances, and debts for certain criminal restitution orders. You remain liable for these debts after your chapter 7 case if you do not pay them during your case.

After the discharge, secured creditors may retain some rights to repossess or foreclose on property securing a debt. Depending on your goals and circumstances, you may wish to keep certain secured property (such as an automobile) by agreeing to reaffirm the debt or redeem the property securing the debt. Redemption allows you to buy back your property by paying for the property in a lump sum, at the value of the property, not the amount of the debt. Most debtors do not have the ability to redeem due to lack of cash, but if you do have exempt cash, you should consider redemption as a viable and good option. Also, see our discussion on reaffirmation at the end of Chapter 11.

A reaffirmation agreement is a contract between you and your creditor that obligates you on the loan and requires you to continue paying all or a portion of the money you owe, even though the debt would otherwise be discharged in the bankruptcy. A reaffirmation means that you continue to be personally liable for that debt and that your bankruptcy case will not discharge the debt. In return, the creditor promises not to repossess or take back the vehicle or other property so long as you continue to pay the debt.

You also may enter into an agreement to retain collateral and continue paying your secured creditor as if there were no bankruptcy and without the necessity of a reaffirmation agreement or a redemption. Called a *voluntary retain and pay* agreement, this type of arrangement serves the interests of both parties: The lender does not lose money and incur increased costs due to repossession and you retain the property. You may repay any debt voluntarily, whether or not a reaffirmation agreement exists.

Even if you receive a discharge in a chapter 7 bankruptcy, the court may revoke it on the request of the Trustee, a creditor, or the U.S. trustee if these parties can prove the discharge was obtained through fraud or for other causes such as fraudulent activities or material misstatements to the court.

The Henri Family: Uninsured Medical Expenses

Jean-Pierre and Marie Henri emigrated from Haiti in 1998 determined to make a better life through hard work. With only $500, the Henri family settled in Dorchester, Massachusetts, and for a year they lived with relatives. They received work permits and found jobs at minimum wage.

Marie has worked as a licensed nurse practitioner at a nursing home making $9.00 an hour. Jean-Pierre has worked as a driver for a private livery service, working all the hours he could, making an average of $400 per week. When they had children, they found an apartment for $1,100 a month. Their three children, who are now six, eight, and ten years old, attend public school. As both parents work full-time, the children attend an after-school program at their church that costs $150 a week and a summer program that costs $300 a week. Neither employer provides health insurance. After paying the bills each month, the Henri family has no disposable income and they have no savings. Jean-Pierre recently began a course at a technical school at night to learn to be a plumber.

Sickness in the Family

Last year, the Henris' middle child, Jean-Luc, passed out during recess at school and was taken to the emergency room. The doctors diagnosed him with a congenital heart defect and told the family that Jean-Luc needed heart valve replacement surgery within a month. After surgery, he would have to stay in the hospital for three weeks and then remain at home for three months. Marie quit work to take care of him. With the loss of Marie's income, the family's monthly living expenses exceeded its income by several hundred dollars a week. The family began to use their credit cards to fund the shortfall and pay for necessities such as food, transportation, and clothes.

Hospital administrators discussed the costs of Jean-Luc's medical care with Jean-Pierre and Marie and directed them to a state-assisted program that the Henris thought would take care of the bills. The doctors and hospital treated the Henri family wonderfully and the surgery was a success. The total cost of Jean-Luc's care was $689,000. Although the state paid over $400,000 of the total bill, the Henris owed $289,000. Even after a low-income discount from the hospital, the Henris still owed over $260,000.

Saddled by Enormous Debt

Jean-Pierre and Marie were desolate, conflicted, and scared. The hospital continued to send them monthly bills and called them three times a week. When they missed payments on their credit cards, the credit card companies began to call, charged them late fees, and raised their interest rates. Soon they were facing a debt of $260,000 to the hospital and over $20,000 to the credit card companies.

At a cousin's suggestion, they met with an attorney at a local legal services center who reviewed with them their liabilities, assets, income, and expenses. She recommended that they file for bankruptcy under chapter 7 and seek a discharge of their debts to the hospital and the credit card companies. She told them that they would have to pay a filing fee of $299, which could be paid in four installments. The legal services center would discount the customary fee of $1,200 to $600 based on their limited income, but they would still have to pay $50 for credit counseling before filing for bankruptcy and then another $100 for a personal finance course once the bankruptcy case was underway.

Jean-Pierre and Marie told the attorney that they were hard-working, religious people, and that they had a moral objection to filing for bankruptcy. They were also embarrassed and concerned that Jean-Pierre's boss would find out and terminate him or that bankruptcy would affect Jean-Luc's future care at the hospital. The lawyer told them to cut up their credit cards and not to use them anymore. She explained that the phone calls would persist and that lawsuits would be filed. The attorney did not see another option for the Henris but to file for bankruptcy.

Ready to File Bankruptcy

After two months of saving for the costs of filing the bankruptcy petition and lawyers' fees, the Henris reluctantly filed for bankruptcy. To prepare for filing, they met with the paralegal at the legal services center for two hours. The paralegal gave them an overview of bankruptcy and they learned that the Department of Justice could audit them. They were warned to be completely accurate and truthful when providing all necessary information. They were asked for details about their assets and liabilities, income, expenses, and personal history and the paralegal requested copies of their bills, wage stubs, and bank account statements. The lawyer finished the chapter 7 petition and documents within 24 hours and filed their bankruptcy documents electronically.

The lawyer showed them the completed paperwork: the joint chapter 7 petition, the income and expense forms, the schedules of assets, and the acknowledgments of disclosures. The Henris signed a form acknowledging all of the documents. They signed Form B 22A, also known as the means test form. Because their income was below the applicable median income of their state based on their family size and earnings for the six-month period before bankruptcy, the Henris did not have to fill out the entire form and itemize their expenses. As below median income debtors, their case would not be challenged as an abuse of bankruptcy law.

Other documents called the Schedules of Assets required that they list everything they own. They listed a few items of personal property: a 1999 Ford Taurus with over 100,000 miles, household goods, furnishings, clothes, their wedding bands, and a small balance in their bank account. They did not list any real estate. The lawyer also added an expected tax refund from the IRS in the sum of $600 as an asset. All of their assets were claimed as exempt under federal exemptions set forth in the Bankruptcy Code. The lawyer explained to the Henris that their case was routine and would likely be closed with only administrative action. She said that they would not have to go to court and appear before a bankruptcy judge.

Bump in the Road: Late Rent Payments

Suppose that during Jean-Luc's illness and before the bankruptcy case, the Henris fell behind two months in their rent and the landlord brought eviction proceedings in the Housing Court against them. The Henris and a lawyer from the legal services center would object in Housing Court to the eviction, giving the reason of a sick child. The judge would likely continue or delay the matter for 30 days on the condition that the Henris pay the two months of overdue rent plus the landlord's attorneys' fees of $850.

With another large bill looming, the lawyer might suggest that the Henris file bankruptcy to stay in the house. If the Housing Court did not enter a judgment of possession before the filing of their bankruptcy petition and the Henris could pay the overdue rent to the bankruptcy court within 30 days of their case, bankruptcy would stop the landlord from evicting

(Continued)

them. Suppose the Henris were able to borrow $2,200 from relatives, pay the money into court, and execute a certification form under the penalty of perjury that the arrears were paid into the court.

The landlord might object, but in this hypothetical case, the bankruptcy court ruled that the Henris could cure the default in this manner without paying the landlord's attorneys' fees and costs. The landlord and his attorney would become unsecured creditors for the $850, the clerk of the bankruptcy court would pay the rent to the landlord, and the Henris would obtain a discharge of the obligation imposed by the Housing Court.

Meeting of Creditors

In January, the Henris received a form in the mail telling them they had a meeting of creditors on February 1, 2010, at the U.S. Bankruptcy Court downtown. This document is known as the Notice of Automatic Stay and Meeting of Creditors.

The Henris called their lawyer and asked if the hospital was going to show up at the meeting and object to their bankruptcy. The lawyer explained that the purpose of the meeting was for their bankruptcy trustee, who administers their case, to question them under oath about what they owned and their income and expenses, and to make sure that they did not have any assets available for distribution to creditors. On the morning of the meeting, the lawyer met the Henris in front of the courthouse and told them not to worry because theirs was a routine case. They entered a room filled with 75 people (50 of them looked as nervous as the Henris and the other 25 looked like lawyers). A woman at the front of the room called names and people would sit at a table with their lawyers and the woman for about five minutes.

The woman called Marie and Jean-Pierre Henri. They sat at the table and the woman introduced herself as Margaret Casey, the trustee of their case. She checked their licenses against the names on the petition. She asked them to stand, raise their right hands, and to swear that they would tell the truth. The trustee asked if they owned any real estate or assets other than those listed in their schedules and if they had any other debts besides the hospital and the credit cards. Marie and Jean-Pierre replied "no." The trustee asked how they got into financial trouble. Marie cried and the trustee offered her a glass of water. The attorney then explained their situation.

Bump in the Road: Job Loss!

Suppose that Jean-Pierre's boss told him that he learned of the bankruptcy and that he was being terminated because he filed for bankruptcy. Is that legal? The answer is no if the termination was due to the bankruptcy filing. Bankruptcy Code Section 525(b) prohibits a private employer from discriminating against an employee based on bankruptcy. Jean-Pierre's lawyer could write the employer a letter, advising him that she would be seeking an immediate injunction against termination. At this point, the employer would likely reconsider the termination and Jean-Pierre would have his job back.

The trustee asked if there were any creditors there who wanted to question the Henris. Nobody spoke up, as no one from the hospital or credit card companies was there. The trustee said that she hoped their son was better now, that she had no further questions, and that she was closing out their bankruptcy as a no-asset case. Although they didn't fully understand, the Henris felt relieved. Their lawyer explained that the trustee meant she would not object to their exemptions, would not try to sell any of their property, and would not object to the discharge of their debts.

After the Meeting of Creditors

After the meeting, the lawyer told the Henris that the Court would mail a discharge notice in about two months. The lawyer explained that the hospital and credit card companies could file a complaint against them seeking to declare their debt "excepted" from or not part of the bankruptcy discharge but she thought it unlikely. The lawyer further said that the hospital and their employers could not discriminate against them simply because they had gone bankrupt. On April 5, the Henris received in the mail the Discharge of Debts form. The form enjoined the creditors from collecting all debts from the Henris. The Discharge of Debts means the Henris were released from the debts owed to the hospital and the credit card companies.

Bump in the Road: Jean-Luc Is Denied Medical Treatment!

Suppose that after the bankruptcy discharge, Marie took Jean-Luc to the doctor and presented her insurance card. The doctor's receptionist told her that they would not treat Jean-Luc unless Marie voluntarily paid $500 toward the old doctor's bill. At this point, Marie should call her lawyer. The lawyer would then warn the doctor that this demand violated the bankruptcy discharge injunction and that the Henris would sue to enforce the discharge as well as for emotional distress damages.

Out of Bankruptcy

Relieved and grateful, Marie baked their lawyer some cookies and dropped them off at the legal services center. Jean-Pierre's employer never said anything to him about bankruptcy. Having completed his plumber's training course, Jean-Pierre took a full-time job at a plumbing company for a salary of $600 per week, plus health insurance for his family. When Marie took Jean-Luc for his next checkup, she gave the receptionist a health insurance card and paid only a $10 co-pay for his visit. Jean-Pierre and Marie benefited greatly from the bankruptcy and health care systems of the United States for giving their son his health back and the family a fresh start.

Bump in the Road: Creditor Wants to Be Repaid Notwithstanding Bankruptcy!

Suppose that one of the credit card companies sent a reaffirmation agreement to the Henris, asking that they reaffirm the $1,500 debt in exchange for a new credit card with a $500 limit (see Chapter 11 for more information on reaffirmation agreements). Should they sign the reaffirmation agreement? The answer is *no*. Although debtors often sign reaffirmation agreements for the purpose of retaining collateral and reestablishing credit, it rarely makes sense to reaffirm an unsecured debt such as a credit card that bankruptcy wipes out. It only makes sense if the credit card company brings timely action to except the debt from discharge and succeeds because the Henris would have to pay in full outside of bankruptcy. Here, the Henris would pay too much for the privilege of getting a new credit card.

The Robinson Family: Job Loss, Credit Card Debt, and Real Estate Gone Bad

Bill and Leslie Robinson were high school sweethearts who grew up outside of Doylestown, Pennsylvania. They married when they were 19 and Leslie worked as a receptionist at a large newspaper to pay for Bill's tuition as he earned a degree in software engineering. After graduation, Bill had a difficult time finding a job, so they used their credit cards to pay for many expenses. Six months after graduation, Bill became a program writer for a software company earning a salary of $58,000 a year. Bill's salary increased to $78,000 over the next two years. Leslie had since started work at a newspaper, earning approximately $35,000 a year. Bill and Leslie bought a two-bedroom, townhouse condominium for $425,000 in a new, upscale development. They borrowed $20,000 from Leslie's parents and put down another $30,000 from their savings, leaving them only $5,000 in savings. They obtained a mortgage for $375,000 from National Bank. Their monthly mortgage payment, with taxes, plus the condo fee was $3,600. Leslie became pregnant and they had a healthy baby boy. After taking eight weeks off from the newspaper, she returned part-time, three days a week to avoid full-time day care expenses. The newspaper reduced her salary to $28,000 a year and day care on an annual basis cost $8,000.

The Perfect Storm

After a foreign corporation acquired Bill's company in 2008, the software company shut down Bill's department and laid him off. He borrowed $25,000 from his 401(k) plan and depleted their savings to make the mortgage payments. Again, they relied on credit cards for many expenses. By the time Bill found another job, they owed $50,000 in credit card debt. Bill finally got a job as a programmer for a financial services company after nearly a year of being unemployed. The Robinsons thought their problems were solved as Bill's starting salary of $65,000 quickly increased to $80,000.

However, the minimum monthly payments on their credit card debts reached $800 a month due to high interest rates and they could not reduce the principal by only making minimum payments. The condominium fee continued to increase every year. The Robinsons could make their monthly mortgage payment but were unable to save any money. They explored refinancing their condominium in an attempt to consolidate their debts, but the lender rejected their application because the appraiser valued the property at $274,000 due to the drastic reductions in the local real estate market.

The payment obligations stressed out and drained the Robinsons. At the end of each month, they had to decide which bills to pay and which bills to leave unpaid. They could not afford any new purchases and had to charge food and diapers on their credit cards.

In the middle of November, Bill was laid off again. He advertised himself as a computer repair technician in the local paper and got a couple of jobs, but not enough to pay their debts. Then the other shoe dropped. The newspaper laid off many employees, including Leslie. Every night, they received telephone calls from different credit card companies. They had no savings, they had reached the credit limit on all but one credit card and they used their sole remaining credit card to pay for all of their expenses through cash advances. Needless to say, they couldn't make their mortgage payments. They could not believe how fast their lives were falling apart.

Surrender the Condo

Leslie's father, an accountant, analyzed their financial situation. He told them that it was inevitable that the condominium would be foreclosed and that they must find a new place to live. He referred them to a bankruptcy lawyer. The lawyer reviewed their assets, liabilities, income, and expenses. He advised them to file for chapter 7 bankruptcy sooner rather than later. He advised them to agree to surrender the condominium to the bank, and that any deficiency after foreclosure would be discharged in bankruptcy, along with their credit card debts. The lawyer prepared a deed-in-lieu, an agreement in which the homeowner gives back the property to the lender and they prepared to surrender the townhouse to the bank. In exchange for the deed, the lawyer negotiated an agreement with the bank to allow the Robinsons to stay in the house for 60 days while the bank marketed the property for sale and they tried to find a new place to live.

Bankruptcy Is a Must!

Leslie's father gave the Robinsons the lawyer's fee in the amount of $1,200 and the filing fee of $299. The Robinsons met with the lawyer's paralegal and provided all of the information requested and attended credit card counseling that cost $50 for a 15-minute consultation. The counselor advised that they had no other alternative but to file for bankruptcy and gave them a credit counseling certificate for filing with the court. The lawyer's paralegal prepared the bankruptcy documents.

Even though neither Bill nor Leslie had jobs and were collecting a minimal amount of unemployment benefits, the law considered the Robinsons to be above median income debtors because their income over the six-month period preceding bankruptcy exceeded the state's median income amount. In addition, because they no longer paid the mortgage due to the deed-in-lieu of foreclosure, the Robinsons' expenses were less than their current monthly income as it appeared on Form B 22A. Thus, at first blush, the bankruptcy documents suggested that they could pay some money each month to creditors.

The Bankruptcy Filing

The Robinsons' Schedule A showed no real property owned because of the deed-in-lieu of foreclosure. On their Schedule B, the lawyer listed $50 in their checking account, assorted household goods and furnishings with a value of $1,500, wearing apparel with a value of $1,000, professional books and tools with a value of $500, and jewelry with a value of $750. Leslie asked how the lawyer came up with the values for their property because they had paid over $4,000 for their furniture, they had a lot of clothes, and Bill had paid $2,500 for Leslie's engagement ring. The lawyer told them that the appropriate value for a bankruptcy case is liquidation value, or the price they could get at a yard sale, not fair market value or the price they had originally paid.

The Robinsons also listed their two vehicles, a 2005 Jeep Cherokee with a value of $7,500 and their 2006 Saturn with a value of $4,000. They still owed outstanding loans on each vehicle. The Robinsons included Bill's 401(k) account, which had a balance of $3,500, and a college trust fund for the baby that Leslie's father had established. Although Leslie was trustee of the college fund, she could not touch the college fund. The lawyer told them they had to list the college fund, but like the 401(k) account, bankruptcy would not affect these assets.

The Robinsons claimed all of their property as exempt under the Bankruptcy Code's federal exemption scheme. The Robinsons listed the potential deficiency claim (the bank's claim for the difference between the sale price and the loan) owed to the bank after sale of the townhouse as an unsecured claim in an unknown amount. They also were required to list the debts owed to their family members as well as all of their credit card debts. The Robinsons had to file a Statement of Financial Affairs form, which includes a series of questions about prebankruptcy events. They had to state their income for the past two years and the details of any transfers they made, including the deed-in-lieu of foreclosure to the bank. The Robinsons had to file a Statement of Intention form regarding secured debts. They indicated that they would surrender the Jeep to the vehicle lender and reaffirm the loan on the Saturn so that they could keep one car. They signed their certification that all documents were accurate and that they understood the relief they were requesting. For a review of the different types of forms mentioned in this paragraph, see Chapter 11.

Bankruptcy Stops Collection Activity

The lawyer filed the petition and other documents electronically that afternoon. When the debt collectors called that night, Leslie told each one that they had filed a chapter 7 petition. One creditor asked for the docket number of the case and the others just hung up. A creditor called a week later, and Leslie asked if they had received the notice of automatic stay. The person on the phone said yes, but he wanted to talk about the Robinsons entering into reaffirmation agreements on their car loans. Leslie referred the creditor to their attorney.

Meeting of Creditors

When they received the notice of the Section 341 meeting of creditors, the Robinsons called their lawyer who told them to relax and plan on answering the trustee's questions truthfully and to the best of their ability. He said he would jump in on any questions as needed. At their meeting of creditors, the trustee had many questions about their finances. She wanted to know why they did not file under chapter 13 and propose a repayment plan if they had income left over every month. The trustee also wanted to know how they had amassed over $55,000 in credit card debt and had nothing to show for it. She also wanted to see evidence of the money Bill had been earning doing computer repairs during the 60 days preceding the filing date.

The lawyer told the trustee about their volatile job histories, the layoffs, the necessity of using credit cards for living expenses, and their inability to pay their mortgage. He said that their current monthly income (CMI) was misleading because they had nothing at the end of the month and continued to experience a substantial shortfall due to unemployment. The lawyer explained to the trustee that for many of the credit cards, over half of the balance was accrued interest because the balances were quite old. He would supply information and documents about Bill's freelance computer repairs. The trustee reviewed the bankruptcy documents, as well as the deed-in-lieu of foreclosure and agreement to occupy the townhouse for 60 days rent-free, and the appraisal report and asked the lawyer to submit additional information about Bill's repair earnings in 10 days. Satisfied after reviewing all the information, the trustee filed a report of no assets with the Court within 30 days of the meeting.

Bump in the Road: The U.S. Trustee Is on Their Case!

After reviewing the documents regarding Bill's computer repair services, the trustee was skeptical of the lawyer's explanation and might have concluded that Bill had additional cash income that he had not reported. Suppose she referred the Robinson case to the U.S. Trustee's Office, the agency of the Department of Justice in charge of administering bankruptcy cases.

After an analyst reviewed the filings, an attorney from the U.S. trustee's Office would send the Robinsons' attorney a letter requesting further documentation of income and expenses and proof of the purchases the Robinsons had made with their credit cards during the two years before bankruptcy. The U.S. trustee's attorney would object to discharge of the bankruptcy case if Bill had additional income during the six months before bankruptcy that he had not disclosed or move to dismiss the case as an abuse of bankruptcy laws if the Robinsons would not adequately explain the hundreds of credit card purchases and new credit cards the two years before bankruptcy.

The lawyer might then call the Robinsons into the office to explain the U.S. trustee's inquiries and ask them to assemble their records within 10 days. After the lawyer and his paralegal reviewed the Robinsons' records, the lawyer would then write to the U.S. trustee explaining how it was necessary for them to live off their credit cards during periods of unemployment. In the best case, the U.S. trustee's attorney would determine that neither a complaint objecting to discharge nor a motion to dismiss was warranted now that she had all the facts.

After the Meeting of Creditors

A week later, the lawyer discussed with the Robinsons the reaffirmation agreement the vehicle lender had sent to him. He explained that they had three options with respect to the vehicle loans: surrender the vehicles to the lender, pay the value of the cars in cash to the lender (known as redemption), or pay the entire debt as scheduled as if no bankruptcy were filed (known as reaffirmation). Reaffirmation and redemption are discussed in detail in Chapter 11. Bill asked if they could turn in the Jeep and keep the Saturn by continuing to make the payments on the Saturn each month. The lawyer told them yes, and if they did so, the lender could not repossess the car as bankruptcy could not be considered a default. With a reaffirmation agreement, they could reestablish their credit as the lender would report timely payments to the credit reporting agencies. The lawyer advised them not to reaffirm. He explained that their expenses still exceeded their income and they would likely default. They would owe the whole balance despite bankruptcy.

The lawyer reviewed a redemption financing agreement they were offered from a new lending company that would pay the old lender the value of the new car then give the Robinsons a new loan to a redemption financing company at an interest rate of 25 percent. The lawyer advised against this redemption due to the high interest rate. The Robinsons decided to surrender the Jeep and not to reaffirm or redeem the Saturn, but to take their chances in continuing to make the monthly car payments. With Bill's computer repair jobs and Leslie's new part-time work at a retail store, they continue to make the car payments without consequence.

Bump in the Road: A Credit Card Company Threatens to Sue!

Suppose that during the bankruptcy proceedings, one of the credit card companies continued to put pressure on the Robinson case. The company would have been listed as an unsecured creditor in Schedule F of Form 22. Suppose that after the meeting of creditors, the credit card company sent a letter to their lawyer indicating that it intended to file a complaint to except the credit card company's debt from the Robinsons' discharge pursuant to a section of the Bankruptcy Code that states that "cash advances aggregating more than $750 . . . within 70 days [prior to bankruptcy]" are excepted from discharge. The Robinson's lawyer would know that it would cost more in attorneys' fees to litigate the credit card company's complaint than the amount sought. The Robinson's lawyer might work out a deal with the credit card company that the Robinsons would pay $1,200 to the credit card company in exchange for them agreeing not to sue and a full release of liability. The $1,200 could be paid out over the course of a set time period to relieve pressure on the Robinsons if the lender agrees to installments.

The Robinsons took the personal financial management course as required to receive a discharge in bankruptcy. They opted for the longer course of three, two-hour sessions, and paid $200 for the course in cash. The Robinsons learned about budgeting, the cost of credit cards, and how to save money. Ten weeks after the meeting of creditors with the trustee, the Robinsons received their bankruptcy discharge and breathed a sigh of relief. Though saddened by the loss of their house, bankruptcy wiped out their debts and the Robinsons benefited greatly.

Bump in the Road: Student Loan Creditors Make Demands!

Suppose Bill owed $20,000 in student loans, including Pell Grants, Stafford loans, and loans from a local bank guaranteed by the U.S. Department of Education. If he defaulted on his student loans, an agency representative might call the Robinsons' bankruptcy lawyer and say that Bill could apply for a variety of plans to consolidate his loans, including one to pay only his net cash flow every month. The lawyer would discuss the options with Bill and advise him that the general rule is that bankruptcy does not discharge student loans unless repayment would cause undue hardship to the debtor or debtor's dependents. (The standard is strict and usually the Bankruptcy Court will allow a discharge of a student loan only if a person is permanently disabled.) The lawyer might recommend that Bill contact the Department of Education to try to work out a repayment plan based on cash flow.

(Continued)

Suppose the Robinsons had experienced a tragedy, such as if the doctors diagnosed their child with a chronic serious illness and a huge liability for medical care. If that were the case, Bill could file a complaint seeking that his student loans be discharged. He would have to obtain reports from doctors and pay his lawyer fees for the case, but he would likely succeed in getting his student loans discharged under such a scenario.

Lessons Learned

These two examples, and possible bumps in the road, represent typical issues that arise in consumer chapter 7 bankruptcy cases. The scenarios are meant to highlight what individuals must do before and during the bankruptcy case, what can go right in bankruptcy, as well as what can go wrong. Bankruptcy exists to help honest but unfortunate people who have run into difficult times, people like the Henris and Robinsons. People and families do survive the bankruptcy process and can then thrive after bankruptcy.

Points to Remember

- Prepare for the commencement of your case by compiling all records, including bills, proof of income, bank account statements, and lists of assets and liabilities. Have assets of significant value appraised.
- Consult with a reputable and honest bankruptcy lawyer who specializes in representing debtors in consumer (i.e., not bankruptcy for businesses) cases. Your lawyer should know the law, rules of procedure, and local practices and the other significant players, such as the trustees and the U.S. trustee.
- Make sure that you have fulfilled all of your duties as debtors, including completing all necessary documents and timely filing them, appearing at the meeting of creditors, and responding to any requests for further information or documents requested by the trustee. Failure to fulfill your duties can result in dismissal of your case.

- Although the bankruptcy case will remain on a debtor's credit report for up to ten years, creditors are free to deny credit to any debtor or any other individual. But as debtors cannot obtain another chapter 7 discharge for eight years after their previous chapter 7 bankruptcy case, lenders soon offer credit to recent bankruptcy debtors. Use the new credit wisely based on lessons learned from the previous chapter 7 bankruptcy filing.

18

Two Trips through Chapter 13 Bankruptcy

It is never too late to be what you might have been.

—George Eliot

In this chapter, we present the stories of individual debtors who owe consumer debts and file for bankruptcy under chapter 13 of the Bankruptcy Code. Even though your situation is not identical to these stories, these stories are meant to bring to life what you would encounter if you filed for bankruptcy under chapter 13. We have also included bumps in the road to demonstrate alternate scenarios that some debtors encounter in bankruptcy cases.

All of the bankruptcy forms mentioned in this chapter are available at www.uscourts.gov. (See Appendix A or www.wiley.com/go/roadoutofdebt for more information.)

Chapter 13 Basics

Chapter 13 of the Bankruptcy Code, Debt Adjustments for Individuals with Regular Income, differs from chapter 7 in a number of ways. Unlike a debtor in a chapter 7 case, a chapter 13 debtor files a plan under which he or she proposes to pay all or a percentage of his or her debts over a period of three to five years depending on his or her income. People in default on their mortgages or who have nonexempt assets and need to pay their debts over time are the primary debtors in chapter 13 bankruptcy cases.

Advantages and Disadvantages

Chapter 13 has many advantages. However, you must also carefully consider some disadvantages before commencing a chapter 13 case. You should additionally evaluate the differences between the types of bankruptcy relief available under the different chapters and weigh the advantages and disadvantages of each chapter while you consider your overall financial situation.

Several important reasons may persuade you to choose chapter 13. Most important, in chapter 13, you can retain all property while performing under the chapter 13 plan. Thus, if you have nonexempt property and you want to retain it, chapter 13 may be the best chapter for you. A self-employed individual who operates a non-incorporated business may continue to operate the business and include the business's debts in the chapter 13 plan. Moreover, since defaults in home mortgages can be paid over the term of the plan, you may be able to save your home from foreclosure in a chapter 13. You can reduce certain mortgages and liens to the value of the property and pay them over the term of your chapter 13 plan.

Judicial liens on real estate that impair your exemptions can be avoided and recharacterized to unsecured claims. Furthermore, you can pay prepetition tax claims (tax claims that the government made prior to your filing) with legal priority over the term of the plan. One of the most significant advantages of chapter 13 is that, in addition to the automatic stay for you as the debtor, a codebtor stay extends to individuals who are also liable with you on consumer debts throughout the term of the chapter 13 plan.

Some disadvantages exist in the chapter 13 case. First, during the years that you are paying debts under the plan, you are under the jurisdiction of the bankruptcy court. Not only does the bankruptcy court scrutinize your financial life, but your finances are subject to monitoring by the chapter 13 trustee and creditors. Thus, if you fail to make a payment under the plan, the trustee and creditors can seek to dismiss your chapter 13 case resulting in the lost opportunity for a discharge, which comes at the end of plan payments.

In addition, if during the term of the plan your income or assets increase, creditors and other parties to your case can request that the plan be modified to increase payments. Chapter 13 cases are more costly than chapter 7 cases. You must pay a trustee's commission— approximately 10 percent of the plan disbursements over the life of the plan. Your attorneys' fees are higher for chapter 13 cases than chapter 7 cases, usually ranging from $2,500 to $3,500 plus filing fees, depending on the jurisdiction.

Eligibility Requirements

You must meet eligibility requirements to file chapter 13. First, you must meet the monetary limitations and can owe no more than $1,081,400 in secured debts and $360,475 in unsecured debts. These limitations are adjusted every three years according to the Consumer Price Index. Second, you must receive the credit counseling briefing from an approved agency within 180 days prior to the filing of the chapter 13 petition, unless the bankruptcy court excuses the requirement if you are disabled or on active military duty. The court may also grant an extension of time because of emergency circumstances. In addition, if you had a case dismissed within the 180 days prior to the filing of the current petition because of your willful failure to abide by a court order, or if you dismissed your case voluntarily after a request for relief from stay, you must wait 180 days to file for chapter 13 relief.

The Procedure

You commence your chapter 13 case by filing a voluntary petition with the $279 filing fee in the bankruptcy court. Although the court may allow the fee to be paid in four installments, you may not obtain a fee waiver as in chapter 7. As a chapter 13 debtor, you have to complete a means test form (Form B 22C) indicating whether your income is above or below median compared to the applicable state, and also showing the amount of disposable income you have to fund a plan.

You must also file the credit counseling certificate, schedules of assets, liabilities, income and expenses, and a statement of financial affairs. You then must file a chapter 13 plan within the first two weeks of the case, unless bankruptcy court extends the time. Within a week before the Section 341 meeting of creditors, you must submit to the chapter 13 trustee your federal tax returns for the most recent year. At the Section 341 meeting, you, or in a joint case, you and your spouse, take an oath to tell the truth and the trustee asks questions about your assets, liabilities, income, and expenses and the plan.

An automatic stay is put into effect upon the filing, which prevents most collection efforts against you and your property, such as legal actions, wage garnishments, and telephone contact. Exceptions from the stay include collection of domestic support obligations from property that is not property of the estate, withholding of pension loan or domestic support obligations from your wages, criminal actions against you, or eviction proceedings if there was a judgment obtained by a landlord prior to bankruptcy.

Individuals who are liable with you for consumer debts, namely those incurred primarily for personal, family, or household purposes, also enjoy the protection of the automatic stay. Creditors may also seek an order of the bankruptcy court granting relief from the automatic stay. If you fail to make timely home mortgage payments after the commencement of the chapter 13 case, the bankruptcy court will often grant relief from stay for a creditor to continue foreclosure proceedings.

However, if you had a bankruptcy case dismissed within a year of a repeat filing, the automatic stay only lasts for the first 30 days, unless the court finds that the second case was commenced in good faith and extends the stay for cause, such as a change in your financial circumstances making the second case feasible. If you have two cases dismissed within a year of a repeat filing, the automatic stay does not go into effect, unless the court enters an order effectuating the stay, upon a finding the subsequent case was filed in good faith.

The Plan and Plan Confirmation

As a chapter 13 debtor, you must file a plan that properly treats the debts owed according to the legal priority of creditors' claims. Priority claims, such as taxes, must be paid in full over the term of the plan. A plan can cure a default in a mortgage or lease if you pay the amount in arrears over the plan term, while maintaining regular payments. Although home mortgages cannot be modified under a chapter 13 plan, and vehicle purchase loans obtained within 910 days prior to commencement of the case must also be paid in full, some types of secured claims can be modified and you need only pay the value of the collateral plus market interest rate over the term of the plan.

The plan need not pay unsecured claims in full as long it provides that you will pay all projected disposable income over an applicable commitment period, and as long as unsecured creditors receive at least as much under the plan as they would receive under chapter 7. In chapter 13, *disposable income* is defined as income (other than child support payments received by you) less amounts reasonably necessary for the maintenance or support of you or your dependents and less charitable contributions up to 15 percent of your gross income. If you operate a business, the definition of disposable income excludes those amounts that are necessary for ordinary operating expenses.

The *applicable commitment period* refers to the required duration of the plan, and it depends on your current monthly income. The applicable commitment period must be three years if current monthly income is less than the state median for a family of the same size and five years if the current monthly income is greater than a family of the same size. The plan can be a period shorter than the applicable commitment period if you propose to pay unsecured debts in full.

The trustee and creditors have the right to object to the plan. Within 30 days after the commencement of a chapter 13 case, you must make the first payment called for under a plan, even if the court has not yet confirmed it. Within 45 days after the meeting of creditors, the bankruptcy court holds a confirmation hearing. Many courts do not hold an actual hearing if there has been no objection to the plan.

The four most frequent objections made to plans include: the plan is not committing all of your projected disposable income for the applicable commitment period; the plan is not properly treating creditors' claims; the plan is not feasible; or that you do not pay your creditors as much as they would receive on liquidation of your nonexempt assets. If the court denies confirmation of a plan, the judge will usually give you time to file an amended plan. Also if your financial circumstances improve during the case, the court can compel you to increase plan payments. Many debtors consent to a direct deduction from their wages for plan payments because they find helpful. However, if a debtor defaults in making plan payments, the trustee will file a motion to dismiss the chapter 13 case. Unless you can cure the default, the bankruptcy court will likely dismiss the case.

In a chapter 13 case, creditors must file proofs of claim with the bankruptcy court in order to receive distributions under the plan. If a debtor or the trustee disagrees with the amount claimed, they can file an objection and the court will determine the appropriate amount.

The Discharge

Under chapter 13, you are entitled to a discharge upon completion of all payments as long as you:

1. Certify that any domestic support obligations that came due prior to making such certification have been paid
2. Have not received a discharge in a prior case filed within two years for prior chapter 13 cases and four years for prior chapter 7, 11, and 12 cases
3. Have completed an approved course in financial management (if the U.S. trustee or bankruptcy administrator for your district has determined that such courses are available to you)

The court also will not enter the discharge, however, until it determines that there is no pending proceeding that might give rise to a limitation on a debtor's homestead exemption, meaning the amount of equity on your primary residence after your mortgages that is protected from creditors.

The discharge releases you from all debts provided for by the plan or disallowed, subject to certain exceptions. The discharge provides an injunction that prevents creditors provided for in the chapter 13 plan from pursuing you on the discharged obligations. Exceptions from discharge include certain long-term obligations (such as a home mortgage), debts for alimony or child support, certain taxes, debts for most government-funded or guaranteed educational loans or benefit overpayments, debts arising from death or personal injury caused by driving while intoxicated or under the influence of drugs, and debts for restitution or a criminal fine included in a sentence on your conviction of a crime.

To the extent that you do not pay debts that are excepted from discharge in full under the chapter 13 plan, you will still be responsible for these debts after the chapter 13 case has been concluded. Debts for money or property obtained by false pretenses, debts for fraud or defalcation while acting in a fiduciary capacity, and debts for restitution or damages awarded in a civil case for willful or malicious actions by you that cause personal injury or death to a person will be discharged unless a creditor timely files and prevails in an action to have such debts declared excepted from the discharge. The discharge in a chapter 13 case is somewhat broader than in a chapter 7 case. Debts dischargeable in a chapter 13, but not in chapter 7, include debts for willful and malicious injury to property (as opposed to a person), debts incurred to pay nondischargeable tax obligations, and debts arising from property settlements in divorce or separation proceedings.

After confirmation of a plan, circumstances may arise that prevent you from completing the plan. In such situations, the court may grant you a hardship discharge. A *hardship discharge* is available only if:

1. The debtor's failure to complete plan payments is due to circumstances beyond your control and through no fault of your own
2. Creditors have received at least as much as they would have received in a chapter 7 case
3. Modification of the plan is not possible

Injury or illness that precludes employment sufficient to fund even a modified plan may serve as the basis for a hardship discharge. The hardship discharge is more limited than the regular chapter 13 discharge and does not apply to any debts that are nondischargeable in a chapter 7 case.

A Note of Caution

Because of the complexities of chapter 13, in particular the requirements for treating claims, the elements necessary for plan confirmation, and the scope of the chapter 13 discharge, anyone contemplating chapter 13 should consult an attorney skilled in the specialty of chapter 13 cases before going down the road of chapter 13.

The Delgado Family: Spending Freely, Saving Nothing

Jim and Stephanie Delgado liked the good life. Jim began working in his father's Chrysler dealership right after graduating from college and married Stephanie, an art gallery salesperson, the next year. Jim's family owned and operated two Chrysler franchises and sold Chrysler, Dodge, and Jeep vehicles in a suburb outside of Phoenix, Arizona. During the 1980s, the dealerships flourished and made great profits. His father promoted Jim to executive vice president with a handsome salary.

After their third child was born, Jim and Stephanie built a 10-room house in Scottsdale, with a three-car garage, a pool, and an apartment for the children's nanny. Construction of the house cost over $750,000, which they funded with all of their savings and a $60,000 loan from the company. After construction, their mortgage on the house was over $500,000, and their monthly mortgage payment was $3,900. As their property was assessed for $800,000, real estate taxes totaled over $20,000 a year.

Jim and Stephanie had no money worries and spent freely. They sent their children to private schools, belonged to an exclusive country club, went on expensive vacations, and were generous in donating to various charities. Jim and Stephanie did not save much money. They expected a sizable inheritance from Jim's father. Unbeknownst to them, Jim's father will left all of his estate to charity in his will.

The Family Business Suffers

Around 2005, the automobile businesses began to sustain losses. With sales down, the company sold several vehicles without repaying Chrysler. Jim's father made personal advances to the dealerships to fund operations and mortgaged the real estate on which the dealerships operated. In 2008, one of the dealerships couldn't pay its franchise fee to Chrysler and it was shut down in a matter of weeks. When Chrysler filed for chapter 11 bankruptcy reorganization, Jim met with the automobile executives and tried to persuade them that the Jeep franchise could operate at a profit. The executives disagreed, rejected the franchise agreements, and closed the Jeep dealership, too. They continued to sell used cars, but the commission Jim earned was 20 percent of his prior $250,000 salary.

Jim's father had a massive heart attack and died. With no one to bail them out, Jim and Stephanie fell behind on their $350,000 mortgage. They made attempts to reduce the expenses, took their children out of private school, laid off the nanny, and canceled the country club membership. Stephanie went back to work at the art gallery, earning approximately $35,000 a year and Jim found a job at another car dealership as a commissioned salesman, earning approximately $60,000 a year. Their credit card debts reached more than $50,000 with minimum monthly payments over $2,500 due to interest rates of 30 percent because of recent missed and late payments. They owed other miscellaneous unsecured debts to creditors, such as their landscaping service, the pool service, and a carpenter who had done some work on their house.

Chrysler made demands on Jim personally for the $60,000 from sales of vehicles for which he owed the proceeds to Chrysler and failed to deliver to Chrysler. To make matters worse, Jim hadn't paid any taxes on his income in a year, and the IRS sent him a notice of assessment for $20,000 plus interest and penalties. When their mortgage company sent a notice that a foreclosure sale would be held in six weeks because of four unpaid mortgage payments, Jim and Stephanie decided that it was time to see a lawyer.

Answering Tough Questions

A bankruptcy lawyer asked Jim and Stephanie what their financial goals were and whether their marriage was solid. They told him that their main goal was to save their house, as they had substantial equity in it, and that they were committed to stay together despite the stress of financial problems. The lawyer agreed that the equity in the home was worth trying to save and asked about their other debts. They prepared a declaration of homestead on their home for their signature. He explained that once recorded with the land registry, the declaration of homestead would protect $150,000 in equity from their creditors. The attorney inquired about their monthly income over the past six months and concluded that despite their decrease in income, they were still above median income debtors.

The attorney advised the Delgados that the best way to accomplish their goal of saving their home was to file a chapter 13 individual reorganization case.

The lawyer explained that chapter 13 of the Bankruptcy Code had eligibility requirements: an individual or husband and wife had to have regular income and no more than $1,081,400 in secured debts and $360,475 in unsecured debts. The bankruptcy court would dismiss their case at the outset if they owed more than the chapter 13 debt limitations. Before the case was commenced, they would have to obtain credit counseling briefing and a certificate stating they had completed the counseling. The attorney would file the chapter 13 petition, and within 15 days, the Delgados would have to sign sworn schedules of their assets, liabilities, and a statement of their financial affairs. The trustee at the Section 341 meeting of creditors would question them under oath about their filings and if they did not tell the truth, they would suffer consequences, including dismissal of their case, loss of the protection of the automatic stay, conversion to a chapter 7 bankruptcy case, loss of nonexempt assets, and/or criminal prosecution for a federal crime.

Bump in the Road: A Creditor or the Trustee Objects at Hearing

One bump in the road would be if objections were filed to a chapter 13 plan. Three such objections could be:

1. The IRS objected because the Delgados owed tax returns for the current year and despite their extension, the bankruptcy accelerated the due date for their returns.
2. The mortgage company objected on the grounds that the amount owed on the mortgage arrearage provided in the plan did not include attorneys' fees and other charges incurred during foreclosure proceedings.
3. The trustee objected on the grounds that the Delgados' income and expenses as stated in their schedules were unrealistic and that the plan was not feasible.

In each of these scenarios, the Delgados' lawyer would file responses to the objections and the bankruptcy judge would schedule a hearing to rule on them.

With the necessary tax returns reflecting no tax due to the IRS, an itemization of charges for the mortgage company, and an agreement with the trustee that they would dismiss the bankruptcy case if they fell behind on plan payments, all three objections would be withdrawn or overruled.

The lawyer would report the agreements to the judge, and an amended plan including the mortgage charges and a stipulation with the trustee would need to be filed within two weeks.

They would have to bring their payment advices—wage stubs or other evidence of income—to the Section 341 meeting. The lawyer warned them that the bankruptcy system expects full disclosure and truth. The number of people who were in the Section 341 meeting shocked the Delgados. After a few minutes, though, they realized that everyone was there for their own cases and paid no attention to them.

The lawyer further explained that the bankruptcy judge would have to approve their chapter 13 plan and that their creditors would have the right to object to the plan on the grounds that treatment of their claims was improper. Most important, a trustee would have the right to object to the plan's treatment of creditors and would investigate the Delgados' finances and budget, and if their plan was confirmed, the trustee would supervise their payments under the plan for five years. The attorney advised them that they would have to commit to a plan period of five years due to their above-median-income status.

The projected disposable income test was more complicated. Chapter 13 debtors are required to submit all of their projected disposable income over the life of the plan to the payment of their unsecured creditors.

Although some courts had used a mechanical approach in applying this test, multiplying the previous six months of debtors' monthly income over the term of the plan, the Supreme Court of the United States rejected that test, and directed that courts adopt a forward-looking approach and consider what actual income a debtor expects to receive during the plan.

Because Jim's income as a commission salesman was volatile and Stephanie's income prospects were uncertain, their lawyer indicated that he could persuade the chapter 13 trustee and the court that their income would not likely increase during the plan term. He recommended the filing of a plan paying unsecured creditors 10 percent of their allowed claims. They recognized that their chapter 13 plan was a five-year commitment and that if their income increased, they may be required to modify the plan and increase the amount to be paid to unsecured credit. Their plan would relieve them from their financial problems with the least risk and retention of all assets.

Put to the Test

The attorney also provided the Delgados with an explanation of the two legal tests for confirmation of a chapter 13 plan: the best interests test and the projected disposable income test. The second test comes into play if the trustee or a creditor objects to the plan. He told them that the best interests test means they would need to submit payments of at least the amount that their creditors would get in a chapter 7 bankruptcy case. He did not think that this test was a problem for their case because the value of their property was less than the amount of their mortgage plus the amount of their homestead exemption of $150,000 under Arizona law.

The projected disposable income test was more complicated. In the 9th Circuit, where Arizona is, this test means their current monthly income earned in the past six months is multiplied over the term of the plan in order to determine how much creditors would receive. This was good news for the Delgados. It meant that they could propose a plan with a payment of zero percent to their general unsecured creditors. However, because the Supreme Court is reviewing the 9th Circuit test with the forward-looking test of other courts, the lawyer drafted a plan proposing a 10 percent dividend to unsecured creditors. A 10 percent dividend means creditors are paid 10 percent of their claim over the term of the plan. The Delgados agreed to file a chapter 13 plan along the lines their lawyer suggested. Although they recognized that chapter 13 was a five-year commitment, it would relieve them from their financial problems with the least risk and retention of all assets.

After the meeting, the lawyer had commissioned an appraisal of the property. After an inspection and review of comparable listings and sales, the appraiser valued the house at $450,000 due to the

Bump in the Road: Trouble Sticking to the Plan

The Delgados dutifully made their monthly plan payments and regular mortgage payments for five months. Suppose Stephanie got sick and could not work and the Delgados started missing mortgage payments. Soon, their lawyer would receive a motion for relief from the automatic stay in which the mortgage company would seek authority from the bankruptcy court to continue a mortgage foreclosure.

The Delgado's lawyer advised them that he would file an objection to the motion for relief from stay and the bankruptcy judge would hold a hearing. At the hearing, the mortgagee's lawyer argues that cause existed for relief from stay, because the Delgados failed to make regular postpetition payments. He further points out that they are now three months in arrears postpetition. The lawyer for the Delgados argues the mortgagee's position was not in jeopardy due to equity in the property, explains that the Delgados had fallen behind due to a decrease in income, indicates that Jim's sales for the past month had increased, and proposes to amend the plan to include the three months of postpetition arrears in an amended plan.

The judge accepts the Delgado's proposal. The judge orders that if they fall behind in payments again, he will allow the motion for relief from stay without a further hearing upon the filing of an affidavit of default by the mortgagee's attorney. The mortgage company could then recommend foreclosure without any action from the court. Jim and Stephanie leave the courtroom with the determination to get second jobs to make sure that they do not default again and lose their house.

drastic decrease in real estate values in Arizona. The Delgados have $100,000 in equity in their residence.

Based on Jim and Stephanie's unsecured debts, totaling approximately $160,000, their lawyer advised that he would draft the plan proposing to pay their unsecured creditors 10 percent of their unsecured claims, or $16,000. Because only creditors that timely filed a proof of claim within approximately three months after the filing (and six months for the taxing authorities) could participate in the plan, the plan could be amended in some jurisdictions to save the Delgados money if all creditors did not file claims. In other jurisdictions, creditors that filed claims would receive bigger dividends. Because of the homestead declaration, the equity in their home was not available to creditors. However, the Delgados would have to pay the IRS in full as well as the full amount of the mortgage arrearage over five years.

Bump in the Road: A House They Can't Afford

What if, three months after the hearing, the Delgados defaulted on their mortgage again? The mortgage company's attorney would file an affidavit of default. The lawyer would propose an amended plan providing for a sale of the property within six months. The mortgage company would file an objection, stating that the Delgados already filed an amended plan, and did not merit another chance. The bankruptcy judge would decide that although they have equity in the property, the Delgados can not afford to keep the house. He would order the Delgados to hire a real estate broker and list the property at a price of $469,000. The judge would give them three months to complete a private sale of their house. A buyer would make a low offer of $445,000. Their lawyer advises the Delgados to accept the offer, even though it is less than the appraised value.

Because the Delgados have declared a homestead, all of the proceeds of the sale would be exempt—meaning that the Delgados would keep the net proceeds after payment of the broker's fee, mortgage, and real estate taxes of approximately $90,000. The Delgado's lawyer would file the appropriate documents with the bankruptcy court to obtain approval of the sale. Other interested parties could make higher offers for the property, but if no objection or higher offer is filed with the court, the court could approve the sale shortly thereafter. The Delgados's lawyer also would explain that after the sale, they could convert to chapter 7 bankruptcy. In the chapter 7 bankruptcy, the Delgados would receive a discharge in bankruptcy of all of their unsecured debts, with the exception of the IRS. They could likely work out a repayment plan with the IRS for its claim after bankruptcy.

The lawyer files a motion to sell real estate free and clear of liens and a notice of intended sale soliciting higher offers with the bankruptcy court. He serves these papers on all of the Delgados' creditors. After no one files objections or higher offers, the bankruptcy judge approves the sale without a hearing. Their case is converted to a chapter 7 bankruptcy. The Delgados appear before their chapter 7 trustee at the Section 341 meeting and explain that their chapter 13 case failed due to their inability to maintain mortgage payments, that they sold their house, and that all proceeds from the house were exempt from their chapter 7 bankruptcy. The chapter 7 trustee files a no-asset report. Two months later, the Delgados receive their discharge in the mail. With the $90,000 in exempt homestead proceeds, the Delgados pay off the IRS and rent a three-bedroom foreclosed house on a golf course in Scottsdale for $2,200 a month. Their children are able to stay in the same public school.

The cost of the chapter 13 bankruptcy plan would include the lawyer's fee of $3,500, which could be spread over a year and paid under the plan, a filing fee of $279, which had to be paid up front, payments to creditors and a 10-percent fee on disbursements to the chapter 13 trustee for administering the plan. Their monthly payment to the chapter 13 trustee under the plan would be approximately $900 per month and they must continue to pay their current monthly mortgage and real estate tax payments directly to the mortgage company and the city. During the first year of the plan, the monthly payment is $1,200,

Bump in the Road: Sued in Bankruptcy Court!

Chrysler Credit Corporation received notice of the Delgado bankruptcy and timely filed (within 60 days after the Section 341 meeting of creditors) an adversary complaint seeking to except their debt from the bankruptcy discharge. In the complaint, Chrysler pleaded two counts that the debt should be excepted from discharge pursuant to two different sections of the Bankruptcy Code Sections 523(a)(a)(2)(A) and (a)(4). It first argued that Jim defrauded Chrysler when he executed the 2008 floor plan agreement because Jim knew that his company was in dire financial straits from the outset and intended to use proceeds of the collateral in breach of the floor plan agreement. Chrysler's second theory was that Jim acted in a capacity of trustee for Chrysler, so that when Jim failed to remit the proceeds of vehicle sales to Chrysler under the floor plan agreement, Jim converted the proceeds and used them for improper purposes. Chrysler claimed his actions constituted a defalcation while he was acting as a fiduciary to Chrysler rendering the debt nondischargeable in bankruptcy.

The Degado's lawyer's fee of $3,500 did not include adversary proceeding but he would require a $5,000 retainer with a $350 per-hour fee to represent them in the adversary proceeding.

Ending #1: Stephanie's father gave them the loan. Chrysler found evidence that Jim approved the out of trust sales that defrauded Chrysler. Jim's lawyer advised him to settle. They offered Chrysler $20,000 to be paid over the five-year term of the chapter 13 plan. Chrysler accepted the offer, and the bankruptcy judge approved the agreement that they filed with the court.

Ending #2: If Jim testified in court that he knew of and approved the out of trust sales, the bankruptcy judge likely would enter a judgment for Chrysler in the amount of the entire debt plus interest from the date of the filing of the complaint which debt would survive bankruptcy. Some judges, however, would simply rule that the entire debt was not dischargeable in bankruptcy, and direct the parties to litigate the amount due in a state court.

(Continued)

Ending #3: If the bankruptcy judge was convinced that Jim did not know about the sales out of trust, the bankruptcy judge would have found that Jim did not have the requisite specific intent to injure the Chrysler credit. In this situation, Jim would win at the trial and the entire debt owed to Chrysler would be declared discharged in bankruptcy.

as it includes the attorney's fee spread over 12 months. After five years, their debts to Chrysler, the IRS, and all of their unsecured creditors would be discharged, and they would have saved their home.

Ann Wolfe: Divorce, Business, and Real Estate Woes

Ann Wolfe never thought her life would encounter so many twists and turns. When Ann first married Jeff, they loved life and each other and decided to start their own landscaping business in a booming suburb of central Massachusetts. Ann designed the landscapes and managed the business affairs while Jeff and several employees did the labor to plant her designs.

Soon after the birth of their second child, they felt increased pressure on themselves and their business. Jeff drank heavily and did not show up for jobs. The employees slacked off without Jeff's supervision and customers complained. When Jeff crashed his truck and the police charged him with his third drunk-driving offense, Ann decided to end things. She filed for divorce and obtained a restraining order against Jeff.

Fortunately, they could return the company's leased equipment, the business had no debts, and they did not owe much on their credit cards. The divorce court found that their business had no value and that Jeff had no prospects for financial improvement they awarded Ann only $150 per week for child support. Jeff paid for the first year, but then stopped paying. Ann kept her head above water by doing design work for other landscapers, but the cost of living in Massachusetts was too high and she decided to move to Naples, Florida.

A Change

Ann worked as an independent contractor for other landscape designers, charging a hefty hourly rate because of the high demand for her services due to the housing construction boom. After two years, Ann had saved enough money to put a down payment on a small ranch house on Collier Boulevard on Marco Island. Ann decided to give it another try and start her own landscaping design business and signed a five-year lease of an elegant storefront in Old Naples.

Clients flocked to Ann's new business. In her third year, Ann netted $100,000 in salary. She decided to buy a new house in the gated community of Mirror Lakes and to landscape it as a showpiece to attract new clients. The house cost $575,000. Ann used the proceeds of the sale of her Marco Island house to make a $30,000 down payment and financed the rest with a mortgage. The bank also gave her an equity credit line of $60,000 secured by a second mortgage, which she used to fund the landscaping and construction of a pool. Confident of her increasing income, Ann spent most of her savings and tapped out the equity credit line to buy new furnishings for the house. She paid more than $3,000 for her monthly mortgage payment.

A Tough Economy Hits Hard

When the economy slowed, Ann's new clients decreased and several of Ann's regular maintenance customers sold their homes due to financial problems. Ann obtained a $50,000 line of credit, secured by the company's trucks and accounts receivable of the business from Commercial Bank. The bank required as a condition of the loan that Ann refinance her home mortgage. The house needed painting so Ann used the opportunity to increase her first mortgage to $405,000 and her equity line to $75,000. She used the $40,000 of her new equity line proceeds to paint the house and buy a new Chevrolet Tahoe. Originally, her monthly mortgage payment went down to $2,900 even though the mortgages were greater. But after two years, her interest-only mortgage reset and her new monthly payment increased to $4,000.

As the housing market continued to deteriorate and construction of new homes stopped, Ann's customers decreased dramatically. She didn't have enough money to pay the rent on the office or warehouse and both landlords served her notices of eviction. One of her suppliers sued her personally and got an attachment on her house for $10,000. Ann had to close her business.

Her world fell apart fast. Due to defaults in the vehicle leases, the trucks were repossessed. Ann's income dried up, so she started to use her credit cards to buy food and clothes and other necessities. She used her credit card to make three monthly mortgage payments.

Ann asked the bank for help, but the banker would not give her an extension. She fell behind on her mortgage. Ann saw a real estate broker about selling her house but learned that the most she could get for the house would be $375,000 and it could take up to two years to sell.

Ann got a job working for a large hotel in Naples in its grounds department for a monthly salary of $4,000 but could not pay her monthly debt service. When Ann received the bank's notice of foreclosure on her house, she did not know what to do.

Turning to a Lawyer for Help

Ann called a bankruptcy lawyer recommended by her union. The lawyer told her to bring in all of her bills and legal papers. She met with a paralegal for three hours. The lawyer then reviewed the information Ann had given to the paralegal and asked Ann what she hoped to accomplish. She said she could not afford to move. More important, she said that she loved her house and had invested over $100,000 in the landscaping and outdoor space and wanted to keep it.

The lawyer told her that she was lucky that she had obtained a job because only a person with regular income was eligible for chapter 13 bankruptcy. Because of her situation over the past six months, her income calculation on Form B 22C qualified her as a below median income debtor, meaning that she could pay her debts over a three-year bankruptcy plan. He counseled her that chapter 13 bankruptcy was her best option because she could avoid the creditor's judicial lien on her property and avoid her equity credit line. The lawyer required a $2,500 fee plus a $279 filing fee for the bankruptcy court upfront. Ann asked where she could get that kind of money. The lawyer said he could not advise her to borrow more money to pay his fee.

Ann told the lawyer she would need some time to figure out where to get the money for the fees. She learned her union would pay half. After six weeks, Ann had been able to save enough for her half. The paralegal completed the petition, schedules of assets and liabilities, income, and expenses, and statement of financial affairs with the information Ann had provided. All of Ann's exemptions were under Florida law. On Schedule C, Ann claimed the value of her residence as exempt because the Florida Constitution provides homestead protection for the entire value of any equity in a person's home.

However, because the first mortgage exceeded the value of the house, Ann did not have equity in her house even with the homestead. The lawyer listed all of Ann's other assets, including furniture and clothes, with a value of $5,000 and as exempt under Florida law. Ann was surprised by this low valuation, but the lawyer explained that he valued them at the price she could get for them now in a yard sale. The lawyer also explained that only $1,000 of the equity in her vehicle was exempt. She could retain the car but would have to pay its value to creditors over the term of the plan.

To Ann's surprise, her lawyer told her he could modify Ann's mortgage. Ann told the lawyer that she had read in the newspaper article about bankruptcy that home mortgages could not be changed. The lawyer explained that she read about the general rule, but luckily, she came within a narrow exception because she had pledged her house for a business loan and the bank took other collateral in addition to her house. If she had just had an ordinary mortgage, current law prevents her from modifying the mortgage. In addition, Ann could avoid the equity credit line and judicial lien and treat them as unsecured claims because the equity credit line had no property as security and the homestead defeats the judicial lien.

Bump in the Road: The Bank Doesn't Agree to a Modification

Suppose that Ann and the bank holding the first mortgage could not agree on a voluntary loan modification. What are Ann's options in a bankruptcy case?

As her lawyer had explained, in a chapter 13 bankruptcy, her options are limited. She could pay her regular monthly mortgage payment and cure what she owes on the mortgages over the plan period. However, this is not a feasible option for Ann based on her monthly income.

Ann's second option for treating the mortgage in a chapter 13 case is to pay the full balance of the mortgage over the entire plan term. However, Ann would have to pay more than $6,000 per month, plus the trustee's commission.

Ann's attorney explained that a third option existed but it would cost more in legal fees. Because the first mortgage was secured by other property

(Continued)

in addition to her home, she could convert her chapter 13 case to a case under chapter 11. In chapter 11, she could propose a plan of reorganization in which she would reduce the secured claim of the bank to the value of the house, $375,000, and then restructure the terms of the mortgage. Ann agreed, and the attorney filed the appropriate motion to convert, which was quickly allowed by the court. He filed a plan along the lines he had described and proposed that the mortgage be restructured to a 20-year fixed mortgage with interest payable at a fixed rate 6 percent per year, with payments of $2,686.82 each month. Together with the plan, the attorney filed a disclosure statement backed up by an appraisal of the real estate. The bank had no basis to object to such treatment and the court confirmed the plan.

The lawyer explained that the first mortgage was modifiable in chapter 13 if they did a cramdown in the chapter 13 plan. A *cramdown plan* means that Ann would have to pay the value of the house over the three-year plan term—an impossibility for her. Another option would be to cure the defaults over the term of the plan. If she elected this second option, she would also have to make the regular monthly mortgage payment—another impossibility for her.

The lawyer advised her to explore a modification of the first mortgage under the Home Affordable Modification Program (HAMP), a recently established federal program for distressed borrowers. Participants in that program can negotiate with the lender to restructure the terms of the mortgage, obtain an extension of the loan term of up to 40 years and a decrease in the interest rate. The lawyer submitted on her behalf an application to HAMP. Within three weeks, a modification was approved. Ann's first mortgage was rewritten for a principal amount of the current balance due of $390,000 with interest payable for the first two years of the plan of 3.5 percent. Ann could afford the new monthly payment of $2,000 with her new salary. The rate would go up to 4.3 percent in the third and fourth year, and then it would be 5.2 percent after the fifth year for the next 30 years. Ann was thrilled with this new mortgage. If she made timely mortgage payments for three months, the modifications would be permanent.

The lawyer filed Ann's chapter 13 bankruptcy. Ann's chapter 13 plan provided for:

1. Approval of the HAMP voluntary modification at a lower rate
2. Avoidance by stripping down the undersecured second mortgage from a secured claim to an unsecured claim and payment of a 15 percent dividend on the claim
3. Avoidance of the judicial lien and payment of a 15 percent dividend on the claim as an unsecured claim
4. Payment of 15 percent to other unsecured creditors, including credit card companies, the lease obligations, and suppliers

The reason Ann has to pay the 15 percent dividend to creditors is because she is keeping the vehicle and not all of its value is exempt from creditors. Although she was entitled to exempt $1,000 of the vehicle's equity, the nonexempt equity was $6,000 based on the Blue Book value of the SUV. The $6,000 would be paid to creditors over the plan term. Based on expected creditors' claims of approximately $150,000, a 15 percent dividend should be approved by the bankruptcy court. Ann would also have to pay the trustee's fee resulting in a monthly plan payment of $170 a month for the three-year term that allows, in most cases, at least a partial repayment to most creditors.

Bump in the Road: The Trustee Objects to the Plan!

At the Section 341 meeting of creditors, what if the chapter 13 trustee questions Ann about her new job and her income potential? After reviewing the plan and Ann's testimony, the chapter 13 trustee would file an objection to the plan. The trustee asserted that Ann was not devoting enough of her projected disposable income to unsecured creditors under the plan and that the bankruptcy court should require Ann to pay her unsecured creditors a larger dividend.

Ann's attorney filed a response to the trustee's objection. He stated that Ann's payment terms under the plan were legally proper because the mortgage expenses that existed on the petition date were the applicable expenses in determining Ann's projected disposable income. The court should not look at the expenses as modified or avoided. The bankruptcy court scheduled a hearing based on the trustee's objection.

(Continued)

The court ruled that the Ann's position was legally correct. The mortgage expenses as of the petition date determined Ann's projected disposable income. The court overruled the trustee's objection to confirmation and confirmed the plan. The court added that in the event Ann's income increased because of salary increases during the plan term, the trustee could then seek a modification of Ann's plan and increase the amount she paid to unsecured creditors.

No creditors objected to Ann's plan, and the bankruptcy court confirmed her plan. The hotel was pleased with Ann's performance and she progressed up the ladder of the hotel's grounds department, becoming assistant manager. She received a moderate raise each year and faithfully made her plan payments. At the end of three years, her debts of were discharged. She has continued to make her mortgage payments as modified under HAMP and has kept her beloved home.

Lessons Learned

These two cases show some of the benefits of chapter 13, including the ability to cure mortgage defaults, to strip down totally undersecured mortgages, to avoid judicial liens, and to discharge unsecured claims after payment of a properly calculated dividend over the term of a chapter 13 bankruptcy plan. Many chapter 13 debtors report favorably on the benefits of a chapter 13 bankruptcy. Chapter 13 enables debtors to retain their assets, including most often their house, as long as they continue to make payments, and it grants them relief from overwhelming unsecured debt. Most important, chapter 13 teaches people how to properly budget their income and expenses because they learn to commit their income to a plan for a three-to five-year term.

Points to Remember

- Make sure that you qualify for chapter 13 by having regular income and have secured and unsecured debts that do not exceed the statutory maximum amounts.
- Generally, a home mortgage cannot be modified in a chapter 13 plan but defaults can be cured, and there are exceptions to the general rule.

- The amount you as a debtor have to pay to unsecured creditors under a chapter 13 plan depends on both the amount of your projected disposable income over the plan term and the value of your nonexempt assets. Understand that when you file a chapter 13 bankruptcy, you commit to a definite plan term of three to five years of payments and you are under the jurisdiction of the bankruptcy court during the term of the plan.

CHAPTER

19

A Trip through Chapter 11 Bankruptcy

And that's why earlier today GM did what Chrysler has successfully done and filed for chapter 11 bankruptcy with the support of its key stakeholders and the United States government. In all likelihood, this process will take more time for GM than it did for Chrysler because GM is a bigger, more complex company. But Chrysler's extraordinary success reaffirms my confidence that GM will emerge from its bankruptcy process quickly and as a stronger and more competitive company.
    —President Barack Obama, June 1, 2009, remarks
    about General Motors' chapter 11 bankruptcy filing

When General Motors, Chrysler, and United Airlines filed for bankruptcy, they filed under chapter 11 of the Bankruptcy Code. Most people think about large corporations when they hear chapter 11 bankruptcy because the typical case involves an entity that owns or operates a business. Large and small companies, whether publicly or privately owned, qualify for chapter 11 bankruptcy relief. They can file even when they have sufficient assets to cover their debts.

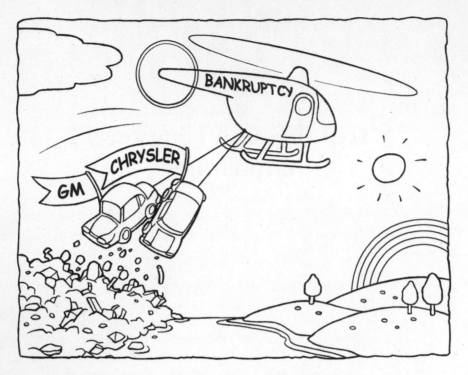

Copyright © 2010 New Way Solutions, www.newwaysolutions.com.

Individuals may also be debtors in chapter 11 bankruptcy cases. Typically, individuals who seek bankruptcy relief under chapter 11 do so because their debts exceed the limitations under chapter 13. An individual chapter 11 case closely resembles a chapter 13 case because debtors must devote their property and their projected disposable income acquired after the beginning of their case to the repayment of creditors for up to five years. The bankruptcy court does not grant individual debtors in a chapter 11 case a discharge of their debt until they complete their chapter 11 bankruptcy plan.

Chapter 11 Basics

Whether involving an individual or businesses, typical chapter 11 bankruptcy cases allow the debtors to continue to operate their businesses or oversee their lives and to stay in control of all of their assets while they restructure their finances. By allowing the debtor to stay in control of the business, chapter 11 reinforces the theory that an operating business's value exceeds that of a business sold off in pieces.

However, if a debtor commits fraud or mismanages assets, the bankruptcy court can terminate the debtor's control and appoint a trustee to take over the business's or the individual's case. Still, the Bankruptcy Code does not require a debtor to retain all assets, and a chapter 11 debtor can sell assets by following proper procedures and obtaining court approval. Over the past decade, chapter 11 cases increasingly involve a quick sale of substantially all assets rather than a reorganization of a business's financial affairs through the more lengthy and cumbersome plan process.

The five biggest chapter 11 bankruptcy filings in history:

Lehman Brothers: Prebankruptcy Assets: $691 billion
Filed: September 15, 2008
Washington Mutual: Prebankruptcy Assets: $327.9 billion
Filed: September 26, 2008
WorldCom: Prebankruptcy Assets: $103.9 billion
Filed: July 21, 2002
General Motors: Prebankruptcy Assets: $91 billion
Filed: June 1, 2009
CIT Group: Prebankruptcy Assets: $71 billion
Filed: November 1, 2009

Source: www.cnbc.com/id/26720522

While in chapter 11, the debtor can use the collateral of its secured lender and even borrow money to operate or exit chapter 11. Unless the court appoints a trustee, during the first 120 days of a chapter 11 case, only the debtor has the exclusive right to file a chapter 11 bankruptcy plan. The plan determines how much creditors will be paid and when they will be paid. The plan must classify claims according to their legal priority. Along with the plan, the debtor, or whoever proposes the plan if the debtor's exclusive period has expired, must file a disclosure statement providing adequate information to creditors to enable them to decide whether to accept or reject the plan. The disclosure statement should describe the debtor's financial problems, assets, and liabilities, treatment of creditors under the plan, alternatives to the plan, and feasibility of the plan. The bankruptcy court will determine if the disclosure statement has sufficient information so that the plan can be circulated for voting.

Creditors are placed in classes according to the type of debt they are owed and other legal rights. The plan, provides how the debtor will pay each class of creditors. Any class of claims that has its legal rights altered by the plan are considered impaired. If a class of claims is not impaired under the plan, that class is deemed to have accepted the plan. If a class is impaired, however, that class of claims votes on the plan. If the plan contains more than one impaired class of claims, at least one impaired class must vote to accept the plan. A class accepts the plan if more than half the creditors in the class and holders of at least two-thirds of that class's debt actually vote to accept the plan. If the plan is accepted by all classes or by at least one impaired class, bankruptcy court approval is still required.

The debtor must demonstrate that the plan is in the best interest of creditors, meaning that under the plan, creditors will receive as much as they would have if the debtor had filed a chapter 7 liquidation case. The debtor must also show that the plan is feasible, meaning that the debtor will not likely need further reorganization after the court confirms the plan. Finally, if a class of claims votes to reject the plan, the bankruptcy court can still confirm the plan if the debtor can show that the plan does not discriminate unfairly against the rejecting class and that the plan is fair and equitable as to the rejecting class. Under a chapter 11 plan, the debtor may obtain a cramdown—a modification of secured claims—by restructuring the debt and paying the value of the collateral over time at a present value rate of interest. The bankruptcy court will hold a confirmation hearing and determine whether to approve the plan. For corporations, partnerships, and business entities, the confirmation of a plan effectuates an immediate discharge of debts. For individuals, the debtor does not obtain a discharge until completion of plan payments.

Chapter 11 has special rules for small-business cases, cases commenced by debtors engaged in a commercial activity with debts that do not exceed $2,000,000. The small-business case rules allow a simpler and quicker reorganization process with increased oversight by the U.S. trustee. Chapter 11 also has special rules for single-asset real estate cases, those in which the debtor's only asset is a parcel of real estate. These cases are treated differently than other chapter 11 cases. The debtor has to file a reorganization plan more quickly in a single-asset real estate case to avoid foreclosure.

Juan and Maria Morales: Measure Twice, File Once

The life of a self-employed home contractor can be tough but also financially rewarding. Contractors frequently encounter problems obtaining customers, paying for supplies, paying their subcontractors, handling delays in construction, paying employees, addressing customer complaints, and collecting what their customers owe them. The details of the business can be overwhelming. With hard work, careful money management, and savvy decisions with real estate opportunities, a contractor can acquire properties and renovate them for sale or self-ownership to complement his everyday work.

Juan Morales embraced his life as a self-employed contractor from Bridgeton, New Jersey. Bridgeton, a small southern New Jersey town, enjoyed a building renaissance in the mid-1980s. Juan settled in Bridgeton after emigrating from Mexico. He worked for several years as a laborer for other contractors and learned plenty by paying particular attention to their work. In the late 1990s, Juan decided to venture out on his own in the hope of making more money and being his own boss. He initially renovated Victorian homes for their owners, and he did well. Because of his success, he purchased multifamily properties, renovated them, and converted them to condominiums or apartments for sale.

Juan also purchased apartment buildings and renovated them for his ownership or to rent to tenants. For some of the apartments in his buildings, he obtained Section 8 designation from the U.S. Department of Housing and Urban Development (HUD), meaning that the federal government would directly pay him the rent of low-income tenants. By 2005 he owned four buildings with four, six, eight, and ten apartments. He also owned a renovated Victorian single-family home with his wife, Maria. Juan and Maria owned all of the real estate holdings individually. Juan's contracting company was unincorporated and operated as a "d/b/a," or doing business as.

Picking Up Business . . . and Mortgages

Juan and Maria took out at least one mortgage on each apartment building they owned. Juan's accountant advised him to keep refinancing for tax purposes and reinvest the proceeds into the building. For two of the buildings, Juan had obtained second mortgages. He used the proceeds of these second mortgages to fund repair and maintenance of the buildings, and occasionally, the operations of his construction company. When the apartments were fully tenanted, the income covered the debt service, the expenses of owning the properties, and generated a small profit each month.

Juan continued to renovate other properties for customers. The business's only assets were Juan's personal tools, a pickup truck, and his sweat equity. Juan operated his construction business out of his home. He employed subcontractors separately for each job and had no salaried employees.

In late 2008, Juan entered into a $500,000 contract as the general contractor for the complete renovation of a Victorian mansion, a project that would require hiring six subcontractors and take nine months. The contract required all subcontractors be licensed by the state and insured. The owners of the mansion reserved the right to disapprove any subcontractor. The project had issues from the beginning. The first phase of demolition took longer than expected. Juan hired a plumbing contractor who did not have insurance or a license from the state, and the plumber hit a pipe from the street causing some flooding in the basement. The owners complained about the water damage, so Juan remedied the problem out of his own pocket. The homeowners made many changes and upgrades to their plans. Juan completed the changes and billed the homeowners for the extras.

Complaining Customers and Tenants

The homeowners of the Victorian mansion complained about the quality of the work and about the delays. Dissatisfied with the progress, they withheld the fifth progress payment. Juan had to pay the subcontractors himself. He continued with the job in the hope of collecting the sums due him, but when the project was 80 percent complete, the owners terminated Juan. They quickly filed a complaint in New Jersey Superior Court for $100,000 in damages for breach of contract and misrepresentations. Juan counterclaimed for amounts due him under the contract and change orders. The state court granted the homeowners an attachment on the Morales's house to secure any judgment.

At the same time, problems developed with Juan's apartment buildings. Two of his tenants lost their jobs and stopped paying rent. When Juan sued them in housing court for eviction and back rent, the tenants counterclaimed asserting that housing code violations existed in the apartments. The housing court stayed the eviction proceedings and allowed the tenants to occupy the apartments at a vastly reduced rent pending a trial. Moreover, unbeknownst to Juan, one tenant sold drugs from the apartment. The police arrested the tenant, but he posted bail and continued to use and sell drugs in the apartment. Another tenant stopped paying rent and moved out of her apartment. Her apartment needed substantial repairs and new appliances and remained vacant. Because of these problems, Juan couldn't pay the mortgage for each building. One of the mortgagees sued and obtained a receiver for one of the apartment buildings. The receiver took control and collected the rents for that building and remitted them directly to the mortgage company.

The appointment of the receiver had a snowball effect. Other banks served Juan with notices of intention to conduct foreclosure sales of the apartment buildings. Juan could see no way to contain the situation himself and decided to consult with a bankruptcy lawyer.

A Turning Point

Juan made appointments with several lawyers. The first lawyer, a consumer lawyer, did not appear to understand real estate ownership or the operations of commercial real estate. The second lawyer bragged about all of the success he had had in bankruptcy cases, but when Juan checked with the bar regulatory agency, he discovered that the lawyer had been suspended from practice several years ago and had pending complaints of unethical conduct against him. Juan interviewed a third lawyer, Steve, who specialized in bankruptcy and seemed to have experience in all types of bankruptcy cases. Juan explained that he wished to retain his home and the apartment buildings and to challenge the case against him by the homeowners.

After the Moraleses obtained their credit counseling briefing, which took about 10 minutes, Steve filed a chapter 11 bankruptcy petition on their behalf. Steve required a $20,000 retainer plus the filing fee of $1,039. After using up the retainer, Steve would bill

$425 an hour and apply to the bankruptcy court for payment of amounts due every three months. Under a written fee agreement, the Moraleses would pay the remaining attorney's fees on confirmation of a plan of reorganization. Steve explained that because the Moraleses owed over $2 million in mortgage debt, they owed too much secured debt to qualify for chapter 13.

Moreover, the case would not be considered a small-business chapter 11 for the same reason. When Juan asked why Maria should be on the bankruptcy petition, Steve explained that she should file because she was also liable on the mortgages. If Maria did not file, the banks could pursue her for payment on the mortgages. Steve also explained to Juan that record keeping during the chapter 11 must be impeccable. Juan had to establish special bank accounts called Debtor in Possession accounts, file monthly operating reports with the U.S. trustee, as well as maintain and show the bankruptcy court that they were current on insurances and tax payments.

Bump in the Road: Juan Fails to File Operating Reports

Suppose that Juan's record keeping was deficient. Juan became so busy getting new contracts that for two months he failed to file his operating reports with the U.S. trustee. The U.S. trustee then filed a motion to convert the chapter 11 case to a chapter 7 liquidation case. The bankruptcy court set a hearing on the U.S. trustee's motion.

Juan brought the outstanding reports to the hearing. The bankruptcy judge would likely admonish Juan that he had to keep current on the reports and that she would continue the motion to convert generally, warning that any further omission by Juan would result in conversion to chapter 7 bankruptcy without further hearing. If Juan failed to file another report, the case would be automatically converted upon the U.S. trustee's report to the bankruptcy court and Juan would lose his construction business. Also, control of the bankruptcy case would go to a chapter 7 trustee who would liquidate all assets.

The lawyer emphasized that Juan and Maria needed to obtain quick appraisals on all of their properties, so that they could accurately list the values on their schedules within two weeks after the filing. The values were also needed to facilitate

Table 19.1   Real Property Ownership

Real Estate Owned	Value	Mortgages, Liens, Total Debt
Home	$475,000	1st mortgage: $393,000 2nd mortgage: $97,000 Attachment: $100,000 **Total = $590,000**
Apartment Building A	$500,000	Mortgage: $510,000 **Total = $510,000**
Apartment Building B	$375,000	1st mortgage: $390,000 2nd mortgage: $50,000 **Total = $440,000**
Apartment Building C	$425,000	1st mortgage: $405,000 2nd mortgage: $72,000 **Total = $477,000**
Apartment Building D	$620,000	Mortgage: $525,000 **Total = $525,000**

the filing of a motion to use cash collateral. In this case, cash collateral primarily consisted of the apartment building rents. Steve explained that obtaining appraisal reports from licensed and reputable experts, although expensive, crucial in a chapter 11 case because the appraisals lay the foundation for the plan's proposed treatment of the mortgage companies' claims and the liquidation analysis in the plan. After obtaining the appraisals, Juan learned that the properties had depreciated due to the economic downturn. Table 19.1 compares the asset and liability of their real estate.

An Emergency Request for Cash

Steve recommended that Juan and Maria's first request to the bankruptcy court should be an emergency motion for use of cash collateral. The motion to use cash collateral requests that the court approve the debtors' continued collection of rents and to use of the rents for payment of expenses of the properties. Bankruptcy courts will allow chapter 11 debtors to use cash collateral—cash that a secured creditor has a lien upon—if the debtor provides the creditor adequate protection so that the value of the secured claim will not decline during the bankruptcy case. In the motion, they would submit a budget for the next three months of the projected income and expenses for each of the properties. The lawyer indicated that he would request that the court approve adequate protection payments to the mortgagees of each property. The adequate protection payments would be for an amount less than the regular monthly mortgage payments based on the appraised value of the buildings and the debtors' proposed restructuring of the mortgage debts. They would propose monthly adequate protection payments ranging from $1,200 to $2,400 to each building's first mortgagee and no payment to the second mortgagees.

The second mortgagees did not have sufficient assets to protect their liens and were considered underwater. The bankruptcy judge found that the properties were not declining in value and therefore the second mortgage lenders were not entitled to any monthly adequate protection payments. However, as a condition of the use of cash collateral, the court ordered that the debtor escrow one-twelfth of the annual real estate taxes and stay current in the payment of all insurance policies on the properties.

After the filing of the emergency motion to use cash collateral, the bankruptcy court held an immediate hearing. The bank's lawyers appeared at the hearing and objected asserting that the debtor proffered inaccurate valuations. Because the banks did not provide their own appraisals, the bankruptcy judge authorized the debtors' use of cash collateral for 30 days, continued the hearing, and directed the banks to obtain appraisals by the next hearing. Because each bank obtained updated appraisal opinions that confirmed those filed by the debtor, the banks withdrew their objections to the use of cash collateral and entered into a stipulation for use of cash collateral pending submission of the debtor's plan of reorganization.

Lien Avoidance: Free the Home from Debt

New Jersey does not have a state homestead exemption, so on Schedule C, Juan and Maria claimed the federal homestead of exemption of $21,625 available to each debtor, for a total of $40,400 in available exempt equity in their home. Steve told Juan and Maria to continue to make their regular monthly mortgage payment to the first mortgagee on their home, but to stop paying the second mortgagee, as it was totally underwater. Steve filed a motion under Bankruptcy Code Section 506(d) and Federal Rule of Bankruptcy Procedure 3016 to value the home and avoid the second mortgage. After reviewing the appraisal, the second mortgagee did not oppose the motion. The second mortgage on the home was avoided and declared an unsecured debt.

Steve then filed a motion to avoid the judicial lien of the homeowners who sued Juan, maintaining that the attachment impaired the debtors' homestead exemption. The homeowners opposed the motion and claimed that the value of the home exceeded the appraisal. In addition, the homeowners filed a complaint to except or remove their debt from the bankruptcy discharge on the grounds that Juan defrauded them in hiring subcontractors who were not licensed and approved by them. The bankruptcy court held an evidentiary hearing on the value of the home at which the Moraleses and the homeowners presented the expert opinions of their respective appraisers. The bankruptcy judge found that the Moraleses' appraisal evidence was valid, rejected several of the comparable sales utilized by the homeowner's appraiser, and allowed Juan and Maria to avoid the judicial lien of the homeowners.

Bump in the Road: Higher Valuations

Suppose that the value of the Moraleses' real estate assets was higher than the appraisal reports obtained at the beginning of the case indicated and that all of the banks' claims were fully secured. How would that change the plan of reorganization? First, with respect to their home, the Moraleses would not be able to avoid the second mortgage and would have to make regular payments to the second mortgagee. The Moraleses could still cure any prepetition arrears on these mortgages in the plan. Moreover, the Moraleses would not be able avoid the judicial lien of the homeowners in full. Instead, the bankruptcy court would determine the extent to which the attachment impaired the debtors' homestead exemption and the homeowners would have a secured claim for the amount not impaired.

As to the apartment buildings, the plan would have to pay the secured claims in full, to the value of the real estate. The plan could modify the terms of the loans on the apartment buildings and provide new interest rates, that could be closer to a market rate, plus a cost adjustment for risk as the Moraleses previously defaulted.

Within three months after commencing the chapter 11 case, the Moraleses submitted a plan of reorganization and a disclosure statement. The disclosure statement summarized the terms of the plan, the reasons for their financial trouble, their liquidation analysis, and the way they intended to implement their plan. The disclosure statement also included projections of the income and expenses of the apartment buildings and Juan's business. The chapter 11 plan provided for a strip down to unsecured status of all of the banks' claims that were no longer secured by property and rewrote the terms of the notes and mortgages that remained secured by the properties. The banks would receive the value of their loan up to the value of the property, but over the new term of 15 years at a lower 5 percent rate of interest. The mortgages that were totally undersecured would be avoided and would be treated as unsecured claims, and receive the same dividend as other unsecured creditors.

The Moraleses would continue to pay their mortgage on their home and repay (over the next three years through the plan) the two months that they fell in arrears. The arrears are the payments they missed before the bankruptcy. The Moraleses indicated in their plan that they intended to object to the mansion homeowners' claim so that the bankruptcy court would determine what, if anything, the Moraleses owed the homeowners. The unsecured claims in the Moraleses' case consisted of deficiency claims from the undersecured mortgages, small credit card balances, and other bills. The Moraleses would pay the unsecured claim's 15 percent dividend under the plan. The plan also provided that in the event the Moraleses earned additional income after confirming the plan enabling them to pay

Bump in the Road: Unpaid Taxes

Suppose that the late operating reports Juan filed demonstrated that he had not paid his postpetition taxes, had allowed his liability insurance to lapse, and had been paying his suppliers and workers for jobs performed during the chapter 11 case. In addition, the reports showed that Juan had no new contracts in the pipeline. In this situation, the bankruptcy court would likely grant the motion to convert the chapter 11 case to a chapter 7 liquidation case and Juan would lose his business.

more than 15 percent, they would modify the plan and increase the dividend.

The Disclosure Statement described the plan and the events that led up to the filing, the operations of the apartment buildings and the construction business, as well as their personal expenditures. It described all assets and liabilities and stated what creditors would get if the case were converted to a liquidation under chapter 7. In the Disclosure Statement, Steve made a persuasive argument that creditors would be better off voting for the plan, explaining that the Moraleses would submit all of their projected disposable income for the next five years to the repayment of creditors.

On the Way to Plan Confirmation

The bankruptcy court approved the Disclosure Statement for circulation to creditors for their vote and set an objection dead-line and a confirmation hearing. None of the secured creditors objected to the plan, which meant that they agreed to the treat-ment of their secured claims. The secured creditors who held deficiency claims cast their votes as unsecured creditors in favor of the plan. Because these banks with deficiency claims held more than two-thirds of the claims and more than one-half in number of the claims, the bankruptcy court considered the plan accepted by the unsecured class.

The homeowners voted against the plan and filed an objection to confirmation of the plan. The bankruptcy court scheduled an emergency hearing to estimate the homeowners' claim for voting purposes. The bankruptcy court determined that the Moraleses owed the homeowners $25,000 at most because they never paid Juan for the changes and extras he did on the mansion. The court ruled that the homeowners did not affect acceptance of the plan by the unsecured creditor class. The court then scheduled a trial for their complaint that the debt owed by Juan arose from fraud and should be excepted from discharge. At the confirmation hearing, Steve presented evidence that Juan's apartment build-ings were now fully tenanted and generating positive cash flow and that he had two renovation jobs under contract that would result in a profit. The bankruptcy court found that the plan was feasible and was in the best interest of the creditors, so it confirmed the chapter 11 plan.

Bump in the Road: Homeowners' Claims against Juan Are True!

Suppose that the homeowners were able to demonstrate that Juan never intended to hire licensed subcontractors as he promised and that the incompetent subcontractors caused the damages. The homeowners claimed Juan walked off the job early without finishing. The bankruptcy court would still estimate the homeowners' claim at confirmation and hold a trial on the complaint of the homeowners to determine whether to except the debt from discharge (i.e., not include it in the debt that would be discharged). Under this scenario, the bankruptcy court would likely find that some amount that the homeowners' claim would be excepted from discharge, and although the debt to the homeowners could be included in the plan, the debt would not be affected by the bankruptcy discharge. The debt to the homeowners would have to be paid in full either through the plan or outside of the plan.

Two months later the court held a trial on the homeowners' dischargeability complaint and Juan's counterclaim. The court found that although Juan breached his contract to hire only licensed subcontractors, his breach did not amount to fraud. The judge further found that Juan did not owe any debt to the homeowners, but the homeowners owed Juan $18,000 for unpaid extras. The bankruptcy judge entered a judgment for Juan in that amount.

Points to Remember

- Don't wait until immediately before a foreclosure or some imminent action to investigate filing for bankruptcy.
- Interview several attorneys and hire a competent bankruptcy lawyer to represent you in any bankruptcy case, especially a chapter 11 reorganization case. Recognize that chapter 11 is not inexpensive, but in the long run, if you are able to meet the requirements of the Bankruptcy Code, you will be able to retain assets and likely pay debts at a discount over time.
- Develop your exit strategy from chapter 11 even before you file the chapter 11 petition by obtaining evidence of value of assets and knowing your liabilities.

- Disclose everything, including all horror stories, to your bankruptcy lawyer so that a strategy can be developed and no surprises disrupt the case.
- During your chapter 11 case, cooperate with the U.S. trustee by filing all required documents, especially monthly operating reports and insurance and tax proofs. If a problem arises in reporting or incurring postpetition debts, make a proposal to the U.S. trustee to cure the defaults in advance to prevent the U.S. trustee's Office from taking action, such as, filing a motion to appoint a trustee or convert the chapter 11 case to a chapter 7 case.

A Trip through Chapter 12 Bankruptcy

You can make a small fortune in farming—provided you start with a large one.

—Anonymous

To meet the economic realities and problems unique to family farming and fishing, chapter 12 of the Bankruptcy Code provides special treatment for the debts of family farmers and fishermen. More streamlined, less complicated, and usually less expensive than chapter 11 bankruptcy cases, chapter 12 eliminates many of the barriers that family farmers and fishermen had faced when seeking to reorganize successfully under either chapter 11 or 13 of the Bankruptcy Code.

Chapter 12 Basics

First enacted in 1986 to redress the plight of the agricultural industry and to protect farmers, chapter 12 bankruptcy cases originally were made available to only family farmers with regular annual income. In 2005, Congress made family fishermen also eligible for chapter 12.

Reorganizations under chapter 12 resemble reorganizations under both chapter 11 and chapter 13.

Chapter 12 has eligibility requirements. In order to qualify as a family farmer or fisherman, one must have regular annual income and have debts that do not exceed the debt limitations presently capped at $3,792,650 in the case of farmers and $1,757,475 in the case of fishermen. Like all bankruptcy chapters, the debtor files the bankruptcy petition and schedules of assets, liabilities, income, and expenses. Involuntary petitions by creditors to put a person or entity into a chapter 12 bankruptcy case are not permitted. In fact, a family farmer or family fisherman may not be the subject of an involuntary bankruptcy case under any chapter of the Bankruptcy Code.

The automatic stay applies to both the debtor and any codebtor upon case commencement. The debtor remains in possession of assets and continues the operation of the farming or fishing business,

unless the bankruptcy court takes control from the debtor for cause. A standing trustee supervises the debtor's case. The debtor must provide documents and information and submit payments under the plan to the trustee.

Under the Bankruptcy Code, family farmers and family fishermen fall into two categories: an individual or individual and spouse, and a corporation or partnership. Farmers or fishermen in the first category must meet each of the following four criteria:

- The individual or husband and wife must be engaged in a farming operation or a commercial fishing operation.
- The total debts (secured and unsecured) of the operation must not exceed $3,792,650 (if a farming operation) or $1,757,475 (if a commercial fishing operation).
- If a family farmer, at least 50 percent, and if a family fisherman at least 80 percent, of the total debts that are fixed in amount (exclusive of debt for the debtor's home) must be related to the farming or commercial fishing operation.
- More than 50 percent of the gross income of the individual or the husband and wife for the preceding tax year (or, for family farmers only, for each of the second- and third-prior tax years) must have come from the farming or commercial fishing operation.

In order for a corporation or partnership to fall within the second category, the corporation or partnership must meet each of the following criteria:

- More than one-half the outstanding stock or equity in the corporation or partnership must be owned by one family or by one family and its relatives.
- The family or the family and its relatives must conduct the farming or commercial fishing operation.
- More than 80 percent of the value of the corporate or partnership assets must be related to the farming or fishing operation.
- The total indebtedness of the corporation or partnership must not exceed $3,792,650 (if a farming operation) or $1,757,475 (if a commercial fishing operation).
- At least 50 percent for a farming operation or 80 percent for a fishing operation of the corporation's or partnership's

total debts, which are fixed in amount (exclusive of debt for one home occupied by a shareholder) must be related to the farming or fishing operation.
- If the corporation issues stock, the stock cannot be publicly traded.

Under chapter 12 bankruptcy, the debtor submits a reorganization plan for repayment of creditors according to the ability to make payments for a period of up to three years, or five years if the court finds cause exists for a longer plan. Chapter 12 cases proceed on the fast track. The debtor must propose a debt adjustment plan within 90 days after the filing of the petition, and a confirmation hearing is held within 45 days. Both of these deadlines can be extended by the bankruptcy court, however. Throughout the case, the requirement that the debtor provide adequate protection to secured claims is more liberal in chapter 12 than in chapter 13.

Under the chapter 12 plan, the debtor may include provisions that restructure both secured and unsecured debts. The debtor has the right to split any secured claim into secured and unsecured portions. The debtor then treats the deficiency as unsecured and can also alter the terms of a secured loan. Unlike chapter 13, a chapter 12 plan may modify and extend the term of repayment of a secured debt over a period exceeding the plan term. The debtor can also modify the mortgage on the personal residence—an ability no debtor has in any other bankruptcy chapter. The debtor can propose a plan to offer the present value of the claim and make payments through installments amortized over a period of time different from the original loan.

Creditors do not have the right to vote on a chapter 12 bankruptcy plan as in chapter 11, but the court still has the duty to determine that the requirements for confirmation are met. In particular, the court seeks to determine that the debtor is contributing projected disposable income to the payment of creditors under the plan. Chapter 12 contains special tax provisions favorable to debtors. One of the most significant provisions of chapter 12 provides that claims owed to taxing authorities arising from the sale of farm assets are treated as general unsecured claims and can be paid the same dividend rate as to the other unsecured creditors. Chapter 12 does not treat these tax claims as priority claims, which must be paid in full in the other bankruptcy chapters.

The Jensens: Making a Silk Purse Out of a Sow's Ear

Anders and Anna Jensen, third-generation farmers, inherited a 150-acre farm in Mitchell County, Iowa, 23 years ago in their first year of marriage. Their farm includes their 20-acre homestead. Anders received a bachelor's degree in Farm Management Agriculture from Iowa State University. Hogs comprised the primary operation of their farming business. As of 2009, their sow herd exceeded 500. They bred their own hogs, fattened them with grain that they grew on the farm, and raised the hogs for sale to slaughter. They also built a farrowing house from which they sold feeder pigs. They operated a farrow-to-finish farm. Selling their hogs constituted their major source of income. They also leased 40 acres of land to a friend for cash rent of $1,500 a month—below fair market value for a lease of farm land in their area. The Jensens also owned several livestock trailers and farrowing equipment.

In mid-2009, two of their hogs came down with swine disease. The sickness spread through the herd and drastically reduced their income and negatively impacted their operations. Their bank refused to finance further operations because of the bad publicity over the swine disease. The Jensens had to kill all of the infected slaughter hogs and others that had been exposed to swine disease. They also had to sell the rest of the slaughter hogs because their funds for operations had evaporated. The proceeds of the sale went to the bank because of its lien on all farming assets to prevent the bank from foreclosing on the farm. Still, even after paying $100,000 to the bank, they owed the bank $200,000. Because payments to the mortgagees depleted their funds, the Jensens could not pay the equipment lenders who repossessed the trailers and other equipment. The Jensens produced only minimal income from selling the babies of the breeding hogs and the small amount of rent from their tenant friend.

During January 2010, the Jensens consulted with their accountant on the filing of their tax returns. On their initial draft federal tax return for 2009, the Jensens reported $124,531 of farm income attributable to the sale of livestock, produce grains, and other products, which included the sale of the healthy hogs. They reported the sale of their healthy hogs as a capital gain of $55,000. As a result of the capital gain, the Jensens owed the IRS $30,550 for their 2009 taxes, which they could not pay.

The Jensens consulted a local bankruptcy lawyer, who advised them to immediately file a chapter 12 bankruptcy. The lawyer explained that chapter 12 contains many favorable provisions for family farmers, including beneficial treatment of tax claims resulting from the sale of farm assets used in the debtor's farming operations during the bankruptcy. The capital gains tax debt from the sale of the slaughter hogs before the bankruptcy would be considered general unsecured claims, which could be paid the same percentage as other unsecured creditors. In other bankruptcy chapters, these tax debts would be considered priority claims, which have to be paid in full.

The Jensens could then sell the breeding hogs during their chapter 12 case and use the proceeds to pay the bank's lien. They could pay the taxing authority and the other unsecured creditors 10 percent over the term of the plan. Moreover, in their plan, they could reject the below-market lease they have with their friend and find a better-paying tenant. The lawyer would also include in the plan a request that the court approve their new agreement with a new business contact, Real Squeal, which would bring their income to a level to fund the plan through a change in their business focus.

Bump in the Road: Tenant Objects to Rejection

Suppose that the tenant objects to rejection of his favorable lease. In this event, bankruptcy law provides two options to the tenant. The tenant can either treat the lease as terminated and file a claim for damages or the tenant can remain on the premises and pay the rent at the contract rate. If the tenant elects the latter option, the Jensens would be bound to accept the lower rent and could not increase their income by finding a new higher-paying tenant.

The lawyer filed the petition and plan on February 1, 2010. The IRS objected to confirmation of the plan because the debtors sought to reduce its claim, but the bankruptcy court overruled the objection and confirmed the plan. In mid-2010, the Jensens sold their breeding sows by public auction, under the authority of the bankruptcy court, and realized $50,000, which they paid to the bank. The balance of the bank's claim in the sum of $150,000 was considered an unsecured claim because the bank no longer had any collateral securing it.

Bump in the Road: Missed Payment to the Bank

Suppose that the Jensens don't pay the bank from the sale of the slaughter hogs but instead use the proceeds of the hog sale for operation of the business. Here, the bank's claim against the Jensens would remain $200,000 and would be unsecured. The bank files a complaint against the Jensens to except the $100,000, the money from the sale of the slaughter hogs, from the bankruptcy discharge on the grounds that the Jensens converted the bank's collateral through the sale. In addition, the bank claims that this conversion constituted a debt for willful and malicious injury that cannot be discharged under Section 523 (a)(6) of the Bankruptcy Code.

The Jensens maintain that they had no intent to injure the bank when they used the proceeds of the bank's collateral to fund their farming operations. The bankruptcy court, however, finds that the Jensens knew they were violating the security agreement with the bank at the time they sold the hogs without remitting the proceeds to the bank. The bankruptcy court enters a judgment excepting $100,000 of their debt to the bank from the bankruptcy discharge. The court's decision means that the Jensens must pay the $100,000 in full to the bank because the bankruptcy case does not affect this debt.

Although they realized a capital gain, the Jensens would not have to pay that portion of their 2010 tax in full. The Jensens entered into a deal with Real Squeal and became custom livestock operators. By paying less than $20,000 over three years under their plan, consisting of the creditors' dividend, the chapter 12 trustee's commission, their lawyer's fee, and the bankruptcy court filing fee, the Jensens saved their family farm and their homestead.

Points to Remember

- When considering whether to file a chapter 12 petition, obtain the advice of a competent bankruptcy lawyer who will advise you on the nonbankruptcy and bankruptcy options for your financial situation.
- Chapter 12 has strict eligibility requirements and unless you are a family farmer or fisherman who qualifies for chapter 12 relief, you do not qualify and the bankruptcy court will dismiss your chapter 12 petition.

(Continued)

- Chapter 12 cases proceed quickly, so you should have an exit strategy formulated even before you file your bankruptcy petition.
- In a chapter 12 case, you have many duties including providing documents and information, cooperating with the chapter 12 trustee, and operating your business as a fiduciary to creditors.
- To obtain a discharge in chapter 12, you must obtain confirmation of a plan of reorganization that meets the requirements of the law and that is approved by the bankruptcy court.

Conclusion:
The Road Worth Taking

A journey of a thousand miles must begin with a single step.
—Chinese proverb

When you start out on the road out of debt, you'll need to take a hard look at your financial situation to determine what remedies and resources to pursue. Picking up this book was a giant step in the right direction. Finishing this book means you now have the knowledge and tools to make informed decisions to get out of debt without the confusion and intimidation that so many people experience.

We've shown you the road out of debt but you must make your own way through the long stretches, turns, roadblocks, and other obstacles that stand in the way of your destination: freedom from debt. As Americans, we are under constant pressure to spend, spend, spend . . . and to use our credit rather than hard-earned cash. Living a life free from debt means you have to resist that pressure and stand your ground as a financially responsible person.

If you decide that bankruptcy is your best route out of debt, you will need to plan. Planning for a bankruptcy case can mean the difference between a successful and unsuccessful case. The choice to file for bankruptcy is a serious one: consider the timing, different

325

types of bankruptcy, the prerequisites to eligibility, and your duties as a debtor in a bankruptcy case. By this point in the book, you know that we strongly recommend consulting with a competent bankruptcy lawyer to best understand your legal rights and obligations. With all this information and advice you now have, we know you can make your best decision on whether bankruptcy is right for you.

If you do file for bankruptcy, creditors will stop calling and writing. However, you must complete your duties as the debtor in a bankruptcy case to ensure that your case won't be dismissed and those calls and visits never restart. Once you've made the decision to file, stick with it to the end. Stay on your road.

Getting out of debt will not be as easy or fun as it was getting into debt. However, you will find more satisfaction and more reward in your freedom from debt than any purchase ever brought you. You are now armed with the information and ability to free yourself from all your debts. We wish you the best of luck as you take your journey on the road out of debt.

APPENDIX A

Helpful Resources

Throughout the book, we have referenced specific bankruptcy forms and other resources you may need as you take the road out of debt. The information and forms are numerous and can be daunting when you're not sure where to begin. Whatever your situation may be, there's good information available out there; you just need to know where to look. We have received invaluable information from the resources listed below.

In addition, links to bankruptcy forms, checklists for evaluating your situation, resources concerning the bankruptcy process, and more are available at the book Web site: www.wiley.com/go/roadoutofdebt.com and www.roadoutofdebt.com.

Auto Debt

American Financial Services Association (AFSA): www.afsaonline.org, "Vehicle Repossession Prevention: Steps Taken by Industry," July 2008

Americans Well-informed on Automobile Retailing Economics (AWARE): www.autofinancing101.org

Edmunds.com: www.edmunds.com, "Stay One Step Ahead of the Repo Man"

Fair Debt Collection.com: www.fair-debt-collection.com

To Find out what Your Vehicle is Worth:

Kelly Blue Book: www.kbb.com

N.A.D.A. Appraisal Guides (widely available at gas stations and convenient stores): www.nadaguides.com

Vehix: 1 (866) MY-VEHIX or www.vehix.com

Autotrader.com: 1(866) Auto-Trader (Mon.-Fri. 8 a.m.-8 p.m., Sat. 8 a.m.-6 p.m. EST) or www.autotrader.com

Bankruptcy and Debt Basics

American Association of Retired Persons (AARP): www.aarp.org

American Bankruptcy Institute: www.abiworld.org

Bankrate.com: www.bankrate.com

The Center for Responsible Lending: www.responsiblelending.org/

Elizabeth Warren's works (Harvard Law professor and bankruptcy expert): www.law.harvard.edu/faculty/directory/facdir.php?id=82)

I Hate Debt: www.ihatedebt.com

Jump$tart Coalition for Personal Financial Literacy: www.jumpstartcoalition.org

Mahalo: www.mahalo.com/how-to-deal-with-debt-collectors

MSN Money: http://articles.moneycentral.msn.com

Practical Money Skills: www.practicalmoneyskills.com

Smart Money: www.smartmoney.com

U.S. Bankruptcy Courts: www.uscourts.gov/bankruptcycourts/bankruptcybasics.html

Bankruptcy Forms

Federal forms: www.uscourts.gov/bkforms/index.html
- Form B 1: Voluntary Petition
- Form B 3A: Application and Order to Pay Filing Fee in Installments
- Form B 3B: Application for Waiver of Chapter 7 Filing Fee
- Form B 6: Declaration Concerning Debtor's Schedules

- Form B 6A: Schedule A, Real Property
- Form B 6B: Schedule B, Personal Property
- Form B 6C: Schedule C, Property Claimed as Exempt
- Form B 6D: Schedule D, Creditors Holding Secured Claims
- Form B 6E: Schedule E, Creditors Holding Unsecured Priority Claims
- Form B 6F: Schedule F, Creditors Holding Unsecured Non-priority Claims
- Form B 6G: Schedule G, Executory Contracts and Unexpired Leases
- Form B 6H: Schedule H, Codebtors
- Form B 6I: Schedule I, Current Income of Individual Debtor(s)
- Form B 6J: Schedule J, Current Expenditures of Individual Debtor(s)
- Form B 7: Statement of Financial Affairs
- Form B 8: Chapter 7 Individual Debtor's Statement of Intention
- Form B 9: Notice of Commencement of Case under the Bankruptcy Code, Meeting of Creditors, and Deadlines
- Form B 12: Order and Notice for Hearing on Disclosure Statement (Chapter 11)
- Form B 13: Order Approving Disclosure Statement and Fixing Time for Filing Acceptances or Rejections of Plan, Combined with Notice Thereof (Chapter 11)
- Form B 14: Ballot for Accepting or Rejecting Plan (Chapter 11)
- Form B 15: Order Confirming Plan (Chapter 11)
- Form B 18: Discharge of Debtor (Individual Debtor Chapter 7)
- Form B 18J: Discharge of Joint Debtors (Chapter 7)
- Form B 18JO: Discharge of One Joint Debtor (Chapter 7)
- Form B 18RI: Discharge of Individual Debtor in a Chapter 11 Case
- Form B 18W: Discharge of Debtor After Completion of Chapter 13 Plan
- Form B 21: Statement of Social Security Number
- Form B 22A: Statement of Current Monthly Income and Means Test Calculation (Chapter 7)
- Form B 22B: Statement of Current Monthly Income (Chapter 11)

- Form B 22C: Statement of Current Monthly Income and Calculation of Commitment Period and Disposable Income (Chapter 13)
- Form B 23: Debtor's Certification of Completion of Instructional Course Concerning Financial Management
- Form B 25A: Plan of Reorganization in Small Business Case under Chapter 11
- Form B 25B: Disclosure Statement in Small Business Case under Chapter 11
- Form B 240A: Reaffirmation Documents
- Form B 240B: Motion for Approval of Reaffirmation Agreement
- Form B 240C: Order on Reaffirmation Agreement

Local forms: Check the Web site of the bankruptcy court serving your area for local forms to help you file and complete your Chapter 11 and Chapter 13 cases. You can find the link to your local bankruptcy court at www.uscourts.gov/courtlinks/.

Consumer Credit Debt

National Foundation for Consumer Credit (NFCC): 1 (800) 388-2227 or www.nfcc.org. See www.nfcc.org/FirstStep/firststep_01.cfm for a list of NFCC-approved counselors.

Association of Independent Consumer Credit Counseling Agencies (AICCCA): 1 (866) 703-8787 or www.aiccca.org. See www.aiccca.org/find.cfm for a list of AICCCA-approved counselors.

Better Business Bureau (BBB): 1 (703) 276-0100 or www.bbb.org. See www.bbb.org/us/ to ensure that other consumers have not had difficulties with the credit counselor you are considering hiring.

Credit Abuse Resistance Education (CARE program): www.careprogram.us

Fair Debt Collection.com: www.fair-debt-collection.com

Federal Trade Commission (FTC): Visit www.ftc.gov or call toll-free, 1 (877) FTC-HELP (1(877)382-4357); TTY: 1 (866) 653-4261 to file a complaint or to get free information on consumer issues.

Stop receiving pre-screened credit card offers by notifying each
of the three major credit bureaus, Equifax, Experian, and
Trans Union, through their Web sites:

Equifax: www.equifax.com

Experian: www.experian.com

TransUnion: www.transunion.com

California Debt Blog: www.californiadebtblog.com

RipoffReport.com: www.ripoffreport.com

Scam Busters.org: www.scambusters.org

Legal Help

Contact the clerk of the bankruptcy court, the U.S. Trustee's Office,
or the office of the bankruptcy administrator in your area and ask for
names of competent consumer bankruptcy lawyers.

No matter how you find an attorney, make sure you are completely comfortable with your decision before signing anything.
Also, remember that the biggest advertisement does not guarantee
the best lawyer.

American Bankruptcy Institute: www.abiworld.org

American Bar Association: www.abalawinfo.org/find1.html and
www.abanet.org/legalservices/findlegalhelp/home.cfm
(American Bar Association list of resources including foreclosure resources and information)

American Board of Certification: www.abcworld.org

American College of Bankruptcy: www.amercol.org

Martindale Hubbell Lawyer Rating Service: www.martindale.com

National Association of Consumer Bankruptcy Attorneys: www
.nacba.org

National Consumer Law Center: www.consumerlaw.org or www
.nclc.org.

National Association of Bankruptcy Trustees: www.nabt.com

National Association of Chapter 13 Trustees: www.nactt.com

Thomson West Publications Attorney Locator Service: www.findlaw
.com and bankruptcy.findlaw.com

Filing for Bankruptcy without an Attorney: This resource provides more detailed information about the procedures for

filing for bankruptcy for the individual who chooses to represent him or herself.

www.uscourts.gov/bankruptcycourts/prose.html

Mortgage Debt

The following resources are useful in dealing with mortgage debt, foreclosure, or mortgage scams.

Bank Fraud Victim Center: http://mortgage-home-loan-bank-fraud.com

California Mortgage Saver: www.california-mortgage-saver.com

Comptroller of the Currency U.S. Department of the Treasury: www.helpwithmybank.gov and www.occ.treas.gov, "OCC Consumer Tips for Avoiding Mortgage Modification Scam and Foreclosure Rescue Scams"

FDIC: www.fdic.gov and www.fdic.gov/consumers/loans/prevention/rescue/index.html, "Beware of Foreclosure Rescue and Loan Modification Scams: If It's Too Good to be True, It Probably Is"

Federal Bureau of Investigation (FBI): www.fbi.gov, "2008 Mortgage Fraud Report 'Year in Review'"

Federal Housing Authority (FHA): 1 (800) CALL-FHA or www.fha.com

Federal Trade Commission (FTC): www.ftc.gov/bcp/edu/pubs/consumer/homes/rea04.shtm

Federal Reserve Board: www.federalreserve.gov/pubs/foreclosurescamtips/default.htm

Foreclosure Self-Defense Blog: http://foreclosureselfdefense.com

Homeowner Crisis Resource Center: www.housinghelpnow.org

Homeownership Preservation Foundation (HPF) and HOPE NOW hotline: 1 (888) 995-HOPE or www.hopenow.com

Making Home Affordable: www.makinghomeaffordable.gov

Nolo Press: www.nolo.com/legal-encyclopedia/bankruptcy-foreclosure-debt/

NeighborWorks America: www.nw.org/network/home.asp

Operation Hope: www.operationhope.org

The Office of the Comptroller of the Currency (OCC): www
.helpwithmybank.gov and www.occ.gov/customer.htm.

U.S. Department of Housing and Urban Development (HUD): 1
(800) 569-4287 or www.hud.gov. See www.hud.gov/offices/hsg/
sfh/hcc/hccprof14.cfm for a list of HUD-approved counselors.

Tax Debt

About.com: http://taxes.about.com

Internal Revenue Service (IRS): 1 (800) 829-1040 or www.irs.gov,
See www.irs.gov/individuals/index.html?navmenu=menu1
for many resources for individuals and www.irs.gov/local-
contacts/index.html for contact information for your local IRS
office. Don't have your most recent tax return? Transcripts
are available for the current and three prior calendar years.
To obtain a copy, contact the IRS by phone or submit Form
4506T by mail or fax.

The Collection Process: www.irs.gov/pub/irs-pdf/p594.pdf

Offer in Compromise Booklet: www.irs.gov/pub/irs-pdf/
f656b.pdf

Taxpayer Advocate Service (TAS): 1 (877) 777-4778 or www
.irs.gov/advocate/. See www.taxtoolkit.irs.gov/help-with-
tax-problems-ii/tas/ for contact and other information.

And for Further Reading . . .

We highly recommend consulting any of the following articles and
books to assist you on your road out of debt; they were essential to
our writing process.

AARP, "Reverse Mortgage Loans: Borrowing Against Your
Home," AARP Report, www.aarp.org.

Atlanta Journal-Constitution, "Economic Slide Touches Many Lives: In
a pinch, many rush to pawn," February 4, 2008, www.ajc.com.

Baird, Douglas G., *The Elements of Bankruptcy*, 4th Edition (Foundation Press, New York, NY, 2006).

Business Week, "A Debt Trap for the Unwary," October 29, 2001,
www.businessweek.com.

CNN, "Why Title Loans Are a Bad Idea," October 8, 2008, CNN
.com.

Caher, James P., and John M. Caher, *Personal Bankruptcy Laws for Dummies*, 2nd Edition (John Wiley & Sons, 2006).

Consumer Federation of America and National Consumer Law Center, "Credit Counseling in Crisis: The Impact on Consumers of Funding Cuts, Higher Fees and Aggressive New Market Entrants," April 2003.

Counin, Deanne, *Guide to Surviving Debt*, 2008 Edition (National Consumer Law Center, Boston, MA, 2008).

Dreher, Nancy C., and Joan N. Feeney, *Bankruptcy Law Manual*, Fifth Edition (Thomson West, St. Paul, MN, 2009).

Elias, Steven et al., *How to File for Chapter 7 Bankruptcy*, 16th Edition (Nolo, Berkeley, CA, 2009).

Epstein, David G., and Steve H. Nickles, *Principles of Bankruptcy Law* (Thomson West, St. Paul, MN, 2007).

Epstein, David G., Steve H. Nickles, and James J. White, *Bankruptcy Practitioner Treatise Series* (West, St. Paul, MN, 1993).

Epstein, David G., Steve Nickles, and James White, *Bankruptcy* (West, St. Paul, MN, 1992).

Foust, Dean, "The Foreclosure 'Rescue' Packet," *Business Week*, June 25, 2007.

Hillman, William C., and Margaret M. Crouch, *Bankruptcy Deskbook*, 4th Edition (Practicing Law Institute, New York, NY, 2009).

Lassman, Donald, and Daniel Austin, *Reaffirmation Agreements* (American Bankruptcy Institute, St. Paul, MN, 2009).

Mann, Bruce H., *Republic of Debtors: Bankruptcy in the Age of American Independence* (Harvard University Press, Cambridge, MA, 2009).

McLeod, William J., *Chapter 13 in 13 Chapters* (American Bankruptcy Institute, St. Paul, MN, 2009).

Nasiripour, Shahien, "Don't Look Back: Major Players Continue to 'Walk Away' from Poor Mortgages," *Huffington Post*, January 25, 2010.

National Taxpayer Advocate, *2009 Annual Report to Congress*, Department of the Treasury, Internal Revenue Service, December 31, 2009, www.irs.gov/advocate/article/0,,id=97404,00.html.

Newman, Michael W., *What You Can Do to Conquer Your Credit and Debt Problems*, 2nd Edition (CreateSpace, Scotts Valley, CA, 2009).

Orman, Suze, *The Road to Wealth*, Revised Edition (Riverhead Books, New York, 2008).

Permanent Subcommittee on Investigations of the Committee on Homeland Security and Governmental Affairs, United State Senate, "Profiteering in a Non-Profit Industry: Abusive Practices in Credit Counseling," April 13, 2005.

Ramsey, Dave, *The Total Money Makeover: A Proven Plan for Financial Fitness* (Thomas Nelson Inc., Nashville, TN, 2009).

Rao, John, and Tara Twomey, *Bankruptcy Basics* (National Consumer Law Center, Boston, MA, 2007).

Silver Lake Editors, *Cramdown, Renegotiating Mortgages, Car Loans, Student Loans, Credit Card Debt, Taxes & Other Obligations in the Age of Wall Street Bailouts* (Silver Lake Publishing, Aberdeen, WA, 2009).

Slurlock, James, *Mixed Out: Hard Times, Easy Credit and the Era of Predatory Lenders* (Scribner, New York, 2007).

Sommer, Henry J., *Consumer Bankruptcy Law and Practice* (National Consumer Law Center, Boston, MA, 2006).

Stanley, Thomas, and William Danko, *The Millionaire Next Door* (Pocket Books, New York, 1996).

Streitfeld, David, "No Help in Sight, More Homeowners Walk Away," *New York Times*, February 3, 2010.

Tripoli, Steve, "Dreams Foreclosed: The Rampant Theft of Americans' Homes through Equity-Stripping Foreclosure 'Rescue' Scams." National Consumer Law Center Report, June 2005.

Trump, Donald, *Never Give Up: How I Turned My Biggest Challenges into Success* (Wiley, New York, NY, 2007).

Warren, Elizabeth, and Amelia Warren Tyagi, *All Your Worth: The Ultimate Lifetime Money Plan* (Free Press, New York, NY, 2006).

Warren, Elizabeth, and Amelia Warren Tyagi, *The Two Income Trap: Why Middle Class Parents Are Going Broke* (Aspen, Cambridge, MA, 2004).

Williams, Jack F., and Susan Seabury, *Thorny Issues in Consumer Bankruptcy Cases* (American Bankruptcy Institute, St. Paul. MN, 2008).

APPENDIX B

Bankruptcy FAQs

This appendix includes 26 of the most frequently asked questions we get about what bankruptcy is and how it works. These are abbreviated answers, so be sure to refer to the main text for more information on any of these topics.

1. What is bankruptcy?

   Bankruptcy refers to a federal code of laws and rules designed to help debtors who have more debt than they can handle. Most notably, bankruptcy laws may provide for some debt forgiveness and typically require that creditors stop all collection efforts against the debtor while the debtor is working out a plan or awaiting a discharge of debts. The bankruptcy laws require that the debtor make full disclosure of all assets, liabilities, and other financial information and either surrender nonexempt assets for liquidation and distribution to creditors or formulate and follow through on a plan of reorganization and debt repayment. Bankruptcy cases are heard and settled by the bankruptcy court, a federal court that is a unit of the U.S. District Court.

2. What are the different "chapters" in bankruptcy for an individual?

   The most commonly filed chapters, and those discussed in this book, include chapters 7, 13, 11, and 12.

   Chapter 7 is the liquidation chapter of the Bankruptcy Code. Chapter 7 cases may be filed by an individual, a corporation, or a partnership. The individual debtor usually receives a discharge, which means that he or she is relieved of the obligation to pay certain types of debts (corporations and partnerships are not eligible to receive discharges). (See Chapter 17 for more information.)

Chapter 13 is the debt repayment chapter for individuals (including those who operate businesses as sole proprietorships) who have regular income and whose debts do not exceed a specific amount. (See Chapter 18 for more information.)

Chapter 11 is the reorganization chapter available to businesses and individuals who have assets or income for use in restructuring and repaying their debts. (See Chapter 19 for more information.)

Chapter 12 offers bankruptcy relief to those who qualify as a family farmer or fisherman. There are debt limitations for chapter 12, and a certain portion of the debtor's income must come from the operation of a farming or fishing business. (See Chapter 20 for more information.)

3. Who is a bankruptcy trustee?

A bankruptcy trustee is appointed in all chapter 7, 12, and 13 cases and in some chapter 11 cases to administer the estate and ensure that creditors get as much money as possible. The trustee also presides at the first meeting of creditors (also called the Section 341 meeting—see Question 22). The trustee can require the debtor to provide information and documents before, during, or after the Section 341 meeting.

Trustees are not necessarily lawyers, and they are not paid by the bankruptcy court. They are appointed by the U.S. trustee. The trustees report to the bankruptcy court, but their fees are paid from the bankruptcy filing fees or from the assets of the estate if any exist.

4. What is the role of the U.S. Trustee's Office in bankruptcy proceedings?

The U.S. Trustee's Office is part of the U.S. Department of Justice. The U.S. Trustee's Office monitors all bankruptcy cases, appoints and supervises all trustees, and identifies fraud in bankruptcy cases. The U.S. Trustee's Office cannot give legal advice, but it can give information about the status of a case.

Debtors may contact the U.S. Trustee's Office if they are having a problem with an individual trustee or if there is evidence of fraudulent activity.

5. What is a discharge?

A *discharge* is a court order that relieves a debtor from personal liability for some specific types of debts. The discharge order permanently prohibits creditors from taking action to collect discharged debts from the debtor and, with very limited exceptions, against income and property that the debtor acquires after the bankruptcy filing. When a debt has been discharged, the creditor can no longer seek repayment. The discharge is the primary benefit most debtors obtain from bankruptcy.

6. Are all debts discharged in bankruptcy?

No. Bankruptcy generally does not discharge secured and nondischargeable debts.

7. Is a discharge guaranteed?

No. In some cases, interested parties, including creditors, can object to a discharge.

In chapter 7 cases, the debtor does not have an absolute right to a discharge. An objection to the debtor's discharge may be filed by a creditor, by the trustee in the case, or by the U.S. trustee.

In chapter 12 and 13 cases, the debtor is usually entitled to a discharge upon completion of payments under the plan, although there are some exceptions.

8. What is the difference between a denial of discharge and a determination that a debt is nondischargeable?

A *denial of a discharge* affects the debtor's entire discharge—and therefore all debts—while a *determination of nondischargeability* affects only a particular debt. When a discharge is denied, the debtor gets no discharge and remains liable for the full repayment of debts. The bankruptcy court can deny a debtor's discharge for various reasons, including the debtor's failure to take the required financial management course; concealed property within one year prior to the bankruptcy or after the case is filed; false statements under oath; false claims; or refusal to obey a lawful order of the court.

On the other hand, if the bankruptcy court determines a particular debt is nondischargeable, then the debtor is obligated to pay that particular debt, but the remaining dischargeable debts are discharged.

9. What is the automatic stay?

Filing a bankruptcy petition automatically stops or "stays" most collection actions against the debtor. (See Section 362(a) of the Bankruptcy Code. Exceptions to the general stay are listed in Section 362(b).) The automatic stay is temporary and will end when a discharge is granted (at which time the discharge protects the debtor) or denied, when the case is dismissed or closed, or if the bankruptcy court grants a creditor or other party relief from the automatic stay for the reasons set forth in the Bankruptcy Code (Section 362(d)).

10. How will bankruptcy affect my credit?

Filing for bankruptcy will show up on your credit report for up to 10 years (under provisions of the Fair Credit Reporting Act, 15 U.S.C. § 1681). If you successfully complete a chapter 13 plan, many credit reporting agencies will report the bankruptcy for seven years. You may have more difficulty or more expense in obtaining credit but will likely still be able to obtain credit, at least on a secured basis.

11. Will I be able to obtain credit after filing for bankruptcy?

The decision to grant or deny credit in the future is strictly up to each creditor and will vary, depending on the type of credit requested. There is no law to prevent anyone from extending credit to a debtor immediately after the filing of a bankruptcy nor is there any law that requires a creditor or potential lender to extend credit to a debtor.

12. How do I get a bankruptcy removed from my credit report?

You cannot change your credit report if the information is correct. The Fair Credit Reporting Act (15 U.S.C. Section 1681) controls credit reporting agencies. If you believe that there is an error in your credit report and want to correct it, you should contact the credit reporting agencies.

Further information may be obtained from the Federal Trade Commission Web site (www.ftc.gov at "How to Dispute Credit Report Errors"). The Federal Trade Commission, Bureau of Consumer Protection, Education Division, Washington, D.C. 20580 may also be contacted. The toll-free telephone number is 1 (877) 382-4357.

13. How will the bankruptcy court protect my identification and other personal information contained in court documents?

Personally identifiable information is a term that is defined in the Bankruptcy Code to broadly include names, addresses, telephone numbers, birth dates, and Social Security numbers. The Bankruptcy Code aims to protect personally identifiable information to the most reasonable extent possible.

The bankruptcy court may order you to file copies of tax returns with the court. If you do so, it is your responsibility to redact or black out personal information from the tax return, such as Social Security numbers, children's names, dates of birth, and financial account numbers.

14. Do I need an attorney to file for bankruptcy?

No. You may file a bankruptcy petition without hiring an attorney. However, filing merely starts the bankruptcy process. Your duties and obligations as a debtor in bankruptcy can be complex and burdensome to many debtors. We highly recommend that you hire a competent attorney to protect your best interests.

15. What if I cannot afford an attorney?

The benefits of having legal representation often justify the cost of hiring a lawyer. Try your best to work out a deal with a lawyer that you can afford. Otherwise, legal service organizations in your area may be able to help with navigating a bankruptcy case at little or no cost.

16. What services can a bankruptcy petition preparer provide?

A bankruptcy petition preparer is a person or firm that is not qualified to act as an attorney, but who fills out bankruptcy petitions and related forms for a fee. Bankruptcy petition preparers can only type the forms and may not provide legal advice to the debtor in any way.

Laws prohibit bankruptcy petition preparers from collecting or receiving any legal fees connected with the filing of a debtor's case.

17. What are exemptions?

Exempt assets are protected by law from liquidation and distribution to a debtor's unsecured creditors.

Section 522(b) of the Bankruptcy Code allows an individual debtor to exempt real, personal, or intangible property from the property of the estate. Typically, exempt assets include the value of a vehicle up to a certain dollar amount, the equity in a home up to a certain amount, and tools of the trade. If no one objects to the exemptions claimed by the debtor, those assets will not be a part of the bankruptcy estate and will not be liquidated and used to pay unsecured creditors.

18. What is the credit counseling requirement and how do I comply with it?

You must receive credit counseling within 180 days prior to filing a bankruptcy petition. Specifically, the law requires you to receive from an approved agency a briefing to outline the opportunities available for credit counseling and creation of a financial management plan. You may attend an individual or group session and may complete training in person, on the phone, or even via the Internet.

19. What is the required financial management course and where can I find a course?

Individual chapter 7 debtors and chapter 13 debtors are required to complete a financial management course in order to receive a bankruptcy discharge. The financial management course will be conducted by a nonprofit company and will provide the debtor with instruction on how to manage his or her finances going forward. The Bankruptcy Code provides very limited exceptions to this requirement.

20. What is the means test?

Individual debtors with primarily consumer debts who file a petition for bankruptcy under chapters 7, 11, or 13 must complete an income-based *means test*. The means test calculates the difference between a debtor's current monthly income (CMI) and his or her allowed expenses. The means test is intended to determine whether a debtor has the means to repay some percentage of his or her nonpriority unsecured debts. This is important because, under chapter 7, most—if not all—of a debtor's nonpriority unsecured debts will be discharged.

21. I'm filling out the bankruptcy forms. How do I know if a debt is classified as secured, unsecured, priority, or administrative?

The type of debt owed depends on the agreement or circumstances which gave rise to the debt. In bankruptcy, debts are divided into four categories: secured, priority, administrative, and general unsecured debts.

Secured Debt: A secured debt is a debt that is collateralized by the debtor's property. A creditor whose debt is secured has a right to take its collateral to satisfy the debt. For example, most people who buy new cars on credit give the lender a security interest (or lien) in the car. The debt is secured by the car and the lender can take (repossess) the car if the borrower fails to make payments on the loan.

Unsecured Debt: A debt for which the creditor has no lien with which to satisfy the debt. The debt is said to be generally unsecured if the claim is also not entitled to any priority of payment under the Bankruptcy Code. For example, the amount owed on a credit card.

Priority Debt: A priority debt is a debt entitled to priority in payment, ahead of most other debts, in a bankruptcy case. Examples of priority debts are some taxes, wage claims of employees, and alimony, maintenance, or support of a spouse, former spouse, or child.

Administrative Debt: An administrative debt is a priority debt created when someone provides goods or services to the debtor's bankruptcy estate (this can happen only after the bankruptcy case is filed). Examples of an administrative debt are the fees generated by the trustee in representing the bankruptcy estate.

22. What is a reaffirmation agreement?

A *reaffirmation agreement* is an agreement by which a chapter 7 debtor becomes legally obligated to pay all or a portion of an otherwise dischargeable debt. Since reaffirmed debts are not discharged, the Bankruptcy Court will normally permit the reaffirmation of secured debts only where the collateral is important to a debtor's daily activities and payments do not inflict an undue hardship on the debtor.

Reaffirmation agreements are strictly voluntary. They are not required by the Bankruptcy Code or other state or federal law. Debtors need not reaffirm a debt in order to repay it; the law does not prohibit a debtor from repaying a discharged debt voluntarily—it only prohibits a creditor from collecting the debt. But there may be valid reasons for wanting to reaffirm a particular debt. For instance, many debtors do not want to surrender their property—especially a home or a car—but cannot afford the lump sum payoff that is typically required to redeem that property.

If a debtor reaffirms a debt and fails to make the payments as agreed, the creditor can take action against the debtor to recover any property that secures the debt, and the debtor will be personally liable for any remaining debt to that creditor, notwithstanding the discharge.

23. What does it mean to redeem collateral?

Outside of bankruptcy, a creditor can repossess property that secures its loan in the event that the borrower defaults on the repayment obligation. Property with liens attached is called *collateral*. The secured creditor has the right to sell collateral and use the proceeds to satisfy its claim.

An individual chapter 7 debtor can keep certain kinds of collateral—tangible, personal property intended primarily for personal, family, or household use—by paying the holder of a lien on the property the amount of its allowed secured claim.

24. What is the meeting of creditors?

Section 341 of the Bankruptcy Code requires that the U.S. trustee convene and preside over a meeting of a debtor's creditors. This meeting of creditors, or Section 341 meeting, is held in every bankruptcy case. You must attend the meeting; in many cases it is the only meeting or hearing that you must attend.

The meeting of creditors permits the trustee or representative of the U.S. Trustee's Office to review your petition and schedules with the debtor face-to-face. You are required to answer questions under penalty of perjury concerning the your conduct, assets, liabilities, financial condition, and any matter that may affect administration of the bankruptcy estate or the debtor's right to a discharge.

If you fail to appear at the meeting, a representative of the U.S. Trustee's Office may request that the Bankruptcy Court dismiss the case, order the debtor to cooperate, or hold you in contempt of court for willful failure to cooperate.

25. What if a creditor continues to try to collect on a debt even after bankruptcy has been filed?

If the automatic stay (see Question 9) is in place and a creditor continues collection actions against you or your property, that creditor violates the automatic stay. Request an injunction or monetary sanctions against the creditor and inform the U.S. trustee or trustee appointed to the case.

26. What does it mean if a case is dismissed?

A dismissal order ends the bankruptcy case before a discharge order has been given. When the court dismisses the case, the automatic stay ends and creditors may start to collect debts again. An order of dismissal does not free the debtor from any debt. The most common reason for dismissing a case is because the debtor has failed to satisfy a filing requirement. Unless the debtor appeals the order or seeks reconsideration of the order of dismissal within 10 days, the clerk will automatically close the case.

Notes

Introduction

1. U.S. Courts Bankruptcy Statistics, www.uscourts.gov/bnkrpctystats/statistics .htm#june.
2. *Wall Street Journal*, "Is the Negative Savings Rate a Negative for the Economy?" July 12, 2007, http://online.wsj.com/article/sb118398853722660848.html.
3. Mortgage Bankers Association, "Delinquencies and Foreclosures Continue to Climb in Latest MBA National Delinquency Survey," May 28, 2009, www .mortgagebankers.org/NewsandMedia/PressCenter/69031.htm.
4. National Center for Health Statistics, www.cdc.gov/nchs/; www.cdc.gov/nchs/ data/nvsr/nvsr54/nvsr54_20.pdf.; www.divorcemag.com/statistics/statsUS .shtml; www.infoplease.com/ipa/A0908742.html.
5. U.S. Courts Bankruptcy Statistics, www.uscourts.gov/bnkrpctystats/statistics .htm#june.
6. "Britney Lost Her Panties...and Now She May Lose Her Shirt," Fox News, November 17, 2007, www.foxnews.com/story/0,2933,311802,00.html.
7. See *Lincoln* by David Herbert Donald (Simon & Schuster, New York, NY 1996).
8. Bob Thomas, *Walt Disney, An American Original* (The Walt Disney Company, New York, NY, 1994).
9. Lifecare Poll: www.lifecare.com/news/archives/stress_0606.html; the prenup audit by Daniel Kadlec, Monday, June 28, 1999; www.time.com/time/magazine/article/0,9171,991358,00.html.

Chapter 3: Fighting Back

1. *MacDermid v. Discover Fin. Servs.*, 488 F.3d 721 (6th Cir. 2007).

Chapter 4: Budgeting Your Way Out of Debt

1. Stanley, Thomas J. and William D. Danko, *The Millionaire Next Door* (New York: Pocket Books, 1996).

Chapter 5: The Danger of Quick Fixes

1. www.federalreserve.gov/pubs/FEDS/2009/200933/200933pap.pdf.
2. www.consumerdirect.gov.uk/before_you_buy/thinking_about/pawn-broking/.

3. For information on Internet and other scams call the Better Business Bureau or visit www.bbb.org/us/Consumer-Alerts/.
4. www.merchantcircle.com/blogs/Wells.Fargo.Home.Mortgage.-.Reverse.Mortgage. Team.484-630-2826/2009/11/Breaking-News-HECM-Loan-Limit-Extended-through-2010/469896; http://assets.aarp.org/www.aarp.org_/articles/money/financial_pdfs/hmm_hires_nocrops.pdf.

Chapter 6: Debt Counselors: How to Tell the Bad from the Good

1. www.cbsnews.com/stories/2002/12/19/eveningnews/main533702.shtml, December 2002, on CBS News by Correspondent Mika Brzezinski about credit counseling.
2. www.ripoffreport.com/Credit-Debt-Services/Family-Credit-Counse/family-credit-counseling-corpo-23q4q.htm.
3. www.ripoffreport.com/Consumer-Credit-Counseling-Debt-Settleme/Credit-Debt-Services/Consumer-Credit-Counseling-Hes-FPMMM.htm.
4. The Web site ripoffreport.com chronicles many of the abuses and wretched tricks of credit counselors and debt negotiation companies.
5. "One in Three Parents Losing Sleep Over Their Finances," www.savethechildren .org.uk/en/41_7527.htm; "Debt Problems Impact Your Health," www.msnbc .msn.com/id/25060719/.
6. www.ftc.gov/bcp/edu/pubs/consumer/credit/cre26.pd and www.ftc.gov.

Chapter 11: The Way Out of Auto Debt

1. "Repossessors, Interrupted," *Boston Globe*, May 23, 2007.

Chapter 12: The Way Out of Tax Debt

1. *Wall Street Journal*, "Nurse Outduels IRS Over M.B.A. Tuition: How One Woman Went to Tax Court and Won Deduction," January 9, 2010.
2. IRS Small Business/Self-Employed Division, *Collection Activity Report* NO-5000-108, Monthly Report of Offer in Compromise Activity FY 2008 Cumulative Through September—National Total.

Chapter 14: 21 Bankruptcy Myths

1. Himmelstein, David U., et al, "Medical Bankruptcy in the United States, 2007: Results of a National Study." Elsevier, 2009.

Chapter 16: Understanding the Bankruptcy Process

1. *Man v. Chase Manhattan Mortgage Corp.*, 316 F.3d 1 (1st Cir. 2003).
2. *Local Loan Co. v. Hunt*, 292 U.S. 234, 244 (1934).

Glossary

A

Acceleration The right of the lender to demand payment on the outstanding balance of a loan before the expiration of the term of the loan due to some default of the borrower.

Adjustable-rate mortgage (ARM) A mortgage with a variable interest rate (not fixed) that changes based upon the interest rate changes of a certain market index, such as the London Interbank Offered Rate (LIBOR) or the U.S. Constant Maturity Treasury (CMT), and a premium or margin in addition to the market interest rate. Lenders usually structure these mortgages with attractive lower payments and interest rates at the beginning of the loan to entice prospective borrowers. When rates change, ARM monthly payments increase or decrease at intervals determined by the note; the change in monthly payment amount, however, is sometimes subject to a cap. Also referred to as adjustable mortgage loans (AMLs) or variable-rate mortgages (VRMs).

Adversary proceeding A lawsuit arising in or related to a bankruptcy case that begins by filing a complaint with the court, that is, a trial that takes place within the context of a bankruptcy case.

Amortization A method of calculating interest that enables you to reduce your debt gradually through monthly payments. The payments may be principal and interest or interest only. The monthly amount is based on the schedule for the entire term or length of the loan.

Annual percentage rate (APR) A measure of the cost of credit expressed as a yearly rate. It includes interest as well as other charges. Because all lenders, by federal law, follow the same rules to ensure the accuracy of the annual percentage rate, it provides consumers with a good basis for comparing the cost of loans, including mortgage plans. APR is a higher rate than the simple interest of the mortgage.

Appraisal (Real Property)   A document from a professional that gives an estimate of a property's fair market value based on the sales of comparable homes in the area and the features of a property and other factors; an appraisal is generally required by a lender before loan approval to ensure that the mortgage loan amount is not more than the value of the property.

Assessed value   The value that a public official has placed on any asset (used to determine taxes).

Assets   Property of all kinds, including real and personal, tangible and intangible; any item with measurable value.

Automatic stay   An injunction that automatically stops lawsuits, foreclosures, garnishments, and most collection activity against the debtor the moment a bankruptcy petition is filed.

Avoid lien (also lien avoidance)   The process in bankruptcy of obtaining the release of a lien through either the approval by the court of a stripdown of a secured claim or the court's determination that the lien impairs an exemption of property.

B

Balance sheet   A financial statement that shows the assets, liabilities, and net worth of an individual or company.

Balloon mortgage   A mortgage that typically offers low interest rates for an initial period of time (usually 5, 7, or 10 years); after that time period elapses, the entire balance is due or is refinanced by the borrower.

Balloon payment   The final lump sum payment due at the end of a balloon mortgage.

Bankruptcy   A legal procedure for dealing with debt problems of individuals and businesses; specifically, a case filed under one of the chapters of title 11 of the United States Code (the Bankruptcy Code).

Bankruptcy administrator   An officer of the Judiciary serving in the judicial districts of Alabama and North Carolina who, like the U.S. trustee, is responsible for supervising the administration of bankruptcy cases, estates, and trustees; monitoring plans and disclosure statements; monitoring creditors' committees; monitoring fee applications; and performing other statutory duties.

Bankruptcy clerk's office   The office responsible for the management and safe keeping of the documents filed in a bankruptcy case or adversary proceeding in the district where the case is pending. Debtors file their bankruptcy petitions at the clerk's office. The clerk keeps the docket for each case, a claims register, correct copies of court documents filed in a case, as well as an index of all cases and adversary proceedings filed. Additionally, the clerk notifies creditors of deadlines within a case or proceeding.

Bankruptcy Code   The informal name for title 11 of the United States Code (11 U.S.C. §§ 101-1330), the federal bankruptcy law.

Bankruptcy court   A unit of the district court responsible for the administration of bankruptcy cases.

Bankruptcy estate   All interests of the debtor in property at the time of the bankruptcy filing. The estate technically becomes the temporary legal owner of all of the debtor's property.

Bankruptcy judge   A judicial officer of the U.S. district court who is the court official with decision-making power over federal bankruptcy cases.

Bankruptcy petition   The document filed by the debtor (in a voluntary case) or by creditors (in an involuntary case) that opens the bankruptcy case. (There are official forms for bankruptcy petitions.)

Bankruptcy trustee   An individual appointed in all chapter 7 and chapter 13 cases to represent the interests of the bankruptcy estate and the debtor's creditors.

Borrower   A person who has been approved to receive a loan and is then obligated to repay it and any additional fees according to the loan terms.

Budget   A detailed record of all income earned and spent during a specific period of time.

C

Cash-for-keys   A deal with the lender for a small payment to assist the debtor in vacating the debtor's place of living.

Chapter 7   The chapter of the Bankruptcy Code providing for liquidation; that is, the sale of a debtor's nonexempt property and the distribution of the proceeds to creditors. In order to be eligible for chapter 7, the debtor must satisfy a means test. The trustee will evaluate the debtor's income and expenses to determine if the debtor may proceed under chapter 7.

Chapter 7 trustee   A person appointed in a chapter 7 case to represent the interests of the bankruptcy estate and the creditors. The trustee's responsibilities include reviewing the debtor's petition and schedules, liquidating the property of the estate, and making distributions to creditors. The trustee may also bring actions against creditors or the debtor to recover property of the bankruptcy estate.

Chapter 11   A reorganization bankruptcy, usually involving a corporation or partnership. A chapter 11 debtor usually proposes a plan of reorganization to keep its business alive and pay creditors over time. People in business or individuals can also seek relief in chapter 11.

Chapter 12   The chapter of the Bankruptcy Code providing for adjustment of debts of a family farmer or a family fisherman as those terms are defined in the Bankruptcy Code.

Chapter 13   The chapter of the Bankruptcy Code providing for adjustment of debts of an individual with regular income, in which debtors pay debts according to a chapter 13 plan often referred to as a *wage-earner plan*. Chapter 13 allows a debtor to keep property and use his or her disposable income to pay debts over time, usually within three to five years.

Chapter 13 trustee   A person appointed to administer a chapter 13 case. A chapter 13 trustee's responsibilities are similar to those of a chapter 7 trustee; however, a Chapter 13 trustee has the additional responsibilities of overseeing the debtor's plan, receiving payments from debtors, and disbursing plan payments to creditors.

Claim   A creditor's assertion of a right to payment from a debtor or the debtor's property.

Coborrower   An additional person that is responsible for loan repayment and also signs the promissory note.

Collateral   Property that is promised as security for the satisfaction of a debt or the payment of a loan. For example, on a home loan, the home is the collateral and can be taken away from the borrower if mortgage payments are not made.

Comparative market analysis (COMPS)   A property evaluation that determines property value by comparing similar properties sold within the last year.

Confirmation   Approval of a plan of reorganization by a bankruptcy judge.

Consumer debts   Debts incurred for personal, as opposed to business, needs.

Contested matter   Those matters, other than objections to claims, that are disputed but are not within the definition of adversary proceeding contained in Rule 7001.

Contingent claim   A claim that may be owed by the debtor under certain circumstances that have not yet occurred (e.g., when the debtor is a cosigner on another person's loan and that person may fail to pay in the future).

Conventional loan   A private sector loan, one that is not guaranteed or insured by the U.S. government.

Convertible ARM   An adjustable-rate mortgage that provides the borrower the ability to convert to a fixed-rate mortgage within a specified time.

Credit   An agreement that a person will borrow money and repay it to the lender over time.

Credit counseling   Education on how to improve bad credit and how to avoid having more debt than can be repaid. Also refers to two events in individual bankruptcy cases: (1) the individual or group briefing from a nonprofit budget and credit counseling agency that individual debtors must attend prior to filing under any chapter of the Bankruptcy Code; and (2) the instructional course in personal financial management in chapters 7 and 13 that an individual debtor must complete before a discharge is entered. There are exceptions to both requirements for certain categories of debtors, exigent circumstances, and if the request for counseling is timely made, or if the U.S. trustee or bankruptcy administrator have determined that there are insufficient approved credit counseling agencies available to provide the necessary counseling.

Credit history   A record of an individual that lists all debts and the payment history for each. The report that is generated from the history is called a credit report. Lenders use this information to gauge a potential borrower's ability to repay a loan.

Credit report   A report generated by a credit bureau that contains the borrower's credit history for the past seven years. Lenders use this information to determine if a loan will be granted.

Credit reporting agency (also Credit bureau)   A company that maintains national credit-reporting databases. The three major companies are Equifax, Experian, and Trans Union.

Credit score   A score calculated by using a person's credit report to determine the likelihood of a loan being repaid on time. Scores range from about 360 to 840—a lower score meaning a person is a higher risk, while a higher score means that there is less risk.

Credit union   A nonprofit financial institution that is federally regulated and owned by the members or people who use its services. Credit unions serve groups that hold a common interest. You have to become a member to use the available services.

Creditor   One to whom the debtor owes money or who claims to be owed money by the debtor.

Creditors' meeting (See Section 341 meeting)

D

Debtor   A person who has filed a petition for relief under the Bankruptcy Code.

Debt-to-income ratio   A comparison or ratio of gross income to housing and nonhousing expenses; guidelines suggest that the monthly mortgage payment should be no more than 29 percent of monthly gross income (before taxes) and the mortgage payment combined with nonhousing debts should not exceed 41 percent of income.

Deed (also title)   A document that legally transfers ownership of real property from one person to another. The deed is recorded in the public record with the property description and the owner's signature.

Deed-in-lieu   To avoid foreclosure ("in lieu" of foreclosure), a deed is given to the lender to fulfill the homeowner's obligation to repay the debt; this process does not allow the borrower to remain in the house but helps avoid the costs, time, and effort associated with foreclosure.

Default   The failure to make timely monthly mortgage payments or otherwise comply with mortgage terms. A loan is considered in default when payment has not been paid after 60 to 90 days. Once in default the lender can exercise legal rights defined in the contract to begin foreclosure proceedings.

Delinquency   Failure of a borrower to make timely mortgage payments under a loan agreement. Generally after 15 days a late fee may be assessed.

Depreciation   A decrease in the value or price of a property due to changes in market conditions, wear and tear on the property, or other factors.

Discharge   A release of a debtor from personal liability for certain dischargeable debts. Notable exceptions to dischargeability are taxes and student loans. A discharge prevents the creditors owed those debts from taking any action against the debtor or the debtor's property to collect the debts. The discharge also prohibits creditors from communicating with the debtor regarding the debt, including through telephone calls, letters, and personal contact.

Dischargeable debt   A debt for which the Bankruptcy Code allows the debtor's personal liability to be eliminated.

Disclosure statement   A written document prepared by the chapter 11 debtor or other plan proponent that is designed to provide adequate information to creditors to enable them to evaluate the chapter 11 plan of reorganization.

Disposable income   Income not reasonably necessary for the maintenance or support of the debtor or dependents. If the debtor operates a business, disposable income is defined as those amounts over and above what is necessary for the payment of ordinary operating expenses.

E

Equity   The value of a debtor's interest in property that remains after liens and other creditors' interests are considered. (Example: If a house valued at $100,000 is subject to an $80,000 mortgage, there is $20,000 of equity.)

Escrow account   A separate account into which the lender puts a portion of each monthly mortgage payment. An escrow account provides the funds needed for certain expenses such as property taxes, homeowners insurance, and mortgage insurance.

Exception from discharge   The status of a debt being declared not dischargeable in bankruptcy either by operation of law or after determination by the bankruptcy court.

Executory contracts   Contracts or leases under which both parties to the agreement have duties remaining to be performed. If a contract or lease is executory, a debtor may assume it (keep the contract) or reject it (terminate the contract).

Exempt property   Property that a debtor is allowed to retain, free from the claims of creditors who do not have liens on the property. For example, in some states the debtor may be able to exempt all or a portion of the equity in the debtor's primary residence (homestead exemption), or some or all tools of the trade used by the debtor to make a living (e.g., auto tools for an auto mechanic or dental tools for a dentist). The availability and amount of property the debtor may exempt depends on the state the debtor lives in.

Exemption   State and federal laws allowing a person to retain assets free from the claims of creditors.

Exploding adjustable-rate mortgages (Exploding ARMs)   Mortgages securing promissory notes that have an interest rate will increase at the end of an introductory period.

F

Fair Credit Reporting Act (FCRA)   A federal act ensuring credit bureaus are fair and accurate in protecting the individual's privacy rights. Enacted in 1971 and revised in October 1997.

Fair Housing Act   A law that prohibits discrimination in all facets of the home-buying process on the basis of race, color, national origin, religion, sex, familial status, or disability.

Fair market value (FMV)   The hypothetical price that a willing buyer and seller will agree upon when they are acting freely, carefully, and with complete knowledge of the situation.

Family farmer or family fisherman   An individual, individual and spouse, corporation, or partnership engaged in a farming or fishing operation that meets certain debt limits and other statutory criteria for filing a bankruptcy petition under chapter 12.

Fannie Mae or Federal National Mortgage Association (FNMA)   A federally chartered enterprise owned by private stockholders that purchases residential mortgages and converts them into securities for sale to investors; by purchasing mortgages, Fannie Mae supplies funds that lenders may loan to potential homebuyers. Also known as a government sponsored enterprise (GSE).

Federal Housing Administration (FHA)   Federal Housing Administration, established in 1934 to advance homeownership opportunities for all Americans, assists homebuyers by providing mortgage insurance to lenders to cover most losses that may occur when a borrower defaults; this encourages lenders to make loans to borrowers who might not qualify for conventional mortgages.

FICO score   FICO is an abbreviation for Fair Isaac Corporation and refers to a person's credit score based on credit history. Lenders and credit card companies use the number to decide if the person is likely to pay his or her bills. A credit score is evaluated using information from the three major credit bureaus and is usually between 300 and 850.

First mortgage   A mortgage with first priority subject to municipal liens.

Fixed expenses   Payments that do not vary from month to month.

Fixed-rate mortgage   A mortgage with payments that remain the same throughout the term of the loan because the interest rate and other terms are fixed and do not change.

Forbearance   An agreement between borrower and lender in which lender agrees not to take legal action when a borrower is late in making a payment for an agreed period of time. Usually this occurs when a borrower sets up a plan that both sides agree will bring overdue mortgage payments up to date.

Foreclosure   A legal process in which mortgaged real property is sold to pay the loan of the defaulting borrower. Foreclosure laws are based on the statutes of each state where the property is located.

Fraudulent transfer   A transfer of a debtor's property made with intent to defraud or for which the debtor receives less than the transferred property's value.

Freddie Mac or Federal Home Loan Mortgage Corporation (FHLM)   A federally chartered corporation that purchases residential mortgages, securitizes them, and sells them to investors; this provides lenders with funds for new homebuyers. Also known as a government sponsored enterprise (GSE).

G

Ginnie Mae or Government National Mortgage Association (GNMA)   A government-owned corporation overseen by the U.S. Department of Housing and Urban Development, Ginnie Mae pools FHA-insured and VA-guaranteed loans to back securities for private investment. As with Fannie Mae and Freddie Mac, the investment income provides funding that may then be lent to eligible borrowers by lenders.

Gross income   Money earned before taxes and other deductions. Sometimes it may include income from self-employment, rental property, alimony, child support, public assistance payments, and retirement benefits.

H

Hazard insurance Protection against a specific loss, such as fire or wind, over a period of time that is obtained by the payment of a regularly scheduled premium.

Home Equity Conversion Mortgage (HECM) (also known as a Reverse Mortgage) As known as a reverse mortgage, it is used by homeowners age 62 and older to convert the equity in their home into monthly streams of income or a line of credit to be repaid when they no longer occupy the home. A lending institution such as a mortgage lender, bank, credit union, or savings and loan association funds the FHA insured loan, commonly known as HECM.

Home equity line of credit A mortgage loan, usually a second mortgage, that allows a borrower to obtain cash against the equity of a home, up to a predetermined amount.

Home equity loan A loan of a fixed principal amount, usually a second mortgage, backed by the value of a home or other real estate.

Homebuyer Education Learning Program (HELP) An educational program from the FHA that counsels people about the home-buying process. HELP covers topics like budgeting, finding a home, getting a loan, and home maintenance; in most cases, completion of the program may entitle the homebuyer to a reduced initial FHA mortgage insurance premium—from 2.25 percent to 1.75 percent of the home purchase price.

Homestead exemption A provision of the law of many states, varying in detail and amount from state to state, and a provision of federal bankruptcy law that allows homeowners to protect the equity in their primary residence from seizure by creditors. In a bankruptcy case, some states give a debtor the option of choosing the state or federal bankruptcy exemptions. In Florida and Texas, the amount a homeowner may exempt is unlimited, but in most states there is a monetary cap on the amount of the homestead exemption a homeowner may claim. In some states the exemption is automatic, whereas in others, a declaration of homestead must be recorded in the appropriate land records registry.

Housing counseling agency Provides counseling and assistance to individuals on a variety of issues including loan default, fair housing, and home buying.

HUD (U.S. Department of Housing and Urban Development) Established in 1965, HUD works to create a decent home and suitable living environment for all Americans; it does this by addressing housing needs, improving and developing American communities, and enforcing fair housing laws. The HUD is an excellent resource for housing information and for recommendations on housing couselors.

HUD-1 Settlement Statement (Also settlement sheet or closing statement) Itemizes all closing costs and must be given to the borrower at or before closing. Items that appear on the statement include real estate commissions, loan fees, points, and escrow amounts.

Hybrid adjustable-rate mortgages (Hybrid ARMs) Mortgages that have fixed payments and fixed interest rates for a few years, and then turn into adjustable loans with interest rates that change or float after the initial period. Known as hybrid because they contain both traditional fixed-rate mortgage features and simple ARM features. Lenders refer to some as 2/28 or 3/27 hybrid ARMs: the first number refers to the number of years the loan has a fixed rate and the second number refers to the number of years the loan has an adjustable rate. Lenders offer other hybrid ARMs called 5/1 or 3/1 hybrid ARMs: in these, the first number refers to the number of years the loan has a fixed rate, and the second number refers to how often the rate changes (e.g., 1 for once a year).

I

In forma pauperis A latin phrase for a chapter 7 debtor who cannot afford the court costs and fees; he or she can ask the bankruptcy court to waive them.

Interest A fee charged for the use of borrowed money.

Interest-only mortgages These mortgages allow you to pay only the interest on the mortgage loan for a predetermined period of time, usually up to 10 years. The term of the loan is divided into two periods: interest-only period and interest-and-principal period. The initial payments do not pay down the principal of the loan at all, which allows you to have lower monthly payments over the interest-only period. However, once this initial interest-only period expires, the payments increase significantly to include repayment of the principal. Payments in the second period are greater than those of a traditional fixed-rate mortgage over the same period because the principal now must be paid over a condensed time period. The longer the interest-only period, the higher the payments will rise after its expiration.

Interest rate The amount of interest charged on a loan payment expressed as a percentage.

J

Joint petition   One bankruptcy petition filed by a husband and wife together.

Judgment   A court order deciding a case or controversy. A legal decision; when requiring debt repayment, a judgment may include a property lien that secures the creditor's claim by providing a collateral source.

Jumbo loan (also known as a nonconforming loan)   A loan that exceeds Fannie Mae's and Freddie Mac's loan limits. Freddie Mac and Fannie Mae loans are referred to as conforming loans.

L

Late charges   The penalty the homeowner or borrower must pay when a mortgage or credit card payment is made after the due date grace period.

Lender (also loan officer)   A person or company that makes loans for real estate and other purchases.

Liabilities   A person's financial obligations such as long-term or short-term debt, and other financial obligations to be paid.

Lien   A legal claim against property that is designed to secure payment of a debt or performance of an obligation and must be satisfied when the property is sold. A claim of money against a property, wherein the value of the property is used as security in repayment of a debt. A debtor in a bankruptcy case may still be responsible for a lien after a discharge. Examples include a mechanic's lien, which might be for the unpaid cost of building supplies, or a tax lien for unpaid property taxes. A lien is a defect on the title and needs to be settled before transfer of ownership. A lien release is a written report of the settlement of a lien and is recorded in the public record as evidence of payment.

Line of credit   An agreement by a financial institution such as a bank to extend credit up to a certain amount for a certain time to a specified borrower.

Liquidation   A sale of a debtor's property with the proceeds to be used for the benefit of creditors.

Loan   Money borrowed that is usually repaid with interest.

Loan origination fee   A charge by the lender to cover the administrative costs of making the mortgage. This charge is paid at the closing and varies with the lender and type of loan. A loan origination fee of 1 to 2 percent of the mortgage amount is common.

Loan servicer   An agent for a holder of a mortgage that collects monthly mortgage payments and disperses property taxes and insurance payments if held in escrow. Loan servicers also monitor nonperforming loans, contact delinquent borrowers, and notify insurers and investors of potential problems. Loan servicers may be the lender or a specialized company that just handles loan servicing under contract with the lender or the investor who owns the loan.

M

Market value   The amount a willing buyer would pay a willing seller for a home. An appraised value is an estimate of the current fair market value.

Maturity   The date when the principal balance of a loan becomes due and payable.

Means test   Section 707(b)(2) of the Bankruptcy Code applies a means test to determine whether an individual debtor's chapter 7 filing is presumed to be an abuse of the Bankruptcy Code requiring dismissal or conversion of the case (generally to chapter 13). Abuse is presumed if the debtor's aggregate current monthly income over five years, net of certain statutorily allowed expenses is more than (1) $10,950, or (2) 25 percent of the debtor's nonpriority unsecured debt, as long as that amount is at least $6,575. The debtor may rebut a presumption of abuse only by a showing of special circumstances that justify additional expenses or adjustments of current monthly income. See Chapter 16 and Appendix B for more information.

Median income debtor   If a person's income is below the median income for his or her state, the person may file a chapter 7 case without applying the means test.

Modification   When a lender agrees to modify the terms of a mortgage without refinancing the loan by changing the loan's term, interest rate, or other feature.

Mortgage note (also Note)   A legal document obligating a borrower to repay a loan at a stated interest rate during a specified period; the agreement is secured by a mortgage that is recorded in the public records along with the deed.

Mortgage   A lien on the property that secures the promise to repay a loan. A security agreement between the lender and the buyer in which the property is collateral for the loan. The mortgage gives the lender the right to collect payment on the loan and to foreclose if the loan obligations are not met.

Mortgagee   The lender in a mortgage agreement.

Mortgagor   The borrower in a mortgage agreement.

Motion to lift the automatic stay   A request by a creditor to allow the creditor to take action against the debtor or the debtor's property that would otherwise be prohibited by the automatic stay.

N

Negative amortization   Negative amortization occurs when the monthly payments do not cover all of the interest cost. The interest cost that isn't covered is added to the unpaid principal balance. This means that even after making many payments, the borrower could owe more than he or she did at the beginning of the loan.

Net income   Your take-home pay; the amount of money that you receive in your paycheck after taxes and deductions.

No-asset case   A chapter 7 case in which there are no assets available to satisfy any portion of the creditors' unsecured claims.

Nondischargeable debt   Debt that cannot be eliminated in bankruptcy. Examples include a home mortgage, debts for alimony or child support, certain taxes, debts for most government-funded or guaranteed educational loans or benefit overpayments, debts arising from death or personal injury caused by driving while intoxicated or under the influence of drugs, and debts for restitution or a criminal fine included in a sentence on the debtor's conviction of a crime. Some debts, such as debts for money or property obtained by false pretenses and debts for fraud or defalcation while acting in a fiduciary capacity, may be declared nondischargeable only if a creditor timely files and prevails in a nondischargeability action.

Nonexempt asset   Property of a debtor that can be liquidated to satisfy claims of creditors.

Note (also mortgage note)   A legal document obligating a borrower to repay a mortgage loan at a stated interest rate over a specified period of time.

Notice of default   A formal written notice to a borrower that there is a default on a loan and that legal action is possible.

O

Objection to discharge A trustee's or creditor's opposition to releasing a debtor from personal liability for certain dischargeable debts. Common reasons include allegations that the debt to be discharged was incurred by false pretenses or that debt arose because of the debtor's fraud while acting as a fiduciary.

Option adjustable-rate mortgages (also Option ARMs or Cash Flow ARMs) Offer the borrower four monthly payment options: a minimum payment option, an interest-only payment option, a payment option so the loan is paid off over 15 years and a payment option so the loan is paid off over 30 years. Lenders also call these mortgage loans "pick-a-payment" or "pay-option" ARMs. Payments on the minimum payment option of option ARMs and cash flow ARMs do not usually cover the accruing interest on the mortgage loan so that the borrower encounters negative amortization (what is owed on the loan grows even though payments are being made).

P

Public Access to Court Electronic Records (PACER) These electronic records kept by the bankruptcy clerk include general case information, the docket, and claims register. These electronic records allow access to the records via the Internet.

Partial claim A loss mitigation option offered by the FHA that allows a borrower, with help from a lender, to get an interest-free loan from HUD to bring their mortgage payments up to date.

Partial payment A payment that is less than the total amount owed on a monthly mortgage payment. Normally, lenders do not accept partial payments. The lender may make exceptions during times of difficulty. Contact your lender prior to the due date if a partial payment is needed.

Payment advices Evidence of payment received from an employer, such as pay stubs. Debtor must provide all payment advices received within 60 days of filing a bankruptcy petition.

Personal property Any property that is not real property or affixed to real property. For example, furniture is not affixed, however, a new light fixture would be considered attached and part of the real property.

Petition   The document that initiates the filing of a bankruptcy proceeding setting forth basic information regarding the debtor, including name, address, chapter under which the case is filed, and estimated amount of assets and liabilities.

Points   A point is a fee that a borrower pays a lender, typically equivalent equal to 1 percent of the principal amount of the mortgage loan. For example, if you get a mortgage loan for $95,000, one point means you pay $950 to the lender, usually as a closing cost. Lenders frequently charge points in both fixed-rate and adjustable-rate mortgages in order to increase the yield on the mortgage and to cover loan closing costs. These points usually are collected at closing and may be paid by the borrower or the home seller, or may be split between them.

Predatory lending   Abusive lending practices that include making a mortgage loan to someone who does not have the ability to repay. It also relates to repeated refinancing of a loan charging high interest and fees each time.

Prepayment   Payment of the mortgage loan before the scheduled due date; may be subject to a prepayment penalty.

Prepayment penalty   A provision in some loans that charges a fee to a borrower who pays off a loan before it is due.

Principal   The amount of money borrowed to buy a house. This does not include the interest paid to borrow that money. The principal balance is the amount of principal owed on a loan at any given time.

Priority claim   The entitlement of a claim in a bankruptcy case to payment prior to other claims.

Private mortgage insurance (PMI)   Insurance purchased by a buyer to protect the lender in the event of default. The cost of mortgage insurance is usually added to the monthly mortgage payment. Mortgage insurance is generally maintained until over 20 percent of the outstanding amount of the loan is paid or for a set period of time (seven years is normal). Mortgage insurance may be available through a government agency, such as the Federal Housing Administration (FHA) or the Veterans Administration (VA), or through private mortgage insurance companies (PMI).

Promissory note   A written promise to repay a specified amount over a specified period of time.

Proof of claim   A written statement using an official form that describes the reason a debtor owes a creditor money (also typically sets forth the amount of money owed).

Property of the estate   All legal or equitable interests of the debtor in property as of the commencement of the bankruptcy case.

Property tax   A tax charged by local government and used to fund municipal services such as schools, police, or street maintenance. The amount of property tax is determined locally by a formula, usually based on a percent per $1,000 of assessed value of the property.

R

Reaffirmation agreement   An agreement between a debtor and a creditor, frequently a secured creditor, to continue paying a dischargeable debt after the bankruptcy case is filed, usually for the purpose of keeping the collateral or mortgaged property that would otherwise be subject to repossession.

Real Estate Settlement Procedures Act (RESPA)   A law protecting consumers from abuses during the residential real estate purchase and loan process that requires lenders to disclose all settlement costs, practices, and relationships.

Real property   Land, including all the natural resources and permanent buildings on it.

Redemption   A procedure in a chapter 7 case whereby a debtor satisfies and removes a secured creditor's lien on collateral by paying the creditor the value of the property. The debtor may then retain the property free of lien. It also may refer to a procedure to pay off a secured creditor outside of bankruptcy.

Refinancing   Paying off one loan by obtaining another; refinancing is generally done to secure better loan terms (like a lower interest rate).

Reinstatement period   A phase of the foreclosure process during which the homeowner has an opportunity to stop the foreclosure by paying money that is owed to the lender.

Repayment plan   An agreement between a lender and a delinquent borrower in which the borrower agrees to make additional payments to pay down past due amounts while making regularly scheduled payments.

Reverse mortgage   Used by homeowners age 62 and older to convert the equity in their home into monthly streams of income or a line of credit to be repaid when they no longer occupy the home.

S

Sale leaseback   When a seller deeds property to a buyer for a payment, and the buyer simultaneously leases the property back to the seller.

Schedule   An official bankruptcy form submitted by the debtor with the bankruptcy petition (or shortly thereafter) listing the debtor's assets, liabilities, and other financial information.

Second mortgage   An additional mortgage on real property after the first mortgage. In case of a default, the first mortgage must be paid before the second mortgage. Second mortgage loans are more risky for the lender and usually carry a higher interest rate.

Section 341 meeting (also creditors' meeting)   A meeting of creditors at which the debtor is questioned under oath by creditors, a trustee, an examiner, or the U.S. trustee about his or her financial affairs.

Secured creditor   An individual or business that holds a claim against the debtor that is secured by a lien on property of the estate. The property subject to the lien is the secured creditor's collateral.

Secured debt   A debt for which the creditor has the right to pursue specific pledged property upon default, such as a real estate mortgage. Examples include home mortgages, auto loans, and tax liens.

Security   The property that will be pledged as collateral for a loan.

Servicer   A business that collects mortgage payments from borrowers and manages the borrower's escrow accounts.

Settlement statement (also HUD-1 Settlement Statement)   A document required by the Real Estate Settlement Procedures Act (RESPA). An itemized statement of services and charges relating to the closing of a property purchase, sale, or refinance. The buyer has the right to examine the settlement statement one day before the closing.

Simple adjustable-rate mortgages (Simple ARMs)   In interest rate on a mortgage that adjusts from the outset of the loan according to an index. Payments change at each adjustment. Lenders may impose the adjustments quarterly, yearly, or another term set forth in the loan documents.

Strip down (also cram down, strip-off)   The ability under bankruptcy law to avoid a lien over the objection of the secured creditor and reduce allowed secured claim to the value of the collateral, causing the balance due to be an unsecured claim.

T

Title (or Deed)   A legal document establishing the right of ownership. It is recorded to make it part of the public record.

Traditional fixed-rate mortgage   A mortgage with an interest rate that remains the same throughout the life of the loan, usually 15 or 30 years. Changes may occur to your payments as a result of changes in your taxes or insurance if you have an escrow account with your loan servicer. However, the monthly amount you pay toward the mortgage loan stays constant throughout the whole term.

Treasury Index   An index based on the results of auctions that the U.S. Treasury holds for its Treasury bills and securities. Can be used as the basis for adjustable-rate mortgages (ARMs).

Truth in Lending Act (TILA)   A federal law, 15 U.S.C. Sec. 1601 et seq., obligating a lender to give full written disclosure of all fees, terms, and conditions associated with the loan.

U

U.S. trustee   An officer of the U.S. Department of Justice responsible for supervising the administration of bankruptcy cases, estates, and trustees; monitoring plans and disclosure statements; monitoring creditors' committees; monitoring fee applications; and performing other statutory duties.

Underwater mortage loan   A mortgage loan in which the balance exceeds the value of the property that secured it, or, conversely, a loan in which the collateral is worth less than the loan principal. For instance, if a borrower owes more on his or her mortgage note than the price the home can be sold for, the loan is underwater.

Undue hardship (student loan)   The most widely used test for evaluating undue hardship in the dischargeability of a student loan includes three conditions: (1) the debtor cannot maintain—based on current income and expenses—a minimal standard of living if forced to repay the loans; (2) there are indications that the state of affairs is likely to persist for a significant portion of the repayment period; and (3) the debtor made good faith efforts to repay the loans.

Unsecured claim or debt   A claim or debt for which a creditor holds no special assurance of payment, such as a mortgage or lien. It is a debt for which credit was extended based solely on the creditor's assessment of the debtor's future ability to pay.

V

VA mortgage   A mortgage guaranteed by the Department of Veterans Affairs (VA).

Variable expenses   Costs or payments that may vary from month to month such as gasoline or food.

W

Wage garnishment   A nonbankruptcy legal proceeding whereby a plaintiff or creditor seeks to attach the future wages of a borrower or defendant. In other words, the creditor/plaintiff seeks to have part of the borrower's/defendant's future wages paid to the creditor/plaintiff for a debt owed to the creditor/plaintiff.

Workout   A consensual agreement between a borrower and a lender to restructure a loan to avoid foreclosure, repossession, or lawsuit, usually accomplished by a loan modification, forbearance, or short sale.

About the Authors

The Honorable Joan N. Feeney is a U.S. bankruptcy judge for the District of Massachusetts. She began her term as judge in 1992, served as Chief Judge from 2002 to 2006, and also sits as a member of the First Circuit Bankruptcy Appellate Panel, a tribunal for appeals from bankruptcy courts. Judge Feeney is a member of the International Judicial Relations Committee of the Judicial Conference of the United States. She is a member of the National Conference of Bankruptcy Judges and will serve as its president commencing in 2012. Judge Feeney is also a member of the Board of Directors of the American Bankruptcy Institute and is a Fellow of the American College of Bankruptcy. She co-chairs the M. Ellen Carpenter Financial Literacy Project, a joint venture of the U.S. Bankruptcy Court for the District of Massachusetts and the Boston Bar Association, which teaches high school students about personal finance. Additionally, Judge Feeney coauthors the *Bankruptcy Law Manual*, a two-volume treatise on bankruptcy law published by West. In 2005, Judge Feeney received the Boston Bar Association's prestigious Haskell Cohn Award for Distinguished Judicial Service. Prior to her appointment as judge, Judge Feeney was an associate and partner in the Boston law firm Hanify & King, P.C. and Career Law Clerk to Hon. James N. Gabriel, U.S. bankruptcy judge for the District of Massachusetts. Judge Feeney is a graduate of Connecticut College and Suffolk University Law School. A frequent panelist and lecturer on bankruptcy law topics in Massachusetts and throughout the country, she lives in the Boston area and has two children, Matthew and Caroline.

Theodore "Ted" W. Connolly is a lawyer at the law firm of Edwards Angell Palmer & Dodge LLP, where he has concentrated in bankruptcy and finance law for the past eight years. Before private practice, Connolly was Law Clerk to the Hon. William C. Hillman, U.S. bankruptcy judge for the District of Massachusetts. He teaches at continuing legal education programs for bankruptcy lawyers and writes scholarly articles for publication in legal journals. *Massachusetts Lawyers Weekly* recognized Connolly as one of the state's twenty-five "Up & Coming Lawyers." *Boston Magazine* and *Law and Politics* named him a "Rising Star" in the area of bankruptcy and creditor/debtor rights. Connolly is a graduate of Duke University and Boston College Law School. He lives in the Boston area with his wife, Sharon, and two children, Theo and Corinne.

Index